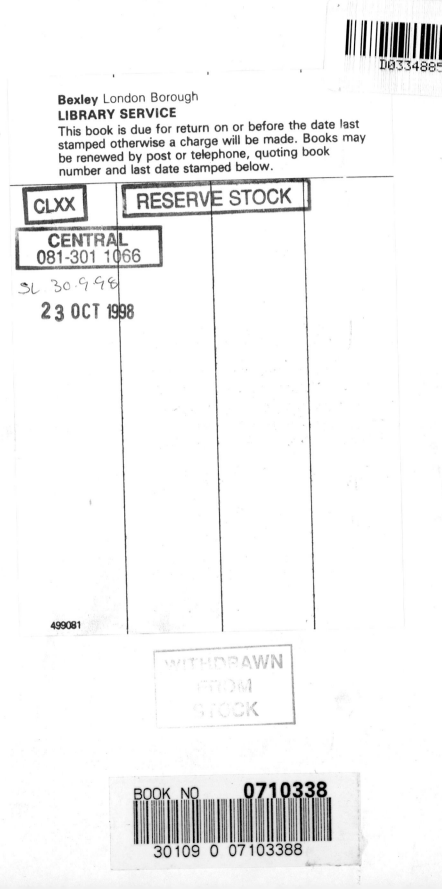

Bexley London Borough
LIBRARY SERVICE
This book is due for return on or before the date last
stamped otherwise a charge will be made. Books may
be renewed by post or telephone, quoting book
number and last date stamped below.

CLXX   RESERVE STOCK

CENTRAL
081-301 1066

SL 30.9.98

2 3 OCT 1998

499081

WITHDRAWN
FROM
STOCK

BOOK NO   0710338

30109 0 07103388

D0334885

THE ENGLISH LANDSCAPE

CLXX

THE ENGLISH LANDSCAPE

PAST, PRESENT, AND FUTURE

Wolfson College Lectures 1983

EDITED BY
S. R. J. WOODELL

CLXX

Oxford   New York
OXFORD UNIVERSITY PRESS
1985

Oxford University Press, Walton Street, Oxford OX2 6DP
Oxford New York Toronto
Delhi Calcutta Madras Karachi
Kuala Lumpur Singapore Hong Kong Tokyo
Nairobi Dar es Salaam Cape Town
Melbourne Auckland
and associated companies in
Beirut Berlin Ibadan Nicosia

Oxford is a trade mark of Oxford University Press

© Wolfson College, Oxford 1985

All rights reserved. No part of this publication may be reproduced,
stored in a retrieval system, or transmitted, in any form or by any means,
electronic, mechanical, photocopying, recording, or otherwise, without
the prior permission of Oxford Univesity Press

British Library Cataloguing in Publication Data
The English landscape: past, present and future:
Wolfson College lectures, 1983.
1. Natural history—Great Britain
I. Woodell, S.R.J. II. Wolfson College
508.41 QH137
ISBN 0–19–211621–5

Library of Congress Cataloging in Publication Data
The English landscape.
(Wolfson College lectures; 1983)
Bibliography: p. Includes index.
1. Landscape—England. 2. Landscape—England—
History. I. Woodell, S. R. J. (Stanley Reginald John)
II. Series.
QH138.A1E54 1985 914.2′02 85–5069
ISBN 0–19–211621–5

Set by Wyvern Typesetting Ltd.
Printed in Great Britain by
Butler & Tanner Ltd.
Frome, Somerset

BEXLEY LIBRARY SERVICE

CARD	CL No.	
SP	911.42 WOO	
PRICE	10 JUN 1986	BK JM
£15		
MSTAT	MAT. TYPE	
2	AD BOOK	
KEYER	TRACE	LANG	CH	PR

0710338

Contents

List of illustrations   vii

Acknowledgements   xi

INTRODUCTION   I
S. R. J. Woodell, *Fellow of Wolfson College, and Lecturer in Plant Ecology,
University of Oxford*

1. SHAPING THE LAND: THE GEOMORPHOLOGICAL
   BACKGROUND   4
   David K. C. Jones, *Senior Lecturer in Geography, London School of
   Economics and Political Science*

2. MAN AND LANDSCAPE IN BRITAIN 6000 BC–AD 400   48
   B. W. Cunliffe, *Professor of European Archaeology, University of Oxford*

3. ANCIENT WOODLAND AND HEDGES IN ENGLAND   68
   Oliver Rackham, *Fellow of Corpus Christi College, University of Cambridge*

4. MAPPING THE MEDIEVAL LANDSCAPE: FORTY YEARS IN
   THE FIELD   106
   M. W. Beresford, *Professor of European History, University of Leeds*

5. THE AGRICULTURAL LANDSCAPE: FADS AND FASHIONS   129
   Joan Thirsk, *formerly Reader in Economic History, University of Oxford, and
   Honorary Fellow of St. Hilda's College, Oxford*

6. CLIMATE AND LANDSCAPE IN THE BRITISH ISLES   148
   Hubert H. Lamb, *Emeritus Professor, Climatic Research Unit, University of
   East Anglia*

7. TOWNS, INDUSTRY, AND THE VICTORIAN LANDSCAPE   168
   F. M. L. Thompson, *Director, Institute of Historical Research, University of
   London*

8. AGRICULTURE, FORESTRY, AND THE FUTURE
LANDSCAPE   188
M. E. D. Poore, *Senior Fellow of the International Institute of Environment
and Development, and formerly Professor of Forest Science, University of
Oxford*

EPILOGUE   202
S. R. J. Woodell

Notes and references   207
Index   237

Illustrations

1.1	The distribution of relief and relief types in England and Wales	6
1.2	The relief regions of England and Wales	7
1.3	Typical granite scenery as displayed on western Dartmoor	8
1.4	Chronology and climatic variability of the Pleistocene	10
1.5	Palaeogeographical reconstruction of the Late Devensian	11
1.6	View of the South Downs near Denton, Sussex	12
1.7	Bamford Edge in the northern Peak District	13
1.8	The Winnats Pass in North Derbyshire	14
1.9	View southwards of upper portion of Borrowdale and Great Gable	15
1.10	Reconstruction of palaeoclimatic change for the eastern sea-board of the North Atlantic	17
1.11	The division into 'Highland' and 'Lowland' Britain	18
1.12	Structural division of England and Wales	20
1.13	The form of the Palaeozoic floor	23
1.14	LANDSAT image of a winter scene	24
1.15	The present distribution of Chalk	26
1.16	Estimated eustatic changes in sea-level	27
1.17	Hypothetical and vertically exaggerated cross-section from Cardigan Bay to London	30
1.18	Cliff-section at Pegwell Bay, Kent	32
1.19	Cross-section through the Chiltern Hills Chalk cuesta	33
1.20	Sarsen stones at Avebury	34
1.21	Glacial limits in the British Isles	37
1.22	The extent of glacial deposits in England and Wales	39
1.23	Patterns of ice-sheet movement and glacial erosion	41
1.24	Major alluvial spreads in eastern England	44
1.25	Cross-section through the floodplain of the Sussex Ouse at Sharpsbridge, Central Weald	46
2.1	Diagram to illustrate the position of man in the environment	49

2.2   Pollen diagrams from Hockham Mere   51

2.3   The effects of Mesolithic clearance on upland forest fringes   52

2.4   Pollen diagrams from Barfield Tarn, Cumberland   54

2.5   Diagram to illustrate the transhumant movements of Neolithic populations
       in Cumberland   55

2.6   Settlement related to soils on Dartmoor   56

2.7   Model to show possible effects of climatic deterioration on the exploitation
       of a moorland fringe zone   58

2.8   Field systems and other landscape features around the hill-fort of
       Danebury, Hampshire   60

2.9   The use of a chalkland landscape in the Iron Age   61

2.10   The parish of Chalton, Hampshire   64

3.1   Ancient Countryside and Planned Countryside   69

3.2   Gamlingay (Cambridgeshire), 1601   71

3.3   Gamlingay (Cambridgeshire), 1900   71

3.4   Lawshall (Suffolk), 1611   72

3.5   Lawshall (Suffolk), 1922   72

3.6   Ancient wood after coppicing   74

3.7   Ancient wood one year after coppicing   74

3.8   Ancient wood in second year after coppicing   74

3.9   Methods of managing trees   75

3.10   Field with many ancient pollard oaks   76

3.11   Secondary woodland, about fifty years old   77

3.12   A fifteenth-century timber building   79

3.13   A great woodbank with external ditch   80

3.14   Giant stool of ash   82

3.15   Herb Paris   82

3.16   Barnsdale Park, Rutland   84

3.17   Epping and Hainault Forests as surveyed in 1772–4   85

3.18   Ancient pollard oaks in a medieval deer-park   86

3.19   Ancient pollard beeches in a former wood-pasture common   87

3.20   Field sizes in Lawshall (Suffolk)   91

3.21   Presence of woodland in Domesday Book England in 1086   95

3.22   Areas of woodland recorded in Domesday England   96

3.23   Distribution of place names   98

3.24	Woods and hedges featured in Anglo-Saxon charters	101
3.25	Regular field patterns (Essex)	103
4.1	Village houses, crofts, and open fields: Laxton (Nottinghamshire)	107
4.2	The unenclosed landscape: Salford (Bedfordshire)	108
4.3	A mixed landscape: Maids Moreton (Buckinghamshire)	109
4.4	An unenclosed landscape: Sutton Coldfield (Warwickshire)	111
4.5	An early enclosed landscape: Whatborough (Leicestershire)	112
4.6	The hedged fields of Whatborough	113
4.7	The dissolution of the medieval landscape: Leicestershire	115
4.8	Reconstruction of a medieval landscape: Bittesby (Leicestershire)	116
4.9	Wharram Percy (Yorkshire): a long-house of the fifteenth century	119
4.10	Wharram Percy (Yorkshire): a reconstruction of the village plan, *c.* 1200	121
4.11	The reconstruction of a landscape: Towthorpe (Yorkshire)	125
5.1	Jojoba	133
5.2	Madder	134
5.3	Safflower	135
5.4	Woad	137
5.5	Sainfoin	138
5.6	Lucerne	139
5.7	Spurrey	141
5.8	Melilot	143
5.9	Great burnet	145
6.1	Departures from today's values of prevailing surface temperatures	151
6.2	The last great ice-sheet over northern Europe and Asia	152
6.3	Old moraine across Glen Strathfarrar, north-west Scotland	153
6.4	Prevailing temperatures in central England over the last 20,000 years	154
6.5	General height of the upper tree line on the Alps over the last 15,000 years	154
6.6	Prevailing temperatures in central England since AD 800	156
6.7	Average positions of the boundary between warm surface water of Gulf Stream origin and the polar water in the North Atlantic at various dates	156
6.8	Dry valley	157
6.9	Part of the Breckland in west Norfolk	158
6.10	Upper forest limit: Cwm Nant Col, near Harlech, in western North Wales	161

6.11   Upper forest limit: Creag Mhigeachaidh (Inshriach Forest, Speyside) on the north side of the Cairngorms   162

6.12   Stumps of full-grown pine trees at about 650 metres above sea level on the northern slope of Cairngorm   163

6.13   Forest remains on the west coast of Wales   164

7.1   The country landscape left by the Victorians: 'Autumn, Kinnordy', by James McIntosh Patrick   170

7.2   'Train Landscape', by Eric Ravilious (1939)   172

7.3   Victorian townscape: Saltaire, Bradford   174

7.4   Towns invading the country: 'London Going Out of Town', by George Cruikshank (1829)   180

7.5   The industrialist in the countryside: Wyfold Court, Oxfordshire   183

7.6   Industry in the Victorian town: Preston   185

Acknowledgements

Sir Henry Fisher, the President of Wolfson College, was very enthusiastic in his encouragement to me to organize this lecture series. I wish to thank him and the Fellows of Wolfson College for their support. Mrs Gillian Moore gave valuable secretarial help, and Dr Chris Lloyd coped admirably with sound recording.

Introduction

S. R. J. WOODELL

A COUPLE of years after my wife arrived in Britain from the United States she commented that sometimes she felt oppressed by the fact that wherever she went not only had people been around for thousands of years, but they had left evidence of their past presence everywhere. This evidence is all around us in the landscape. In the eastern United States, her original home, there is little obvious evidence of thousands of years of pre-European occupation or even of early post-colonization habitation, though recent archaeological work has disclosed more remains than were formerly thought to exist. Both Indian and post-colonization sites are being found. As in Britain natural vegetation underwent drastic change as land came into cultivation. Subsequent abandonment of much of this agriculturally poor land has been followed by recolonization, and much of the north-east is now occupied by secondary woodland, in which evidence of former human activity is hard to find.

She is not the only American I know who has felt this way: many seem to be overwhelmed by this sense of people past. Unlike some, she has now changed her view totally: she has been captured by the fascination that many of us feel at the fact that we are living in a landscape moulded by man over thousands of years. The remains left by people and their activities are the very stuff of landscape history. She now welcomes this, and also welcomes the knowledge that many features of the landscape that we think of as familiar and everyday are man-made, or at least man-modified. Recently, much influenced by Oliver Rackham's book *Ancient Woodland,* she has begun to investigate the history of some ancient woodlands near Oxford; a history that, as Dr Rackham shows vividly in his chapter in the present volume, is inextricably bound up with past human usage of the woodland products.

I have begun with this personal observation because it is illustrative of the route many have travelled, from ignorance or indifference, or even hostility, to a dawning of interest and a desire to know more about the many elements that have contributed to our landscape. It is probably a better-known landscape than any other in the world. It is celebrated in paintings, poetry, prose and music. Its appearance has been carried in the minds of emigrants to all parts of the world, and a desire to see it has been passed on to their descendants. They have even tried to re-create it in some quite unlikely places. It is only when one spends a long period away from the English landscape, as I am doing at present, that one realizes how much it can be missed. No doubt this is true of any home landscape, but does any other nation pass on this nostalgia to its descendants in exile in the same way as the English?

Most people's knowledge is of the landscape as it is now, or was recently. The question of how it came to be as it is was not, until the last few decades, clearly defined or understood. Many who came to these lectures were in search of some of the answers to that question. An interest in the history of our landscape is relatively recent. Most people have accepted the landscape as they know it with little thought as to how it developed. Many people still do: they enjoy its variety and familiar patterns without much awareness of how these patterns were created. We are accustomed to our surroundings as they are. The thought that they were much different once, even more the idea that they might be very different in the future, is somehow alien.

Before the Second World War there were stirrings of interest in the landscape but, as Professor Beresford graphically describes, it was a field of research where few ventured. The event which more than any other aroused interest was the publication of W. G. Hoskins's book *The Making of the English Landscape* in 1955. Many realized for the first time what an amazing store of information exists in documents, books, estate records, county record offices, drawings and paintings, photographs—even the humble picture postcard—and in the landscape itself, which could help interpretation of the past. His book was the forerunner of many. Look in a good bookshop today and you will find shelves of books on the subject. Inevitably television, most notably in a series presented by Professor Hoskins himself, has brought an interest in landscape history to a much wider audience.

When I first suggested a Wolfson Lecture series on this topic one of my reasons was that all the vegetation I study in Britain, as a plant ecologist, has been modified by human activities, and to understand it some knowledge of those activities is required. Nevertheless, as Dr Rackham demonstrates, human influence often merely modifies what was originally there, without destroying it. What was there in turn depended on the climates, and on the soils and parent rocks which comprised the environment. Here then were three topics—geomorphology, climate, and vegetation—which could provide the background to the remaining lectures, in which human influences would be discussed. Another pressing reason for feeling that a series of lectures on the landscape was apposite at this moment was the increasing evidence that the landscape is coming under pressures unlike any that it has faced before. One lecture would have to deal with these pressures and the future of the landscape. A consequence of these pressures is the increasing rate of loss of wildlife habitat and of facets of the plant and animal communities which interest ecologists. Many naturalists delight in seeing and studying native plants and animals in their semi-natural environment and are alarmed at what is happening.

Eight lectures are not enough. Something has to be left out. Many readers will regret the absence of a chapter on the townscape, or of one on country houses and gardens, or on parks. Perhaps the 'built' landscape could be a topic for a future lecture series. I had always envisaged that this series would be about the rural landscape. Most people when they visualize 'landscape' think of the countryside. Many readers will still miss particular topics even within this restricted ambit. One omission I especially regret is the coastal landscape. For many the coast gives British scenery its unique character. I have worked on coastal vegetation and I am very much aware that a significant part of our coastal scenery is profoundly modified by, indeed partly created by, the effects of plants on their physical environment. Salt marshes and sand dunes both depend on plants for their growth. In addition, some of our least disturbed vegetation is in certain coastal areas (and also, unfortunately, some of the most disturbed). Despite this and other omissions, those who were lucky enough to attend the lectures came away with a much enhanced knowledge of our landscape and the forces which have moulded it. Many questions were answered, many myths dispelled.

The three chapters I have mentioned, on geomorphology, climate, and forest vegetation, and in varying degrees all the others, demonstrate that from prehistoric times until the Industrial Revolution and beyond we have been modifying the natural landscape constantly. Sometimes our effects have been slight, sometimes profound, and often they have been subtle and not immediately obvious. Professor Poore rounds off the series with a grim picture of the pressures now being brought to bear on the landscape, especially as the result of current agricultural policies. He is cautiously optimistic about the future. Many of us will echo the doubts he expresses in his final sentence.

I share his doubts, and indeed am less optimistic. I shall outline some of my reasons in an Epilogue. Meanwhile it is our hope that the publication of this series of lectures on the English landscape will help to enlighten many who wonder about its origins and development. A more urgent hope is that, thus enlightened, they will share the concern of many people who for one reason or another are not very optimistic about its future, and perhaps may be moved to take some action.

Middleback, South Australia
August 1984   S. R. J. Woodell

1

Shaping the land: the geomorphological background

DAVID K. C. JONES

IT is well known that landscape is fashioned through the interplay of both physical and cultural influences, except in the most remote and inhospitable regions of the world where 'natural' landscapes still survive which bear a negligible imprint of human activity. The creation of the English landscape is certainly no such exception although, as even the shortest of journeys will soon indicate, it is better to think of landscapes rather than of one 'typical' landscape, for a surprisingly rich diversity is contained within the confines of this small country. Such variety owes much to the vagaries of geological evolution, which has yielded the rock foundations that underlie the contrasting patterns of relief. It is the fashioning of these materials that has produced such distinctive terrains as the dissected 'hard rock' topography of the English Lake Disrict, the granite moorlands of Devon and Cornwall, the sandstone and limestone plateaux of the Pennines, the 'scarp-and-vale' scenery that is so well developed in the English Midlands, and the rolling Chalk downlands of the south. In addition, some of the debris produced by this modelling has contributed to the creation of characteristic 'young' depositional terrains, such as the monotonous till (glacial drift) plains of East Anglia and the low-lying, flat expanses of unconsolidated alluvium that form the Fens, Somerset Levels, and Romney Marsh. It is also evident that prolonged human occupancy has resulted in widespread and profound alterations to both the physical and biological components of 'natural' scenery, causing changes which were slow and modest at first but which increased in pace and severity as the population grew in numbers and technology developed. The major elements of change, frequently over-simplified as the 'clearance of the forests', the 'reclamation of the heathlands', and the 'drainage of the marshes', and to which must be added the more recent impacts of industrialization and urbanization, have combined in a process which may be called the 'diminution of nature', the most extreme examples of which are well displayed in the urban and industrial areas that cover more than 12 per cent of the existing land surface. These anthropogenic changes have been discussed by many writers, most especially W. G. Hoskins in his classic book *The Making of the English Landscape,* and will be amplified by other contributors in this volume. The purpose of this opening chapter is to focus attention on the development of the topographic or geomorphological components of landscape—the flesh and bones which have been variably clothed by nature and by man.

A perspective on topographic development

There is no denying the significance of geological factors in landscape development. The main geological control on landforms include the nature of the rocks in any outcropping sequence; their interrelationships, disposition, and relative resistance to denudation under varying geomorphological regimes, as well as the presence of zones of weakness, such as faults and shatter belts, for it is the contrasts and inequalities of the geological foundations that are exploited by denudation processes to yield patterns of relief.[1] As inspection of a geological map will clearly show, the British Isles have a complex geological fabric testifying to an eventful evolutionary history. The rocks that outcrop at the surface vary greatly in age, indicating that the area has experienced several phases of tectonic deformation, involving both folding and faulting, as well as episodes dominated by major differential vertical movements characterized by the contemporaneous uplift of some regions and the subsidence of others. As a consequence of this inheritance, the present pattern of relief is also complex, thereby contributing greatly to landscape diversity. Despite the fact that the elevational range is limited to a mere 3,162 feet (964 metres), it is still possible to distinguish six main relief types (Figure 1.1) which can be grouped together to form at least twenty-eight relief regions (Figure 1.2).[2] Additional diversity is provided by variations in lithology which give rise to individual topographic features (escarpments and vales), while further landscape distinctiveness is produced by materials which develop into unusually coloured soils (for instance, the orange soils of the Midlands developed on the outcrop of the Keuper Marl) or impart character through their use as building materials (such as flint, Cotswold stone, or the Devonian red sandstone used in and around Hereford). Clearly a detailed examination of the character and evolution of such a varied set of landscapes is beyond the scope of a single short chapter. Indeed, there would appear little need for such a contribution as there already exists an enormous range of descriptive literature on aspects of English topographic landscape and its geological foundations.[3] Instead, attention will be focused on topographic evolution and the main factors that have influenced topographic development.

The shape of the land is essentially a function of the sculpturing effects of geomorphological processes acting on the geological fabric over time periods which are long from a human perspective. The fashioning of the exposed rocks is achieved through the interaction of many agencies: the decomposition and disintegration of rock by weathering activity; gravity-dominated mass wasting processes ranging in magnitude from the imperceptible downslope creep of soils to rapid landslides and falls; fluvial processes associated with running water; the work of ice; the action of waves and currents in coastal and shallow marine environments; wind, and the activities of man.[4] These processes

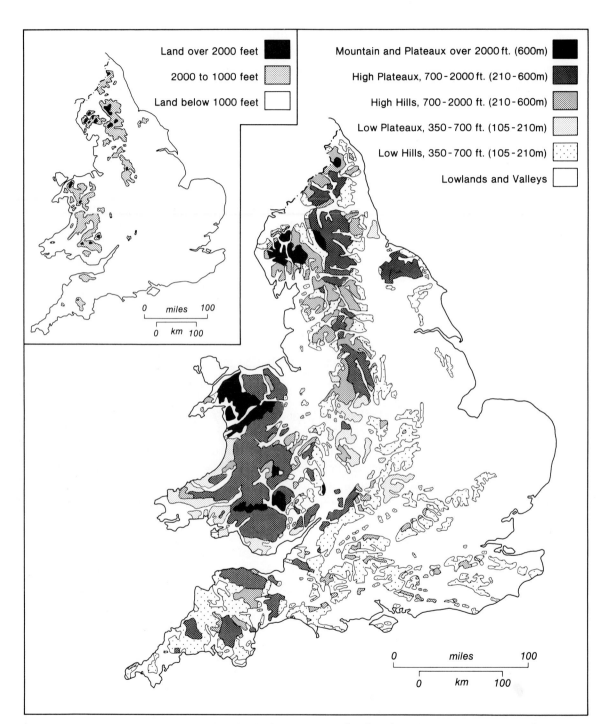

Land over 2000 feet

2000 to 1000 feet

Land below 1000 feet

Mountain and Plateaux over 2000 ft. (600m)

High Plateaux, 700 - 2000 ft. (210 - 600m)

High Hills, 700 - 2000 ft. (210 - 600m)

Low Plateaux, 350 - 700 ft. (105 - 210m)

Low Hills, 350 - 700 ft. (105 - 210m)

Lowlands and Valleys

0   miles   100

0   km   100

FIG. 1.1 The distribution of relief and relief types in England and Wales (based on Warwick 1964).

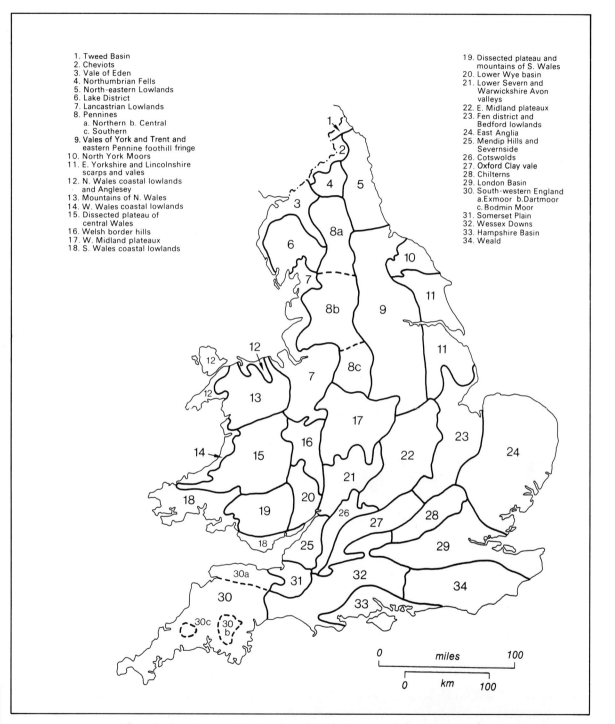

The legend on the map reads:

1. Tweed Basin
2. Cheviots
3. Vale of Eden
4. Northumbrian Fells
5. North-eastern Lowlands
6. Lake District
7. Lancastrian Lowlands
8. Pennines
   a. Northern b. Central
   c. Southern
9. Vales of York and Trent and
   eastern Pennine foothill fringe
10. North York Moors
11. E. Yorkshire and Lincolnshire
    scarps and vales
12. N. Wales coastal lowlands
    and Anglesey
13. Mountains of N. Wales
14. W. Wales coastal lowlands
15. Dissected plateau of
    central Wales
16. Welsh border hills
17. W. Midland plateaux
18. S. Wales coastal lowlands

19. Dissected plateau and
    mountains of S. Wales
20. Lower Wye basin
21. Lower Severn and
    Warwickshire Avon
    valleys
22. E. Midland plateaux
23. Fen district and
    Bedford lowlands
24. East Anglia
25. Mendip Hills and
    Severnside
26. Cotswolds
27. Oxford Clay vale
28. Chilterns
29. London Basin
30. South-western England
    a. Exmoor b. Dartmoor
    c. Bodmin Moor
31. Somerset Plain
32. Wessex Downs
33. Hampshire Basin
34. Weald

FIG. 1.2 The relief regions of England and Wales (adapted from Warwick 1964).

operate in varying combinations and result in the erosion, transport and deposition of material, so as to yield a continuous cover of landforms, some of which are carved out of rock, others fashioned in incoherent superficial sediments. These features display great variation in size, shape, and composition, and it is usual to envisage the topographic landscape as consisting of a hierarchy of landforms, each of the larger forms containing numerous smaller components. Dartmoor, for example, can be considered a landform at one scale, but inspection of the massif reveals a range of smaller landforms including, in descending order of size, ridges and valleys, granite domes, tors, boulder streams, and turf mounds, as is shown in Figure 1.3. Similarly, many prominent escarpment slopes, including the Cotswold edge where it overlooks the Vales of Severn and Evesham, and the

FIG. 1.3 Typical granite scenery as displayed on western Dartmoor. The view is of Staple Tor (1,493 feet; 460 metres) from the west, and shows a granite dome mantled by streams of boulders and surmounted by tors. The jagged silhouette of the tors, the boulder streams and the turf mounds, or *buttes gazonnées*, in the foreground, all testify to the role of periglacial processes operating under past cold climatic conditions in the fashioning of the present landscape.

Lower Greensand ramparts of the Weald (Leith Hill, Hindhead, and so on), are actually complex morphological features composed of landslides, debris cones, gullies, and man-made forms.

Cursory inspection of England's land-surface, with its well-developed valley patterns and drainage networks, might suggest that it is essentially a fluvial landscape largely fashioned under the influence of the contemporary temperate conditions. Such a conclusion would be mistaken, for although fluvial denudation has obviously been important in creating the major patterns of topography, it is now recognized that the actual form of the land and the character of the superficial deposits that extensively mantle the bedrocks owe more to the cold conditions of the Pleistocene (Table 1.1). Recent investigations of shallow marine sedimentary sequences, such as those of the North Sea Basin, have revealed that these deposits contain relatively good evidence for past changes in climate. Studies of these palaeo-environmental records have increasingly highlighted the fact that the Quaternary (the last 1.6 to 2.5 million years (Ma = million years [ago]))[5] appears to have been characterized by repeated dramatic fluctuations in climate from extremely harsh periglacial and glacial conditions to temperate conditions, often a little warmer than those prevailing at present, as is shown in Figure 1.4.[6] Although there is still considerable uncertainty about the number, age, magnitude, and significance of these events, between 16 and 23 cool/cold phases have been identified so far. These climatic changes not only resulted in constantly shifting vegetation belts and considerable oscillations in sea-level in response to the waxing and waning of major ice-sheets, but also profoundly affected the operation of geomorphological processes. Each major alteration of environmental conditions caused variations in the combination of sculpturing agencies that acted on any particular area, as well as on the rates of operation of the individual processes concerned. Thus the dominant influences on landform creation repeatedly changed during the Quarternary, a characteristic most dramatically illustrated by the fact that each advance of the ice-sheets across England was separated by a few tens of thousands of years of temperate conditions. It is not surprising, therefore, that many surface landforms were transient features, for the products of any one geomorphological regime were soon vulnerable to modification by the very different processes associated with the next regime.

The persistence of surface landforms is determined by a large number of variables. Some landforms have relatively short lives (1–1,000 years), either because they are composed of incoherent materials or because their location exposes them to subsequent modification. Others may persist for considerably longer, only to be obliterated by the impact of large-scale 'catastrophic' events (such as floods, major landslides, and so on) or alterations in geomorphological regime due to environmental change (such as glaciation following temperate conditions), while surviving features will be subjected to gradual changes, which will eventually result in their total re-modelling or burial. Thus it should not be particularly surprising that the oldest clearly recognizable depositional landforms in England are a mere 200,000–450,000 years old, although superficial sediments of very much greater antiquity have been identified.

The transient character of many landforms should not be interpreted as indicating that

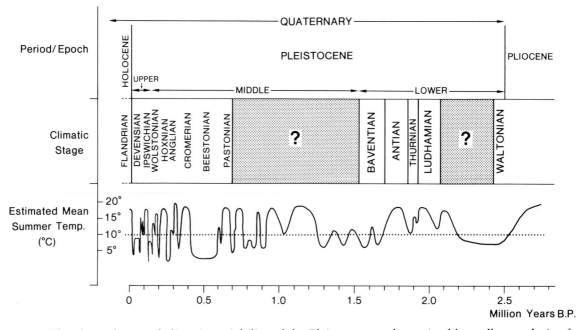

FIG. 1.4 The chronology and climatic variability of the Pleistocene as determined by pollen analysis of deposits in the Netherlands (based on Zagwijn 1975). Correlation of the continental sequence with the English (East Anglian) stages has proved difficult and accounts for the two periods of hiatus. These may, in part, reflect the mixed usage of 'short' and 'long' Pleistocene time-scales. The main point to note is the frequency and magnitude of temperature variations; for the purpose of comparison, the contemporary mean temperatures for lowlands in central England are 15.5–16.5 °C for high summer (July and August), 14.0–15.0 °C for summer as a whole, and 3.5–4.5 °C for winter (December–February).

there are no long-lived or ancient landscape elements. Much of the trunk river network is known to be of great age and thus the major elements of landscape, such as valleys, hill masses, and escarpments, are features of considerable antiquity which have evolved to their present shape and size in response to geomorphological changes—a situation comparable to the way in which cities change in size, shape, and morphology over a period of time. Thus although the surface detail is very young, most of the major components of landscape have been inherited from much earlier evolutionary phases, and have long and complex developmental histories. The granite of Dartmoor, for example, is thought to have been exposed at the surface more than 45 millions year ago (Ma), since which time this upland has continuously evolved to its present form as the surrounding areas have been lowered by denudation.[7] Similarly, the ancestors of the Chalk escarpments that surround the Weald probably first came into existence at about the same time, since when they have retreated many kilometres to their present position and grown both higher and steeper.[8] In addition, certain erosional features may be buried for lengthy periods before re-emerging at the surface as exhumed forms following the removal of the overlying cover of sediments. Such 'stripped stratum planes' are widely developed where there are marked contrasts in the character of outcropping materials. The best example occurs widely in southern England and particularly around the southern outskirts of London. Here the stripping away of the overlying unconsolidated sands and gravels of early Tertiary (Palaeogene) age has revealed a conspicuous inclined marine-trimmed surface developed on the underlying Chalk. This Sub-Palaeogene surface was developed mainly between 52 Ma and 60 Ma, since which time it has been protected by burial until its recent exhumation (see Figure 1.19).[9] Once exposed, however, the lives of such relic features are as transient as other surface landforms, and they are soon either remodelled or destroyed.

Because of these advances in knowledge it is helpful to envisage the landscape as a palimpsest, a continuous patchwork of landforms and deposits of differing antiquity created by varying combinations of processes in response to changing environmental conditions. Under such circumstances, the impact of the most recent evolutionary phases will be writ boldest in the landscape, and evidence of earlier episodes will be fragmentary. As the culmination of the last glacial phase was a mere 18,000 years ago (BP = before the present) when the continental-scale ice-sheet reached North Norfolk (Figure 1.5), it is not

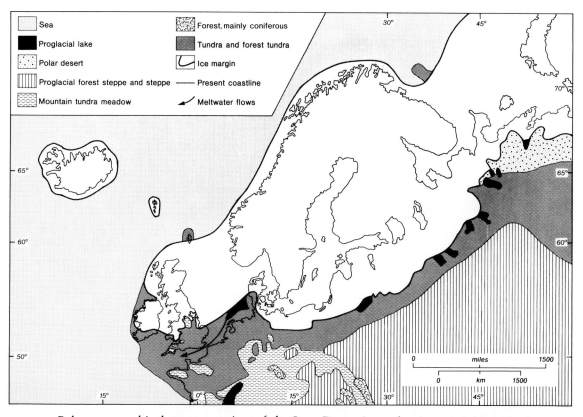

FIG. 1.5 Palaeogeographical reconstruction of the Late Devensian, adopting a minimum ice-coverage interpretation (based on Gerasimov 1969). There is continuing disagreement about the position of the ice-front in the North-Sea Basin.

surprising that evidence for fashioning under cold conditions is widespread, and that the significance of cold-climate relics increases northwards to Scotland, for it was here that the Pleistocene ice-sheets lingered longest. However, even the smooth convexo-concave slopes and dry valleys displayed by the Chalk downlands of southern England (Figure 1.6)—possibly the archetype of English landscapes—appear to have been modelled under the freeze-thaw conditions of the periglacial or tundra environment, as do the gentle tor-surmounted granite domes of Dartmoor (Figure 1.3), and the Millstone Grit and Carboniferous Limestone uplands of the Pennines with their frost-riven edges (scars) (Figure 1.7) and gorges (Figure 1.8). In highland areas the evidence is even more conspicuous, for here heavily ice-moulded landscapes clearly reveal differences in rock resistance to glacial erosion, and pre-existing valleys have been repeatedly excavated by glaciers to form deep glacial troughs, often surmounted by frost-shattered peaks (as in the English Lake District, Figure 1.9).

This discussion about landform creation and survival raises questions as to the scale of denudation that may have been accomplished during the brief duration of the Quaternary

FIG. 1.6 View of the South Downs near Denton, Sussex, showing typical chalkland backslope scenery with winding dry valley. Dry valleys are found on many rock types but are especially well-developed on the Chalk. Several explanations have been advanced for their formation, including climatic change and the lowering of the water-table. The present view is that although a number of factors may have been involved in the creation of dry valleys, much of the visible sculpturing was accomplished under periglacial regimes when permanently frozen sub-soil (permafrost) conditions resulted in the development of surface streams fed by snow-melt in the spring and summer months. The flatness of the valley floor and the marked breaks of slope at the valley margins are the result of ploughing.

FIG. 1.7 Bamford Edge (1,395 feet; 425 metres) in the northern Peak District—the so-called 'Dark Peak'—as seen from the edge of Ladybower Reservoir. The relative relief of this Millstone Grit terrain has evolved since the mid-Neogene, much of it resulting from denudation in the Pleistocene. Both the grit-stone edges, or scars, and the underlying gentler valley-side slopes developed on shales bear the clear signs of fashioning under harsh periglacial conditions.

and the preceding longer span of the Tertiary (Table 1.1). The incompleteness of the record of landforms and deposits makes such a calculation beset with difficulties. One approach is to estimate contemporary mean rates of *overall* landscape reduction based on the measurement of the sediment load of rivers. These vary in the range 0.004 to 0.2 mm a year, equivalent to 4 to 200 metres a million years (Ma) or 4–200 Bubnoff units (1 Bubnoff unit (B) = 1 metre/Ma).[10] There is reasonable agreement that the mean rate is approximately 50B, equivalent to 80-125 metres (260-410 feet) of reduction during the Quaternary, and 3,250 metres (10,660 feet) since the beginning of the Tertiary. Several questions are raised by such calculations. The first concerns the extent to which contemporary measurements are diagnostic of past denudation rates. Some writers argue that present sediment yields are atypically great because of the direct and indirect effects of human activities on the Earth's surface, while others suggest that the dramatic changes in environmental conditions that characterized the Quaternary would have resulted in major pulses of denudation with rates far in excess of those occurring today. The second question concerns the problem of projecting very small annual rates subject to severe instrumentation error, over vast lengths of time. Third is the problem of the extent to

FIG. 1.8 The Winnats Pass in North Derbyshire. This Carboniferous Limestone gorge may originally have been initiated through the collapse of a cave roof but has been largely fashioned by surface waterflows under periglacial conditions. The same may well be true of other famous limestone gorges, including Cheddar Gorge.

which any rate measured during the Quaternary is applicable for what are generally considered to be the less variable conditions of the Tertiary episode of landform creation. Finally, there is the question of whether any single rate is meaningful for the whole of England, because of the differences in resistance of rocks to denudation and variations in the rate of recent vertical movements. All of these points are valid. Nevertheless, it is instructive to note that application of the mean rate (50 B) for the last 1.6 Ma—the minimum estimation for the length of the Quaternary—and the minimum rate (4B) for the remaining time to the beginning of the Tertiary, results in an *overall* lowering figure of 333 metres (1,090 feet). This figure may still appear surprisingly large, but it is merely a mean figure which may represent an over- or under-estimation of reality depending on the nature of exposed rocks, denudation histories, and the magnitude of vertical movements. This tends to be borne out by the results of investigations in areas where landforms or deposits have been preserved which give an indication of the extent of denudation. In the west-country areas of central Dartmoor, the Haldon Hills and the Blackdown Hills, as little as 50–100 metres (165–330 feet) of erosion is claimed to have been accomplished since the earliest Tertiary.[11] Conversely, in central Devon the figure appears closer to 500

FIG. 1.9 View southwards of upper portion of Borrowdale and Great Gable (2949 feet; 899 metres), in the English Lake District, showing typical glaciated hard-rock terrain of Highland Britain. The bedrock slopes are wholly developed on the Borrowdale Volcanics (mainly Andesitic lavas of Ordovician age) and have been profoundly sculptured by repeated glaciation in the Pleistocene so as to produce the general smoothed form. The major glacial trough of Borrowdale (in the foreground) has been partly infilled by alluvium of Holocene age, but still clearly displays the characteristic 'U-shaped' cross-profile of glaciated valleys. A large corrie is visible in the centre of the photograph and another, smaller corrie is located in the bottom right-hand corner. The steeper rock bluffs have been created through the combined effects of glacial plucking and mechanical weathering (freeze–thaw shattering). (Reproduced by kind permission of the Committee for Aerial Photography, University of Cambridge.)

metres (1,650 feet). In south-eastern England, estimations range from a minimum of about 250 metres (820 feet) in the London area to 1,050 metres (3,450 feet) over the central Weald.[12] All of these computations are for areas beyond the reach of the Pleistocene ice-sheets, which suggests that the totals may increase northwards. Irrespective of what the actual figures may turn out to be, the significance of denudation in fashioning the geological fabric to create the present landscape is clearly apparent.

The shaping of the landscape

To gain an understanding of the development of the English topographic landscape we must adopt a long time perspective (Table 1.1). It is essentially a saga in four distinct acts. The first act involves the complex sequence of events that preceded about 70 Ma, during which the main features of the geological fabric were established even though the British Isles, as they exist today, had yet to come into being. This extremely eventful formative phase of geological evolution was brought to a close by the submergence of virtually the whole area beneath the Chalk Sea in Upper Cretaceous times. The second act is concerned with the events of the Tertiary. It began with the emergence of what was to become the British Isles from beneath the Chalk Sea, and the subsequent evolution of the area against a background of crustal movements and under climatic conditions that were distinctly tropical at first and then temperate (Figure 1.10). This change of climate owed more to the opening of the northern North Atlantic Basin post 52 Ma than to the gradual north-eastward drift of the European portion of the Eurasian tectonic plate.[13] The third act was the Pleistocene, during which time the dramatic fluctuations in climate and sea-level,

Table **1.1** The Geological Column (Ages shown are from beginning of Period/Epoch).

Era	Period		Epoch	Age (Ma)
Cenozoic	Quaternary		Holocene/Recent	.01
			Pleistocene	2.5
	Tertiary	Neogene	Pliocene	7
			Miocene	23
		Palaeogene	Oligocene	35
			Eocene	53
			Palaeocene	65
Mesozoic	Cretaceous			135
	Jurassic			195
	Triassic			225
Palaeozoic	Permian			280
	Carboniferous			345
	Devonian			395
	Silurian			435
	Ordovician			500
	Cambrian			600
	Pre-Cambrian			
	Origin of the Earth			4,500

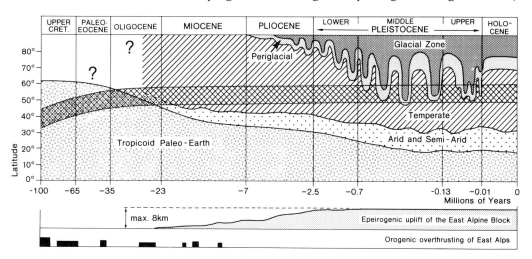

FIG. 1.10 Reconstruction of palaeoclimatic change for the eastern sea-board of the North Atlantic (based on Büdel 1982). The belt of crosshatch represents the changing location of the British Isles over time. It is important to recognize that this is purely an illustrative diagram. None of the boundaries should be interpreted too literally nor the number and extent of glacial oscillations.

together with the effects of repeated glaciation and periglaciation, resulted in major alterations to the pre-existing topography, with widespread valley excavation leading to the creation of the existing topographic landscape. The final act is the Holocene or Recent, the last 10,000 years of temperate conditions, during which time there have been dramatic changes in coastal configuration as a consequence of the rapid rise in sea-level from a minimum of between −100 and −130 metres at 15,000 BP (before the present) and when man has become an increasingly important geomorphological agent in inland areas, to the extent that he is now almost certainly the dominant agent of change.[14]

The development of the geological fabric

The complexities of the geological inheritance need not detain us for too long, for we are not concerned with the details of geological evolution over hundreds of millions of years but rather with the most significant developments which have helped to determine the shape of the present landscape.[15] The apparently random outcrop patterns displayed on the geological map of Britain can be simplified, as was clearly shown by Halford Mackinder in his book *Britain and the British Seas*. Mackinder divided Britain into two parts on the basis of whether the outcropping rocks were older or younger than the end of the Carboniferous period (that is, 280 Ma). The rocks underlying 'Lowland Britain', to the south and east of his famous 'Tees–Exe line' (Figure 1.11), consist of gently tilted or slightly folded young sedimentary rocks: alternations of limestones, sandstones, and clays, which have been exploited by denudation to yield 'scarp-and-vale' scenery with summits that rarely exceed 1,000 feet (300 metres) (Figure 1.1), thereby giving rise to the

Surface of Carboniferous and older rocks

Surface of rocks younger than Carboniferous but underlain by Carboniferous and older rocks

Tees-Exe Line

FIG. 1.11 The division into 'Highland' and 'Lowland' Britain. The distribution of Palaeozoic rocks should be compared with the pattern of relief as shown in Figure 1.1.

so-called 'belted landscapes' of the English Midlands and the Weald. To the north and west of the Tees–Exe line outcrop the older, more resistant, and sometimes highly deformed rocks of 'Highland Britain'. In fact it is possible to distinguish a very generalized decrease in rock age from the north-west to the south-east across Britain, with ancient Pre-Cambrian rocks (older than 1,000 Ma) outcropping in the extreme north-west of Scotland, and young Tertiary sediments, between 35 and 60 Ma, preserved within the London and Hampshire Basins. It was this overall pattern that prompted Mackinder to observe that Britain appeared to have been 'made from the north-west and populated from the south-east.'

Clearly, reality is much more complex. First, the boundary between the rocks of Highland and Lowland Britain is highly irregular (as Figure 1.11 shows), with splinters of older rock emerging through the younger cover in the Midlands (such as the Warwickshire Coalfield, Leicestershire Coalfield, Charnwood Forest), the Bristol area, and the Mendip Hills, while the main mass of Highland Britain is divided into upstanding blocks separated by areas which have foundered, such as the Bristol Channel, the Irish Sea, the Cheshire Basin, and the Vale of Eden. Second, the striking irregularity of the British coastline—a characteristic often noted in the literature—is in fact a feature mainly associated with Highland Britain. Both suggest that structural patterns and variations in rock type are exceedingly important in the creation of topography in these 'older' terrains. Certainly rock variations are great, for not only are there extensive outcrops of sedimentary strata, such as the familiar Carboniferous Limestone and Millstone Grits of the Pennines, but there are also massive igneous intrusions of granitic rocks in the South-West Peninsula (Dartmoor, Bodmin Moor), and areas of volcanic (Cheviot Hills and Lake District) and metamorphic rocks. There thus exists plenty of lithological variety to be exploited by denudation.[16] However, it is the structural patterns that are of even greater significance, for there is an overall concordance between geological structure and relief.

The portion of the Earth's crust which was eventually to become the British Isles has been involved in a number of extremely violent mountain-building upheavals resulting from continental collisions. Two such ancient orogenic episodes are of particular importance—the Caledonian Mountain Building phase (400–500 Ma), which imparted a NE–SW-oriented structural grain (folds and faults) across northern Britain, and the Hercynian or Variscan orogeny (about 300 Ma), which created an E–W or ESE–WNW structural pattern across southern Britain.[17] In their prime, both of these were fully developed mountain systems, equivalent to the Alps or the Iran–Afghanistan ranges. Although they have subsequently been wholly destroyed by denudation, the fundamental structures developed in their foundations still exist, either at the surface or buried under younger rocks, and have continued to exert a significant influence on crustal movements and thereby on landform creation. As is shown in Figure 1.12, exposed structures directly resulting from the Caledonian orogeny are confined in England to the Lake District, although they attain much greater prominence in Wales and Scotland, especially Scotland, where major elements, such as the Great Glen Fault, the Highland Boundary Fault, and the Southern Uplands Fault, have exerted profound influences on the gross patterns of

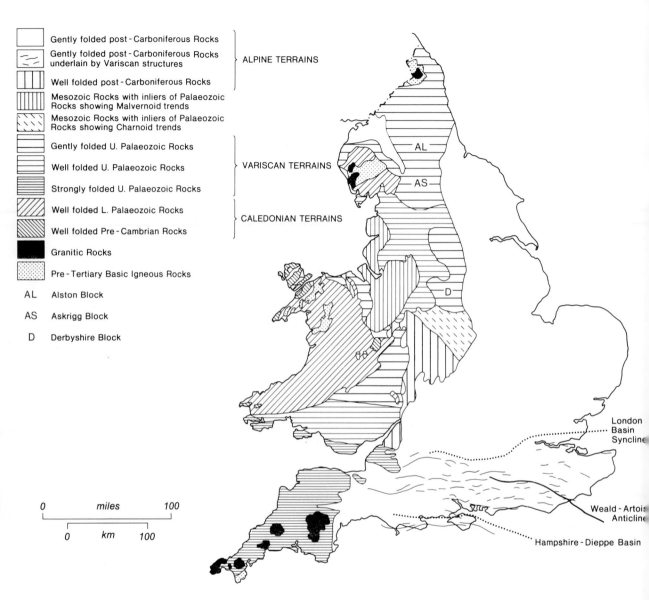

Gently folded post-Carboniferous Rocks

Gently folded post-Carboniferous Rocks underlain by Variscan structures

Well folded post-Carboniferous Rocks

Mesozoic Rocks with inliers of Palaeozoic Rocks showing Malvernoid trends

Mesozoic Rocks with inliers of Palaeozoic Rocks showing Charnoid trends

ALPINE TERRAINS

Gently folded U. Palaeozoic Rocks

Well folded U. Palaeozoic Rocks

Strongly folded U. Palaeozoic Rocks

VARISCAN TERRAINS

Well folded L. Palaeozoic Rocks

Well folded Pre-Cambrian Rocks

CALEDONIAN TERRAINS

Granitic Rocks

Pre-Tertiary Basic Igneous Rocks

AL   Alston Block

AS   Askrigg Block

D   Derbyshire Block

AL

AS

D

London Basin Syncline

Weald-Artois Anticline

Hampshire-Dieppe Basin

0   miles   100

0   km   100

FIG. 1.12 Structural division of England and Wales, the direction of shading approximately conforming to the predominant trend of folds and faults. The narrow lines in southern England represent the most important secondary folds and clearly show how the presence of deeply buried Variscan structures has probably significantly influenced surface flexuring of younger strata (based, in part, on Warwick 1964).

relief and coastline configuration, while lesser structures have been exploited by denudation to yield valley patterns. However, it is important to note that these are merely the *exposed* structures—just a portion of a more extensive network that underlies much of Britain.

The same is generally true of the Variscan episode, which imparted an E–W or WNW–ESE structural grain across a large swathe of what is now central Europe, including southern England, South Wales, southern Ireland and northern France. The folds and faults developed during this mountain building phase are well developed in the South-West Peninsula, although the characteristic graining is complicated here by the presence of a large body of granite. This igneous mass, or batholith, underlies much of Devon and Cornwall, and was originally intruded into the foundations of the mountain chain at depths of around 20,000 feet (6,000 metres)—estimates vary from 16,500–29,500 feet (5,000–9,000 metres)—and has subsequently been partly exposed, or unroofed, by denudation so that the highest extremities now appear at the surface as a number of upland moors (Figure 1.12).[18] Away from the granites, the contorted rocks are well displayed, although present surface exposure merely represents a glimpse of the true extent of the structural pattern, for it is now known to underlie the whole of southern England and the English Channel, with a fragment reaching the surface as the Mendip Hills. Further north, the impact of the Variscan tectonic episode was complicated by the presence of pre-existing structural networks deep in the rock sequence. As a consequence, a confusing array of structures developed with variable trends, resulting from the phenomenon known as 'posthumous folding' or resurgent tectonics.

Posthumous folding occurs where a cover of relatively young surface rocks experiencing compressional stresses are deformed according to the movements of underlying older and long-buried structures, and take on the orientation of the ancient pattern largely irrespective of the direction of the compressive forces. Thus in northern England the Variscan deformation was dominated by the movement of blocks and other underlying Caledonian structures, while in the Midlands and Lancashire, two very ancient Pre-Cambrian trends exerted strong influences—the N–S Malvernoid trend and the NW–SE Charnian trend, both classically exposed in the Pre-Cambrian fragments that reach the surface as the Malvern Hills and Charnwood Forest respectively. The English landscape must, therefore, be envisaged as having developed on a geological fabric criss-crossed by networks of structural axes, which are lines of weakness capable of being both reactivated by later tectonic episodes and exploited by denudation. The full significance of this concept becomes apparent in explanations of the gentle fold pattern of southern England (Figure 1.12). For many years both the major folds (the London Basin Syncline, the Weald–Artois Anticline, and the Hampshire–Dieppe Syncline), together with the numerous minor secondary folds superimposed on the main structures (such as the Weymouth, Pewsey, Winchester, and Fernhurst folds), were believed to represent the 'outer ripples of the Alpine storm' and to have developed as a result of a brief tectonic episode in the mid-Tertiary.[19] Recent research, however, has shown that such an explanation is untenable. It is now thought that while the creation of the Alps may have assisted in the development of the young surface fold pattern of southern England, a far greater influence was exerted by the reactivation of Variscan structures contained in the deeply buried old rocks that underlie the Palaeozoic floor.[20]

The Palaeozoic floor is the boundary between younger strata and Palaeozoic, or even older, rocks as determined by boreholes and seismic investigations. Although the interface should be placed between the Permian and Triassic (that is, 225 Ma), it is convenient here to take the boundary between the Carboniferous and Permian as approximately coincident with the completion of the Variscan tectonic episode. The surface outcrop of this discontinuity outlines the same areas as those used by Mackinder to define Highland Britain (Figure 1.11), but from here the Palaeozoic floor declines to great depths in a number of basins (Figure 1.13): to over −12,000 feet (−3,600 metres) beneath the Isle of Wight; to −8,600 feet (−2,600 metres) in the Cheshire Basin; to −14,000 feet (−4,300 metres) under much of the North Sea, declining to over −19,700 feet (−6,000 metres) in the Central Rift located mid-way between England and Norway; to over −12,000 feet (−3,600 metres) beneath the Celtic Sea and South-West Approaches on either flank of the Cornish Peninsula; and to −6,000 feet (−1,800 metres) in Cardigan Bay (see Figure 1.17).[21] Conversely, the surface must be envisaged as having risen high over the existing uplands of Wales, south-west England, the Pennines, the Lake District, and the Scottish Highlands, for the present land surfaces in these areas are the product of denudation biting deeply into the relatively old rocks underlying the Palaeozoic floor—by an estimated 20,000 feet (6,000 metres) in the case of Dartmoor. Although this surface was originally far from level, much of the present irregularity of over 35,000 feet (10,500 metres) must be the consequence of individual fault-defined blocks moving up or down over the last 250 Ma, a conclusion that has led to the view that most of the major relief units of Britain (such as the Welsh uplands, the Pennines, and the South-West Peninsula) had been defined, or 'blocked out', by an important phase of Permo-Triassic rifting at the close of the Variscan orogeny.[22] Some of the subsequent differential movement of these blocks is explicable in terms of isostatic adjustments brought about through denudation unloading of upstanding areas and sedimentary loading of adjacent basins,[23] but the main cause must have been the imposition of stresses from four main sources: first, the opening of the North Atlantic Basin which began about 170 Ma, although the rift between the British Isles and Greenland did not actively develop until after 52 Ma;[24] second, the foundering of the North Sea Basin, a failed arm of the Mid-Atlantic Ridge system, which has been subsiding for at least the last 160 Ma; third, the development of the Biscay Rift, which resulted in the rotation of the Iberian Peninsula; and fourth, the creation of the Alpine Mountain system over the period 90–20 Ma, due to the rotation of the African block and its collision with southern Europe.[25]

The scale of these events means that consideration of the geological controls on landscape development cannot be restricted to the nature and disposition of the rocks that outcrop beneath the land-surface, but must include the dynamic character of the tectonic setting. The major patterns of relief are not merely an expression of recent denudation, or of the relative resistance of outcropping rocks: they reflect the effects of long-term vertical

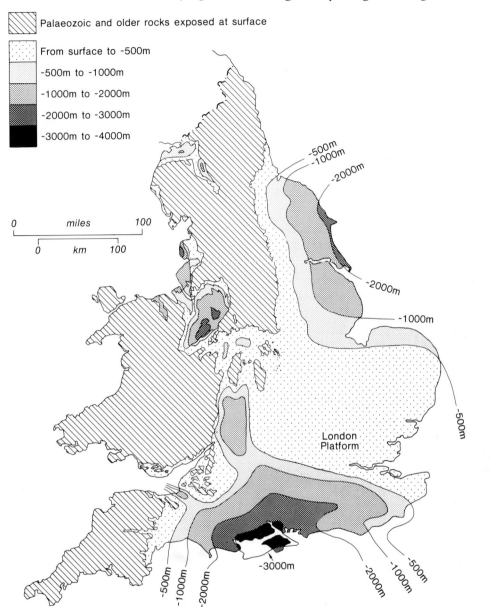

Palaeozoic and older rocks exposed at surface

From surface to -500m

-500m to -1000m

-1000m to -2000m

-2000m to -3000m

-3000m to -4000m

FIG. 1.13 The form of the Palaeozoic floor.

movements, which may have been slow from a human perspective but, when extended over the vastness of geological time, resulted in major displacements. The Pennines are not upstanding merely because of the presence of relatively resistant Carboniferous Limestone and Millstone Grits, but because these particular areas of rock have been differentially elevated with respect to their lateral equivalents which now lie at depth in adjacent basins.

FIG. 1.14 LANDSAT image of a winter (snow) scene covering the area approximately defined by Bournemouth, Worcester, Builth Wells, Swansea, Okehampton and Exeter. Although low cloud and mist obscures central parts of the image, the south coast, Bristol Channel, and River Severn are all clearly visible. The dark area just to the west of the large loop of the Severn is the Forest of Dean, and further north the river is clearly visible passing between the isolated mass of Bredon Hill and the ancient spine of the Malvern Hills. To the south-east of the Severn can be seen the Cotswolds with their irregular west-facing escarpment, the mist-filled Oxford Clay Vale, an extensive area of chalkland with clearly displayed dry valley pattern, and the belted

Furthermore, the creation of persistent upstanding areas—the Pennines and the Welsh massif appear to have been the sites of 'uplands' for most of the last 200 Ma—has influenced subsequent patterns of sedimentation through controls on palaeogeography, thereby determining the distribution of younger rocks, which, in turn, have created the basis for the relief of 'Lowland Britain'. It is important, therefore, to visualize that the English landscape is underlain by a network of major fault-defined blocks that extend beneath the whole of the British Isles and adjacent seas (Figure 1.14); a veritable maze of upward-moving horsts and subsiding grabens, each heavily grained with structural lines produced by long-past episodes of tectonic evolution, which have been in fairly constant motion over the last 200 Ma or more—a process which is now known as 'pulsed tectonism'.[26] The complexities of these foundations are most immediately apparent in the Pennine upwarp, which is not a simple north–south-oriented antiform but a complex assemblage of structures dominated by three variably tilted blocks (Figure 1.12): the Alston and Askrigg Blocks in the north and the Derbyshire Block at the southern end. Elsewhere, simple surface patterns conceal increasing structural complexity with depth.

The closing episode of the long and eventful phase of geological evolution and the beginning of geomorphological development is generally considered to occur in the Upper Cretaceous (70–100 Ma) with the deposition of the Chalk. The Chalk is an extremely pure limestone, up to 1,800 feet (550 metres) thick, thought to have been deposited in *at least* 700 feet (210 metres) of water.[27] The fact that it now forms high ground in southern England (the Chiltern Hills, North Downs, South Downs, Marlborough Downs, for example), reaching 974 feet (297 metres) at Walbury Hill in the Hampshire Downs, gives some impression of the magnitude of subsequent changes in land–sea relationships that have to be envisaged.

The present distribution of Chalk, shown in Figure 1.15, together with its purity, indicates either that most of Britain was submerged by the Upper Cretaceous sea, or that contemporary land areas were providing little sediment because of arid (desert) conditions. Both views have their supporters, but the overwhelming weight of opinion has increasingly favoured a palaeogeographic reconstruction involving almost total submergence, except for some small islands located *above* parts of Highland Britain (Figure 1.15). This reconstruction is not as far-fetched as it sounds, for the differences in elevation

---

landscapes of Weymouth and Purbeck developed on the cores of denuded anticlines. Many lines, or linears, are clearly visible on the image, the most prominent running eastwards across the centre of the image from the South Wales coast via the boundary between the Somerset Levels and the Mendip Hills to the chalklands near the Vale of Wardour. These and other linears in the south-eastern portion of the frame almost certainly represent the expression of reactivated Permo-Triassic rifts. However, the clearest evidence of structural graining occurs in the west, particularly in Devon where the east–west Variscan trend is clearly displayed, and in Wales where strongly developed NE–SW Caledonian trends are visible in the north-west. It is the continuation of these structural networks to the east beneath a cover of younger strata that has led to posthumous folding. (*Reproduced by kind permission of RAE Farnborough.*)

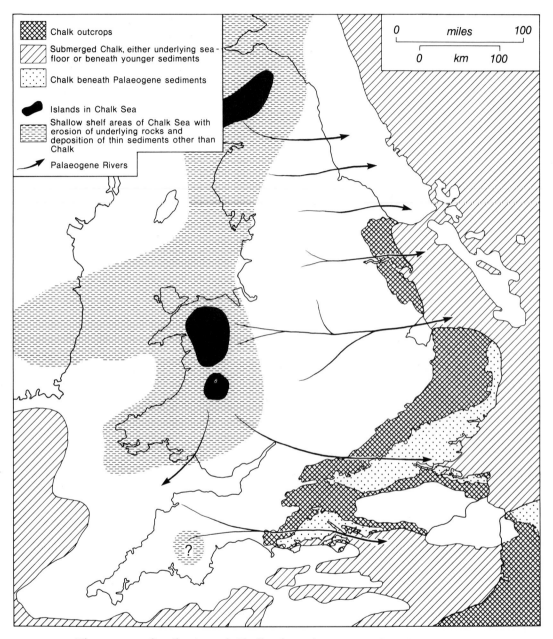

FIG. 1.15 The present distribution of Chalk, the palaeogeography of the Upper Cretaceous (Chalk) sea, and the presumed courses of the early Tertiary (Palaeogene) consequent drainage pattern that developed on the newly emergent Chalk. Areas where Chalk is thought to have been deposited but subsequently removed by denudation are shown in white.

between lowland and upland areas of Britain were certainly much smaller then than they are today, owing to the effects of tectonic activity in the Tertiary. In addition, stratigraphic studies from various parts of the world indicate that the Upper Cretaceous marine transgression appears to have been a global phenomenon, which led to the inundation of many continental areas (Figure 1.16).[28] Thus the idea of an extensive submergence is quite palatable so long as significant post-Cretaceous deformation is accepted.

The Cretaceous submergence is important for two reasons. First, the rise in sea-level, which, in the space of 40 Ma, witnessed an extension of the sea from a restricted and shallow gulf located in the Wealden area to the total inundation of the whole of England, must have resulted in widespread and major marine erosion which planed over the complex structural and lithological patterns created by preceding geological episodes.[29] Second, the subsequent deposition of a thick blanket of Chalk and its associated shallow-water deposits, on top of this marine unconformity, effectively sealed off the past. Thus, ideal conditions were created for a new beginning in landform evolution, for the complexities of the geological fabric were temporarily extinguished and could not re-exert

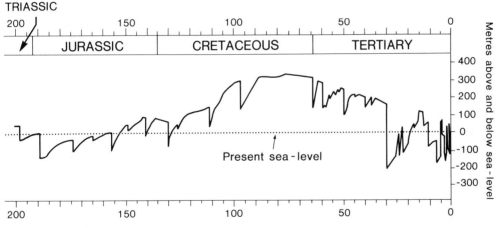

FIG. 1.16 Estimated eustatic changes in sea-level based on seismic investigations of stratigraphy and computation of oceanic ridge volumes (redrawn from Vail, Mitchum and Thompson 1977). The curve should be interpreted as a speculative reconstruction of change, possibly with major errors. Further, the actual fluctuations that occurred at any specific location may have radically departed from the pattern shown, due to local tectonic and isostatic factors. The marked eustatic rise recorded during the Cretaceous is interpreted as a consequence of the formation of the Mid-Atlantic thermal ridge during the early stages of rifting and continental pull-apart associated with the creation of the Atlantic Ocean. The mid-Tertiary fall is considered the product of orogenesis (formation of the Himalayas) and the more recent dramatic fluctuations are interpreted as glacio-eustatic oscillations caused by the growth and decay of continental-scale ice-sheets.

an influence on topographic development until denudation had proceeded through the Cretaceous cover and into the underlying strata.

The Tertiary

About 70 Ma the first important crustal movements of what was to become a fairly long and major tectonic episode led to the emergence of the British Isles. The pattern of uplift was by no means uniform, with individual blocks rising at differing rates and accompanied by the continued downwarping of the basins that underlie the present shallow seas, so that the Britsh Isles began to take on a recognizable form. The shrinking away of the Upper Cretaceous sea progressively revealed a landmass, parts of which had been trimmed smooth by marine agencies, the rest extensively blanketed by a layer of Chalk which thickened away from the former islands. As uplift rates were greatest in the west, the result was an irregular but generally eastward sloping land-surface upon which developed the first drainage pattern. This is envisaged as having included three dominant eastward-flowing trunk rivers, the proto-Dee–Trent, the proto-Thames and the Frome–Solent Rivers (Figure 1.15).[30] These are the ancestors of the present drainage network, for the subsequent 70 Ma of landscape evolution is mainly characterized by subaerial (land) conditions, with continued differential movements dominated by uplift in the west and downwarping in the east. As a consequence of these prolonged subaerial conditions, both the morphological and sedimentological evidence for landscape development are fragmentary, which means that evolutionary interpretations must be largely speculative.

Tertiary landscape evolution is usually considered to include the whole span of landform development from the late Cretaceous emergence to the onset of the Pleistocene (70 Ma–2.5 Ma). The precise duration would have varied slightly over the British Isles depending on the timing of the onset of subaerial conditions. Thus it is considered likely that the shallowly submerged blocks of Highland Britain would have been exposed a little before the areas that now form Lowland Britain. Further, it is worth noting that emergence was a regional phenomenon which did not coincide with either the close of the Cretaceous or cessation in Chalk formation, as deposition of Chalk is known to have continued to the north-east, in the vicinity of Denmark, for some time after 70 Ma, coincident with its removal from parts of Britain.

The great length of the Tertiary landscape development phase (67 Ma) can conveniently be divided into two distinct and unequal parts, the Palaeogene or early Tertiary, and the Neogene or later Tertiary (Table 1.1). The Palaeogene is of considerable importance, not merely on account of its great length (well over 40 Ma) but also because it was characterized by important crustal movements, volcanism, and fairly intense denudation under tropical regimes. The products of this evolutionary phase are classically displayed in southern England where thick Palaeogene sedimentary deposits (mainly sands and clays) rest upon the Chalk in the London and Hampshire Basins (see Figure 1.15), and where the Chalk and other exposed rocks have been thrown into gentle folds ranging in scale from minor ripples to the larger, sharper monoclinal structures of Purbeck and the Isle of

Wight—where the Chalk plunges vertically downwards—and culminating in the Weald–
Artois Anticline which has an amplitude of more than 5,000 feet (1,600 metres). Even
more striking features survive in the South-West Peninsula where three deep down-faulted
basins of Palaeogene age have been identified, the largest of which, the Bovey Basin on the
eastern margin of Dartmoor, is thought to have subsided by about 4,000 feet (1,250
metres) since the Eocene.[31] However, the most dramatic evidence is to be found to the
north-west, in Scotland and Ireland, and serves to provide some indication of what
conditions may have been like in Highland Britain during the early Palaeogene. Both of
these areas experienced widespread volcanic activity between 66 Ma and 54 Ma,
associated with the initial rifting of the northernmost part of the Atlantic Basin, and there
were large volcanoes in Arran and elsewhere, massive dyke development, the outpouring
of basalt lava flows up to 6,000 feet (1,800 metres) thick, and granite intrusions. [32] The
Plateau Basalts still survive as uplands in Northern Ireland and the Western Isles.
However, the fact that these thick lavas were originally poured out over several very
extensive areas and yet survive only as fragments, some of which have foundered by well
over 2,000 feet (600 metres) so as to underlie the sea floor, gives some idea of the scale of
subsequent tectonic activity and denudation.[33] Similarly, the Mourne Granites in Ireland
were originally intruded at a depth of 2,500 feet (800 metres) and now form uplands,[34]
while the granite of northern Arran was emplaced about 58 Ma beneath 8,000 feet (2,500
metres) of strata and yet now forms hills rising to over 2,000 feet (600 metres).[35]

This evidence suggests that any Chalk cover on Highland Britain would have been
rapidly stripped away so as to reveal the underlying heavily grained rocks (Figure 1.14).
Support for this contention is to be found in Northern Ireland, where the basalts are not
everywhere underlain by Chalk, implying that it had been widely removed before the
volcanic episode. Similarly in Devon, the flint gravels that cap the Haldon Hills testify
both to the former existence of Chalk and its removal prior to the mid-Palaeocene, a
conclusion in line with the view that no Chalk has been preserved in the nearby Bovey
Basin.[36] The rapidity of removal is not surprising, for Chalk is prone to attack by both
erosional and weathering processes. The fundamental question that remains to be
resolved, however, is the rate at which denudation proceeded into the underlying, older,
and more resistant rocks, for this would allow the elevation of the base of the Chalk cover,
or Cretaceous sea-floor, to be established. Opinion remains divided on this subject. Early
writers took the view that the Chalk originally lay just above the summits of Highland
Britain, thereby implying a very low rate of landscape reduction during the Tertiary.
Recent research has suggested that areas of moderate relief exposed to subaerial erosion
for the whole span of the Tertiary may have suffered quite significant denudation, so
providing support for the raising of this surface to well above the existing topography, as
is shown in Figure 1.17. Certainly consideration of general erosion rates, as discussed
earlier, suggests that even conservative estimations of denudation support the equivalent
of between 1,000–3,300 feet (300 and 1,000 metres) of overall denudation since the
earliest Tertiary. Although much of this volume can be accounted for in valley excavation,
it is still feasible to envisage the end Cretaceous surface as lying 330 feet (100 metres) or

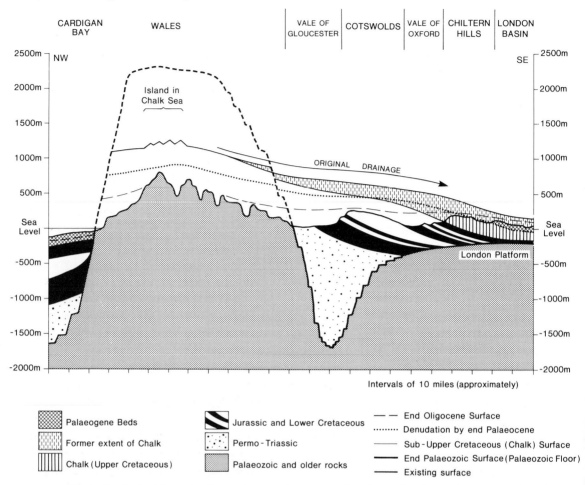

FIG. 1.17 Hypothetical and vertically exaggerated cross-section from Cardigan Bay to London showing the possible relationship of important surfaces to the present topography. Earlier models, e.g.Linton 1951a and Brown 1961, depicted the base of Chalk curving low above the existing summits of Wales. This reconstruction is different in that it attempts to incorporate such ideas as differential movements of fault-bounded blocks, pulsed tectonism in the Tertiary, and intense Palaeogene denudation in Highland Britain.

more above the existing summits. Nevertheless, the relationship of this surface to the present summits remains a matter of speculation.[37]

Denudation of the re-exposed older rocks would have contributed debris via the drainage network to the thick sedimentary sequences that were accumulating in the subsiding basins, and particularly in the shallow sea that overlay the North Sea Basin and periodically encroached over what is now south-eastern England. The remnants of these deposits, which are preserved in the London and Hampshire Basins (Figure 1.15), are important for a number of reasons. First, the nature and interrelationships of the various beds suggest that they were laid down under fluvial and shallow marine conditions over the period 60–35 Ma and in response to frequent changes in coastline position.[38] The main marine transgression was associated with the London Clay Sea (53–49 Ma) which is considered to have inundated the whole area to the south and east of a line joining Lyme Bay to the Wash, including the Weald. The other marine incursions, and there were at least twelve, were apparently mainly restricted to the London and Hampshire Basins, thereby indicating that these synclinal areas, or downwarps, were developing at this time. The complexity of the deduced pattern of sea-level change suggests that tectonic deformation was a major factor, with the basins subsiding and the adjacent areas rising, including the Weald–Artois Anticline. In fact it is possible to argue further, for the deposits in the Hampshire Basin contain sediments which indicate that the Dartmoor Granite had been uncovered by 45 Ma, while those of the London Basin point to the breaching of the Chalk cover on the crest of the growing Weald Arch by about the same time, implying that well over 1,600 feet (500 metres) of rock had already been removed by erosion, including over 1,000 feet (300 metres) of Chalk.[39]

Further evidence for significant early Tertiary denudation is provided by examining the interface between these Palaeogene sediments and the Chalk. This Sub-Palaeogene surface is well displayed at Pegwell Bay, Kent (see Figure 1.18), where tilting due to later tectonic disturbance is clear. In this instance the difference in age of the sediments on either side of the marine-trimmed unconformity is 10 Ma and about 250 feet (75 metres) of Chalk appears to have been removed. Elsewhere in the London and Hampshire Basins, where the time interval is slightly greater, there is evidence for the removal of up to 700 feet (210 metres) of Chalk before burial. The significance of this Sub-Palaeogene surface is not merely confined to the evolutionary perspective but has relevance in the contemporary landscape. It can be clearly recognized fringing the present Palaeogene outcrop where it has been exposed through the stripping away of the overlying cover which has concealed it for between 40 and 60 Ma.[40] Indeed it is now considered likely that much of the overall form of the chalklands reflects the remodelling of this recently exhumed early Tertiary erosion feature (Figure 1.19).

The evidence that the Weald–Artois Anticline was well developed in the early Tertiary is contrary to the view expressed in most traditional texts which consider it a mid-Tertiary (late Oligocene–early Miocene) feature. Certainly the fact that both the Chalk and Palaeogene strata are folded tended to support such a conclusion, while the presence of small east–west secondary folds (Figure 1.12) was seen to be indicative of a brief phase of compression, their lack of development to the north of the London Basin Syncline being interpreted as clear evidence of how the shallowly buried 'London Platform' element of the Palaeozoic floor (Figure 1.13) had restricted the flexuring of surface strata.[41] However, this reconstruction resulted in problems, for much of the drainage pattern of the Weald and Hampshire Basin flows to the sea across these secondary structures, thereby producing widespread discordant relationships (such as those of the Rivers Arun, Adur, and Sussex Ouse). As the natural product of long-term drainage development is concordant drainage, with rivers oriented along synclines, faults, shatter belts, and the

FIG. 1.18 Cliff-section at Pegwell Bay, Kent, showing shallow marine Thanet Sands (Palaeocene) resting on an inclined marine-trimmed unconformity cut in Chalk. This is the Sub-Palaeogene surface shown in Figure 1.19, and has clearly suffered warping since burial about 60 Ma. The equivalent of this feature has been extensively exhumed around the flanks of the London and Hampshire Basins where it produces a clearly identifiable landscape element.

outcrop of less-resistant strata, the frequent occurrence of discordance required explanation. While the similar discordant relationsips that occur widely in other parts of England can simply and easily be explained as the product of the superimposition of rivers from the gently inclined Chalk cover on to pre-existing structures in the underlying rocks, such an explanation could not be applied to south-eastern England because the fold pattern clearly post-dates the deposition of Chalk. As the envisaged rapid growth of folds would surely have displaced the existing drainage pattern, it proved necessary to advocate a convoluted explanation whereby mid-Tertiary drainage derangement resulted in a 'new', east–west-oriented, concordant pattern in the Neogene, which survived until it was largely swamped by a marine inundation in the Plio-Pleistocene. This 'Calabrian' incursion was presumed to have flooded most of southern England, except for an island above the axis of the

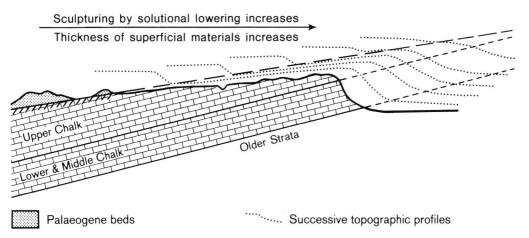

FIG. 1.19 Cross-section through the Chiltern Hills Chalk cuesta showing the relationship of the Sub-Palaeogene surface to the present chalkland topography, and how the lowering of adjacent clay vales during the Neogene and Pleistocene has caused scarp retreat and dramatically accentuated escarpment form.

Weald, and to have planed across the existing land-surface to an elevation of 600–690 feet (183–210 metres). When it withdrew, a new drainage network developed on the marine plane which flowed *down* the slope of the surface and *across* the truncated folds, thereby causing the discordant relationships of today.[42]

The need to abandon this model of landscape evolution has arisen from many factors: a better understanding of tectonic mechanisms; the indications that surface flexure patterns may be related to deeply buried Variscan structures in the Palaeozoic floor; the recognition of an increased variety of stress-inducing mechanisms; the knowledge that the tectonic development of the Alps took 70 Ma; and the fact that evidence for a Plio-Pleistocene marine inundation is poorly preserved and apparently restricted to the London Basin, an area without discordant drainage.[43] As a consequence the fold pattern of southern England is now interpreted as the product of long-lasting pulsed tectonism, beginning in the Late Cretaceous but with major pulses throughout the Palaeogene to the mid-Tertiary.[44] The drainage pattern of the area is also considered to be inherited from the Palaeogene, for although the initial drainage system that developed on the newly emergent Chalk was obliterated by the Palaeogene transgressions, the withdrawal of the sea over the period 49–30 Ma witnessed the re-establishment of a broadly similar pattern, including a proto-Thames and Frome–Solent River, with tributaries draining the flanks of the Weald–Artois Anticline and Hampshire Basin. These are now thought to have been capable of maintaining their courses in the face of pulsed fold growth and to have survived in modified form to the present day as antecedent streams.[45]

The various lines of evidence for landscape evolution during the Palaeogene suggest that by the mid-Oligocene (30 Ma) the general form of Britain had been largely blocked out, much of the tectonic deformation had been completed, and denudation had removed much of the Chalk cover and had already achieved considerable sculpturing of the underlying strata in upland areas. The evidence for tropical conditions is found in laterite deposits sandwiched between basalt layers in Northern Ireland and in the floral remains found in the Palaeogene sediments of the London and Hampshire Basins,[46] as well as in the sarsen stones that litter certain chalklands, particularly the Marlborough Downs, and have been used to such great effect in the megalithic monuments of Stonehenge and Avebury (Figure 1.20). These extremely hard silica-cemented sandstone blocks have been found on the Chalk from Devon to Kent, and are thought to be the remnants of a sheet, or sheets, of surficial duricrust known as 'silcrete'.[47] They are considered to have been formed within Palaeogene sediments by soil processes acting beneath a low-relief ground surface suffering a tropical climate characterized by seasonal rainfall. Their age is uncertain, but many writers favour development during the early Oligocene.[48] Thus the fact that these sarsen stones still litter some of the higher chalklands has been used to suggest that a low-relief Oligocene land surface lay not far above the present highest chalkland summits, that

FIG. 1.20 Sarsen stones at Avebury. These extremely hard cemented sandstone blocks were originally part of extensive sheets of silcrete formed in the Palaeogene by soil processes operating beneath a low relief land surface experiencing tropical climatic conditions. It is usual for them to display irregular surfaces and in many cases root-holes are clearly visible. (Reproduced by kind permission of Fay Godwin's Photo Files.)

is at 820–1,080 feet (250–330 metres). Where such a surface, or surfaces, lay over the rest of England is unknown, for with the exception of the deposits preserved in the London and Hampshire Basins, the only Palaeogene sediments identified occur either off-shore or in deep tectonic basins (such as the Bovey and Petrockstow Basins).[49] In view of the known efficacy of later denudation it appears reasonable to argue that it stood above the present topography, as is shown in Figure 1.17. However, the survival of Palaeogene gravels on the Haldon Hills and ancient soils on the Blackdown Hills[50] suggests that this surface must coincide with the present summits, at least in this area, thereby indicating that the west Dorset–east Devon region was characterized by extremely stable conditions for much of the Tertiary. Such an interpretation would appear to lend support to the widely known hypothesis that the tors of Dartmoor (Figure 1.3), as well as those of the Pennines, are the product of deep weathering under Palaeogene tropical conditions.[51] However, although tors are known to develop under tropical conditions, and probably did develop on Dartmoor and elsewhere during the early Tertiary, there is little evidence to suggest that the present-day tors developed at that time. In fact most of the available evidence suggests that they are of Pleistocene age.[52]

Although the Oligocene may have begun with a tropical climate, two major changes in environmental conditions are thought to have soon occurred: a change to a warm, humid, temperate climate (Figure 1.10) and a marked fall in sea-level (Figure 1.15).[53] The evidence for these changes is heavily based on the results of submarine studies carried out in the North Sea Basin and elsewhere, for the on-shore sedimentological record contained in the Hampshire Basin dies away in the Mid-Oligocene and the preservation of Neogene deposits is restricted to survivals in limestone solution pipes in the Peak District (the Brassington Formation)[54] and Kent (the Lenham Beds).[55] Thus the Miocene and Pliocene continue to be the 'lost phase' of geomorphological development—a 20 Ma gap in the record thought to be characterized by subaerial denudation. There has been much speculation about the nature and scale of Neogene landform evolution, and it is true to say that the significance of this phase has been steadily reduced in recent years as emphasis has increasingly been placed on the role of Palaeogene denudation.[56] Much of the earlier work was dominated by attempts to identify flights of erosion surfaces—consisting of valley-side benches, the flat tops of spurs and ridges, and areas where summits rise to approximately the same elevation—which were then arranged into denudation staircases with each 'flat' or 'tread' representing the product of a phase of stability. The overall conformity of summit levels above 700 feet (213 metres) in Lowland Britain was interpreted as the dissected remains of a low-relief surface produced by Neogene denudation and variously termed the 'Summit Surface', 'Mio-Pliocene peneplain', or 'late Pliocene land-surface'.[57] Study of the higher and more rugged terrains of Highland Britain resulted in the recognition of several equivalent levels, a series of erosional staircases envisaged as having been produced by cycles of landscape reduction, whereby surfaces fashioned during earlier phases were subsequently denuded by later cycles in the creation of new lower surfaces.[58] Such ideas are now largely discredited and instead it is fashionable to envisage that the final episodes of pulsed tectonism in the south, coupled with the change in climate and the eustatic fall in sea-level, resulted in increased fluvial denudation and accelerated river incision, thereby starting a process of relief accentuation which was to be reinforced during the Pleistocene. Thus the patterns of scarps and vales began to develop during the Neogene, and valley-side slopes became steepened. Nevertheless, the topographic landscape at the close of the Neogene would have been much gentler than that of today.

The Pleistocene

The short span of the Pleistocene is undoubtedly the most important of the phases of landform development. The process of relief enhancement begun in the Neogene was dramatically reinforced as a consequence of uplift, rapid changes in climate (Figure 1.4) and frequent reductions in sea-level, sometimes to at least −330 feet (−100 metres). Fluvial denudation caused the widespread lowering of clay vales, which, in turn, resulted in both the emphasizing of escarpments and their retreat (Figure 1.19). Differences in rock resistance exerted an increasing impact on topographic form, and old buried features, such as the Pre-Cambrian rock masses of Charnwood Forest and the Malvern Hills, progressively emerged as their covering of weaker rocks was removed.

The significance of the Pleistocene is due almost entirely to the direct and indirect effects of glaciation. Although significant fluctuations in polar ice-coverage began in the Pliocene (Figure 1.10), they became particularly important in the Middle and Upper Pleistocene (Figure 1.4).[59] Despite much research there remains considerable uncertainty about the pattern and relative significance of events within this recent phase of Earth history, for the correlation of sequences between areas is still fraught with difficulties.[60] Nevertheless, enough is now known to abandon the classic 'four glacial' model of Penck and Bruckner in favour of multi-glacial interpretations. Although up to twenty-three cool/cold phases have been identified, exactly how many of these climatic deteriorations led to glacier and ice-sheet development in Britain has yet to be ascertained, for the natural characteristics of ice erosion have meant that each succeeding ice advance has tended either to mask or to destroy the evidence for earlier advances. To date, firm evidence has been found for five distinct ice advances, four of them involving continental-scale ice-sheets, and there is additional but less secure evidence for two earlier ice advances. The most recent episode, a relatively minor advance in what is known as the Late Glacial, merely resulted in local ice-cap development in Scotland and the Lake District—an episode that has come to be called the Loch Lomond Re-advance. The preceding Last Glacial, or Devensian as it is known in Britain, appears to have resulted in two distinct ice-sheet advances (Figure 1.4), while the earlier Wolstonian and Anglian glaciations apparently had single but rather more extensive ice-sheets, whose margins fluctuated in response to minor variations in climate, thus giving rise to complicated patterns of minor advances, or stadials, separated by retreat phases, or inter-stadials. Evidence for an earlier, Beestonian, ice advance has increased in recent years and there are suggestions for a much older glaciation during the Baventian (Figure 1.4).[61]

Present knowledge about the former extent of these ice-sheets is shown in Figure 1.21,

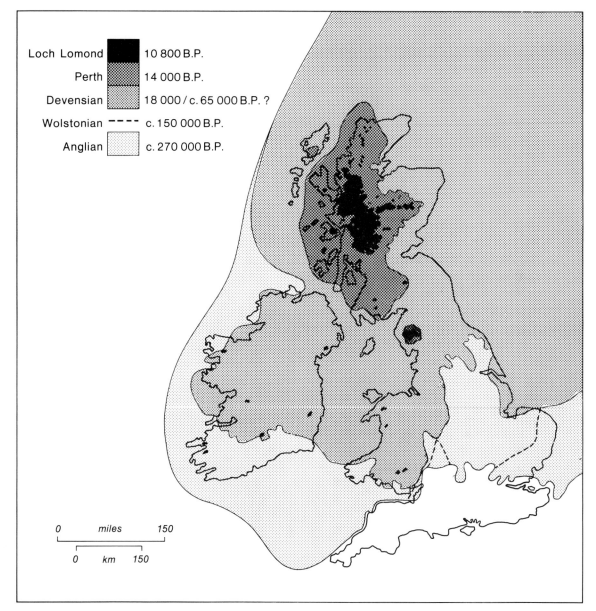

Loch Lomond █ 10 800 B.P.

Perth ▨ 14 000 B.P.

Devensian ░ 18 000 / c. 65 000 B.P. ?

Wolstonian – – – – c. 150 000 B.P.

Anglian ░ c. 270 000 B.P.

0   miles   150

0   km   150

FIG. 1.21 Glacial limits in the British Isles.

together with the estimated dates of their maximum extent. The most recent—the local valley glaciers associated with the Loch Lomond Re-advance—reached their maximum extent at about 10,800 BP.[62] Before the start of ice accumulation in about 11,500 BP it is thought that the whole of the British Isles may have been ice-free for about 1,200 years following the wastage of the ice associated with the previous Devensian glaciation. The extent of Devensian ice shown in Figure 1.21 represents a compromise of various views, as there appear to have been two distinct ice advances which reached roughly similar limits in 18,000 BP and *c.* 65,000 BP—two events which were almost certainly separated by temperate ice-free conditions. The earlier of these two advances is known to have extended slightly further to the south in both eastern England and the Cheshire Basin,[63] but the exact ice limit in South Wales, together with its age, remains a matter of controversy.[64] The so-called 'Lammermuir Limit', which was once thought to be another, and later, advance into northern England, has now been rejected, and even the Perth Re-advance, dated at 14,000 BP (Figure 1.21), is now considered merely to represent a temporary check in the overall wasting progress of the Devensian ice.[65] It is not surprising, therefore, that the extent of the early Devensian ice-sheet shown in Figure 1.5 is also a compromise between 'minimum' and 'maximum' ice-coverage models, the latter envisaging a continuous mass of ice joining Europe to Greenland.

The area covered by Devensian ice in Britain is the area of the Newer Drift (Figure 1.22), and it is in the lowland areas within this zone that the most clearly formed glacial deposition landforms are to be found such as kames, kettles, eskers, moraines, and drumlins. The older drift terrains to the south of the Devensian ice limit do not display these landforms, for they have largely been refashioned by other processes, the former presence of ice being mainly signalled by extensive and thick spreads of till and outwash gravel. The youngest of these earlier advances, the Wolstonian Glaciation, is variously dated between 150,000 BP and 200,000 BP, and is thought to have covered the Midlands extensively, as far south as the Chiltern Hills escarpment (Figure 1.21).[66] However, the authenticity of this glaciation has been challenged in recent years. Its former extension across East Anglia to southern Essex has been rejected in the last decade,[67] its pre-eminence in the Midlands is now questioned,[68] and its extent in the west has yet to be proved.[69] The yet older Anglian Glaciation, of 270,000 BP or earlier, is at present thought to have been the most extensive ice advance, reaching the Scilly Isles in the west and extending as far as north London in the east and possibly even penetrating into the Straits of Dover.[70] The margin of the Anglian ice is the presently accepted Glacial Limit, and suggestion of more extensive glaciation[71] is discounted for lack of credible evidence.

These repeated ice advances and retreats caused dramatic changes to the physical landscape, both directly and indirectly, for during full glacials, ice thicknesses were measurable in thousands of feet; for instance, the surface of the Devensian ice is thought to have been at 5,700 feet (1,750 metres) over the Southern Uplands of Scotland,[72] and this was a relatively small ice-sheet! In highland areas, ice-flow during buildup phases was confined to pre-existing valleys which were dramatically transformed into deep glacial troughs, many containing strings of lakes in over-deepened basins, while obstruction to ice-flow resulted in ice-streams spilling across ridges and divides so as to create new valley patterns, as in the Lake District.[73] Where not confined, the ice produced heavily ice-moulded and smoothed landscapes.

While such smoothed landscapes bear clear testimony to the power of glaciation, the significance of the Pleistocene ice-sheets in fashioning lowland areas is equally great, even

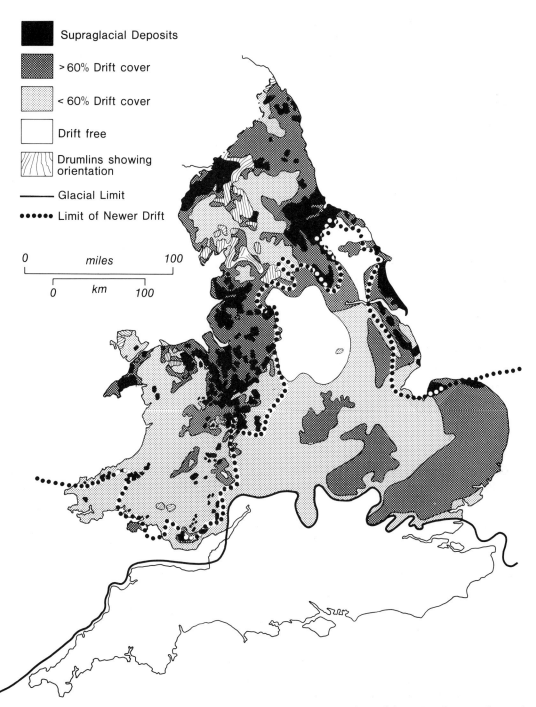

Legend:

- Supraglacial Deposits
- > 60% Drift cover
- < 60% Drift cover
- Drift free
- Drumlins showing orientation
- —— Glacial Limit
- •••• Limit of Newer Drift

Scale: 0 — miles — 100
0 — km — 100

FIG. 1.22 The extent of glacial deposits in England and Wales (adapted from Boulton *et al.* 1977).

though it is often less conspicuous. Clay vales were considerably denuded, as were areas of constricted flow, such as the Vale of York and the Cheshire Plain, and intense denudation also occurred where ice-streams converged, as for example in the case of the Wash (Figure 1.23). Many escarpment zones were also totally refashioned or buried, a feature most clearly displayed by the Chalk escarpment. To the south of the Glacial Limit near Hitchin the Chalk forms the high cuesta of the Chiltern Hills, rising to over 800 feet (250 metres). A few miles to the north it has been lowered by more than 300 feet (100 metres) and largely buried by till, while over most of northern East Anglia and the Wash the Chalk has no surface expression at all.

Episodes of erosion by ice and sub-glacial water flows were followed by extensive deposition of assorted deposits during wastage phases. The volume of such deposits in the British Isles has recently been estimated at 2,000 cubic kilometres.[74] They are especially thick and extensive in Cheshire, Yorkshire, and East Anglia (Figure 1.22), where their removal would result in extensive invasions by the sea. Thus the effects of ice-sheet erosion and deposition on the soft rock terrains of Lowland Britain combined to eradicate pre-existing patterns of topography and drainage in some areas completely and to obliterate others through burial. Even the network of major eastward-flowing trunk rivers which had been slowly evolving over millions of years through drainage adjustments, such as river capture, were to suffer major modification as a consequence of these repeated ice advances. The ancestral Thames used to flow to the North Sea via a route that lay above Hertford and Colchester until it was dammed by the Anglian ice-sheet and deflected to its present position.[75] Similar drainage modifications through pro-glacial lake development have been postulated for many areas, although doubts have been raised concerning the huge size of some of the proposed lakes. The Wolstonian ice-sheet is thought to have dammed the River Soar, a former tributary of the Dee–Trent, resulting in the creation of a huge lake in the south Midlands, called Lake Harrison, which overflowed to the south and south-west and eventually led to the establishment of the Warwickshire Avon, a river which now flows in the opposite direction to the original pre-glacial drainage pattern.[76] The Dee–Trent was similarly dismembered, the Upper Severn headwater tributary being deflected southwards via the Ironbridge Gorge as a consequence of the creation of Lake Lapworth in the Devensian;[77] while in the east Midlands the repeated formation of pro-glacial lakes, such as Lake Humber, led to the progressive deflection of the Trent from its original exit near the Wash to its present route via the Humber.[78]

Although glaciation was the most dramatic feature of the Pleistocene, other important changes were occurring. Each glacial episode was accompanied by a significant fall in sea-level, often by more than 330 feet (100 metres), which led to the repeated exposure of the surrounding sea-floors and the retreat of the coastline to a position west of Cornwall (Figure 1.5). During these phases the river networks extended over the floors of the North Sea and English Channel so as to form what can be called the 'Greater Seine' and 'Thames–Rhine' systems, and it was the latter, swollen with glacial melt-waters and dammed by grounded ice-sheets, that for periods discharged southwards and thereby assisted in the development of the Dover Straits (Figure 1.5). The magnitude, frequency, and duration of sea-level oscillations remains a matter of conjecture, partly because of the complex interrelationships of global and local factors that influence sea-level change, and partly because each fluctuation in sea-level tended to destroy the evidence for previous stands of the sea.[79] Fragments of raised beaches, rarely either above 100 feet (30 metres) or apparently older than the Hoxnian (Figure 1.4), indicate interglacial high sea-levels, while deeply incised trenches (buried channels) beneath the lower courses of existing river valleys point to the incision generated by low 'Glacial' sea-levels.[80] What is clear, however, is that the repeated fluctuations in sea-level stimulated fluvial denudation inland, thereby assisting in the progressive accentuation of relative relief through the Pleistocene. They also resulted in major coastal sculpturing and contributed greatly to the creation of the present coastline; for while the Post-Glacial (Flandrian) rise in sea-level has caused significant coastline modelling in the 'soft rock' and 'drift' terrains of the east, in the west it has often been able to do little more than exhume and re-utilize former shore-line features, such as shore platforms and cliff-lines.[81]

Even more important than these dramatic fluctuations in land–sea relationships were the effects of periglaciation. The advance and retreat of each ice-sheet was first preceded by and then followed by a phase of periglaciation, or tundra conditions, while in extra-glacial England repeated phases of periglaciation were able to operate unhindered by the erosional and depositional impacts of glacial ice. The main features of such conditions are permanently frozen subsoil, or permafrost, and summer thawing of the surface, the latter combining with snow-melt to yield a decidedly unstable or mobile 'active' layer which will flow or slide downslope. Periglacial conditions, therefore, result in both the release of large volumes of water during the spring thaw *and* the supply of considerable quantities of debris to valley floors through surface sludging processes, called solifluction, which are aided by the general lack of vegetation.[82] Thus the cold phases of the Pleistocene were characterized by both valley downcutting and terrace accumulation, with relatively little apparently happening during the more heavily vegetated interglacial episodes.[83] This discovery has disturbed chronological studies considerably in recent years, for the traditional view was that river terraces were the product of high interglacial sea-levels, and were therefore consequences of warm conditions. Now terraces are increasingly recognized as cold-condition accumulations caused by climatically induced variations in river regime (palaeohydrological variations) in which a single major change in environmental conditions can result in the 'complex response' of several terraces.[84]

The evidence for periglacial fashioning is therefore writ large upon the landscape, particularly where permeable strata were made impermeable through permafrost development. Thus the gorges and ravines of the Carboniferous Limestone uplands, including Cheddar Gorge, owe much to the sculpturing achieved by seasonal melt-waters (Figure 1.8). The same is true of the amphitheatre-shaped coombes that scallop the Chalk escarpments and the long and winding systems of relic dry valleys which, although most dramatically developed on the Chalk (Figure 1.6), also occur on other normally permeable limestones and sandstones (such as the Carboniferous Limestone of the Pennines, the Oolites of the Cotswolds, the Lower Greensand cuestas of Surrey and Kent). If a chalkland

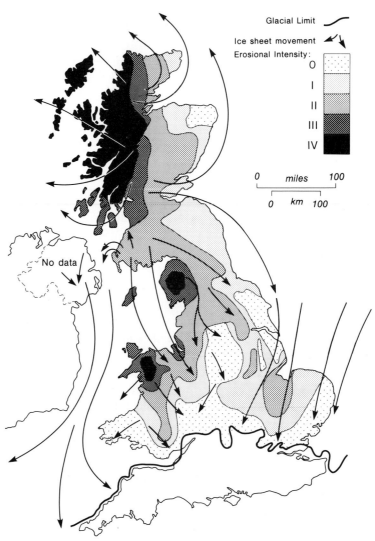

FIG. 1.23 Patterns of ice-sheet movement and glacial erosion (figure adapted from Boulton *et al.* 1977; table giving explanation of zones of erosional intensity is that advocated in Clayton 1974).

Zones of glacial erosion

Zone	Lowlands	Uplands
O	No erosion Head on weathered rocks and slopes Outwash in concavities Rare occurrences of till on weathered rock	No erosion Outwash on valley floors Solifluxion deposits on slopes Boulder fields and tors on divides

I	Ice erosion confined to detailed or subordinate modifications
	  Concavities drift mantled but convexities may show some ice moulding
	  Occasional roches moutonnées
	  Ice-scoured bluffs in favourable locations
		Ice erosion confined to detailed or subordinate modifications
		  Suitable valley slopes ice steepened
		  Entrenched meanders and spurs converted to rock knobs
		  Interfluves still commonly *Zone* O

II	Extensive excavation along main flowlines so that concavities may be drift free or floored by outwash or post-glacial deposits. Isolated obstacles may be given ovoid or cutwater forms if of soft rock, or crag-and-tail with associated scour troughs if hard. Margins of larger masses converted to ice-scoured bluffs or planar slopes	Conversion of pre-glacial valleys to troughs common, but usually confined to those of direction concordant with ice flow Some diffluence; transfluence rare Interfluves may be *Zone* I or even *Zone* O, and separated from troughs by well-marked shoulders
III	Pre-glacial forms no longer recognizable but replaced by tapered or bridge interfluves with planar slopes on soft rocks, and by rock drumlins and knock-and-lochan topography on hard	Transformation of valleys to troughs comprehensive giving compartmented relief with isolated plateau or mountain blocks. *Zone* O may still persist on interfluves at sufficiently great heights
IV	Complete domination of streamlined flow forms even over structural influences	Ice moulding extends to high summits Upland surfaces given knock-and-lochan topography (sometimes of great amplitude at lower levels) Lower divides extensively pared or streamlined

dry valley is viewed in section, as is often possible along the Kent and Sussex coasts, several features are normally visible: the extent of frost-shattered rock; the presence of soliflucted Chalk (Coombe Rock), the layering of the superficial materials beneath the valley floor indicating several phases of slope activity; and the irregularity of some of the junctions (cryurtobation structures) which indicates convection within a mobile layer.[85]

Enormous volumes of material must have moved downslope under periglaciation conditions so as to be reworked by fluvial activity, for solifluction deposits (head) are widespread and sometimes exceed 30 feet (10 metres) in thickness. As most of the surviving deposits appear to be the product of the four most recent cold episodes—Late Glacial Zones I and III (12,300–12,000 BP and 10,800–10,300 BP) and the two main Devensian ice advances (Figure 1.5)—one can only speculate on the total amount of work achieved by an, as yet, unspecified number of arctic phases.

Solifluction activity was not the only feature of the Pleistocene cold environments. Freeze–thaw attack of rock outcrops created cliffs (scars) and screes, and may well have been largely responsible for the exposure and fashioning of tors.[86] Landsliding was widespread along escarpment zones[87] and extensive, and possibly thick, layers of loess were deposited in southern areas as silts were blown westwards from the exposed floor of

FIG. 1.24 Major alluvial spreads in eastern England (from Steers 1964).

the North Sea Basin and from the Continent.[88] Thus, periglaciation had two main consequences: the accentuation of relief in upland areas and an overall smoothing of lowland topography so as to create the periglacially moulded landscapes of extra-glacial England.[89]

The Holocene or Recent

The brief duration of the Holocene, a mere 10,000 years, should not be allowed to conceal the importance of this phase of landform development. The waning of the Devensian ice-sheet resulted in a northward shift in vegetation belts and an exceedingly rapid rise in sea-level from about −330 feet (−100 metres) at 15,000 BP to close to present sea-level at 2,500 BP, although the detailed pattern of change varies regionally depending on the differential effects of local warping due to tectonic movements and isostatic responses.[90] The sea can be envisaged as having advanced quickly over the exposed sea-floors, penetrating the Dover Straits by 9,600 BP and achieving the final separation of England from the Continent in 8,600 BP when the link between northern East Anglia and Holland was finally submerged.[91]

This rapid rise in sea-level resulted in the reworking of the large quantities of loose superficial materials which had been deposited to the south of the Devensian limit, and it was these that were used to create the major coastal sediment structures of Dawlish Warren, Chesil Beach, Dungeness, and Orfordness.[92] The sea also flooded the low-lying areas now occupied by Romney Marsh, Pevensey Levels, the Somerset Levels, and the Fens (Figure 1.24), as well as the lower reaches of river valleys, so as to create an indented coastline of embayments and rias, which subsequently became filled with alluvial sediments. Elsewhere, the reoccupance of former shoreline features allowed the sea to recommence its sculpturing of coastal form. This has been most dramatic in the south and east, where the freshness of cliff-lines (such as the Seven Sisters) and the historical record of 'lost' villages in East Anglia and Holderness, clearly indicate that retreat can be measured in miles.[93] However, the most dramatic example of coastal erosion remains the breaching of the Chalk ridge between Purbeck and the Needles so as to dismember the Frome–Solent River and create the Isle of Wight.[94]

The obvious magnitude of recent changes along the coastline has tended to focus attention away from contemporaneous developments inland. Here the changes in vegetation and climate, together with the explosive growth in the geomorphological impact of man, have combined in further major landform modification. Despite the fact that little integrated work has been undertaken on anthropogeomorphology in this country, it is clear that the 'direct' and 'indirect' effects of man's activities have caused significant changes. The thousands of burial mounds (tumuli) and earthworks represent the relics of early stages of man-made landform creation, which were later to become much more widespread and important, as is testified by the extensive 'ridge-and-furrow' landscapes of the English Midlands, the thousands of small 'marl pits' that pock the land-surface (37,000 have been reported from Norfolk alone), and the creation of the Norfolk Broads through the removal of 25.5 million cubic metres of material by peat digging before AD 1300.[95] However, the major changes were consequent upon the technological developments of the Industrial Revolution: the cuttings and embankments of the canal and railway networks, the canalization of rivers, the excavation of ports, mineral extraction, and urbanization. The ubiquitous colliery spoil heaps, now largely remodelled as a consequence of the 1966 Aberfan disaster, are a testimony to man's recent impact on the physical landscape. Man is now the dominant force in landform change, as is illustrated by the fact that surface mineral extraction alone has accounted for the *annual* removal of over 250 million tonnes of material over the last decade, while about 80 million tonnes of spoil, rubbish, and waste are dumped on the ground surface each year, much of it as 'made ground' or 'reconstituted land'.[96] It is not really surprising, therefore, that the humorous French classification of recent sedimentation into *Poubellien supérieur (à plastique)* and *Poubellien inférieur (sans plastique)*, or Upper and Lower Dustbinian (with and without plastic) is becoming increasingly apt.[97]

The indirect effects of man's activities, while less obvious to the eye, are no less important. Forest clearances and changes in land-use practices (including urbanization) have resulted in marked variations in the patterns of erosion, transportation, and deposition, thereby causing the widespread development of man-modified landforms.[98] Two possibly linked examples of these impacts are the occurrence of truncated or immature soil profiles due to accelerated soil erosion in historic and prehistoric times, and the widespread and extensive development of flood-plains.

It may appear surprising that the formation of flood-plains—among the youngest of landforms—continues to prove a matter of heated controversy. Most English streams wander across broad belts of alluvium contained within valleys which also meander across the landscape. The difference in wavelengths of the stream and valley meanders has been recognized for over a century and eventually led to the widely supported 'underfit stream' model of flood-plain development, in which the creation of meandering valleys was envisaged to have been achieved by swollen rivers which subsequently shrank to their present size, the change in stream competence resulting in sedimentation and the

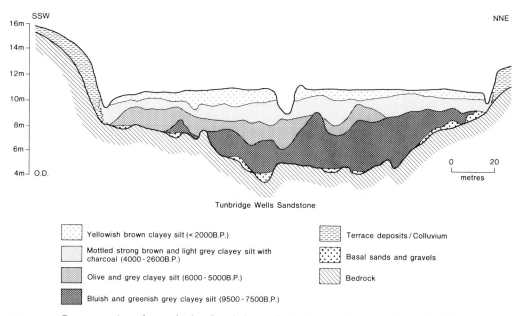

SSW
NNE

Tunbridge Wells Sandstone

Yellowish brown clayey silt (< 2000B.P.)

Mottled strong brown and light grey clayey silt with charcoal (4000 - 2600B.P.)

Olive and grey clayey silt (6000 - 5000B.P.)

Bluish and greenish grey clayey silt (9500 - 7500B.P.)

Terrace deposits / Colluvium

Basal sands and gravels

Bedrock

FIG. 1.25 Cross-section through the floodplain of the Sussex Ouse at Sharpsbridge, Central Weald, showing the irregular sub-alluvial surface and preliminary interpretation of alluvial stratigraphy (from Burrin and Scaife 1984).

accumulation of alluvium.[99] This change in size has been explained by a number of factors, mainly climate-based, such as decreased rainfall, reduced storminess, the disappearance of frozen subsoil conditions, or greater evapo-transpiration, which could, either singly or in combination, have resulted in decreased run-off. Recent research, however, has indicated that some rethinking may be necessary, because of the irregular form of the sub-alluvial surfaces and the character of the fill sequences (Figure 1.25). Most flood-plains apparently began forming about 9,500 BP and attained their present dimensions at some time between 5,000 and 2,000 BP.[100] In the Weald these landforms appear to be composed largely of reworked loess[101] and the depositional sequence, as elucidated by pollen analysis, indicates alternating episodes of accumulation and erosion which may well reflect the impact of man-induced soil erosion.[102] If this conclusion should be borne out by further field studies, then the impact of early man on landforms will have to be re-evaluated and emphasized.

Conclusion

Just as landforms have continued to evolve in response to changing environmental conditions, so interpretations of landform development also must evolve in the light of advances in knowledge. The shape of the topographic landscape of England may have changed only in detail over the last three decades, even along the coast and despite the efforts of man, and yet the shaping of ideas about how it developed has progressed dramatically through the acceptance of new concepts and methodologies, such as the implications of plate tectonics, the application of absolute dating techniques, the better appreciation of the scale of recent environmental change, and the further undersanding of process–form relationships, particularly under cold-climate conditions. Both the English landscape and contemporary interpretations of landscape evolution are therefore palimpsests, with some elements that are 'modern' and others that are relic. For example, the inheritance of upland 'erosion surfaces' still survives in the literature, while the full implications of the ideas of 'complex response' have yet to be ascertained with respect to river terrace development. These trends will continue into the future and may well result in significant reappraisal of the evolutionary sequence outlined above, for there remain considerable areas of uncertainty: for example, the significance of man as a geomorphological agent; the number, age, and geomorphological significance of glaciations in the Pleistocene; the pattern and impact of sea-level change; the significance of fluvial responses to climatic change; the nature of landform evolution in the Neogene; the significance of Palaeogene denudation. Even our understanding of the ways in which the geological fabric has influenced landform development may have to be modified in the near future as a result of the availability of LANDSAT remote sensing imagery which has revealed the presence of hitherto unsuspected structural features (linears).

Much has been written about the English topographic landscape: the shape of the hills and valleys, the variable colour of the soils, the differing nature of the underlying rocks, the character of the rivers, and the beauty of the coastline, where the relationships of geology and scenery are plainly displayed for all to see. As has been shown in this chapter, the scenic diversity that has so often been commented upon in the literature is essentially due to the intraction of two major factors: the complexity of the geological fabric and the variable nature of recent sculpturing episodes. Both of these are explicable in terms of marginality. That portion of the Earth's crust which eventually became fashioned into England was often marginally located with respect to many of the significant formative events that have helped to shape Europe. It was on the fringes of the Alpine upheaval and was partly affected by both the Variscan and Caledonian orogenies. Thus elements of Stille's threefold division of Europe into Palaeo-Europe (Caledonides), Ur Europe (Variscides), and Meso-Europe (intervening areas) are all represented within the confines of this small country. Oversimplified, this means that the Lake District has some geological affinities with Scandinavia, the South-West Peninsula with Brittany and the Ardennes, and East Anglia with the North European Plain. It is the juxtaposition of these zones that is the main cause of both the structural complexity to the west of the Tees–Exe line and the scenic variety. In addition, the area was located near the edge of the Atlantic Rift which has meant both continued tectonic activity and a marginal position with reference to the European mainland. Thus the impacts of Quarternary sea-level change have been particularly significant for landscape development, and the struggle between 'continental' and 'maritime' influences has resulted in frequent and dramatic fluctuations in climate. Finally, the area was located at the edge of the major Pleistocene ice-sheets, so that northern parts of the country bear the scars of repeated glaciation while the southernmost portion has been moulded only by periglacial activity. The gentle topographic scenery of England is thus the product of a long, varied, and often traumatic evolutionary history.

2

Man and landscape in Britain
6000 BC–AD 400

B. W. CUNLIFFE

MAN's power to alter his environment has been used in Britain with increasing effect for the last 8,000 years. In the beginning, simple chipped stone axes and the controlled use of fire enabled the forest cover to be attacked for the purposes of manipulating food supply: nowadays machines mould the landscape, and soil is treated as little more than a convenient medium for holding the chemicals in which crops are grown. To a conservationist there is much to bewail about the present state of the countryside; to an archaeologist and historian the present is merely the best-understood phase of a process, each stage of which holds its own fascination.

Much of the story of the last 8,000 years is the preserve of the archaeologist and the environmental scientist. Collaborative research began in earnest in the 1930s with the Fenland Research programme involving the work of archaeologists, like Grahame Clark, and botanists, most notably (Sir) Harry Godwin. It was a powerful combination of skills which established the direction for much subsequent work and showed that the total output of such a venture was considerably more enlightening than the sum of the individual parts. Nowadays few archaeological projects are designed without an environmental component.

The last decade or so has seen a considerable increase in the range of scientific techniques applied to archaeological research. Pollen analysis continues to be an important tool, particularly in upland areas where preservation is good.[1] The study of the molluscan assemblage in fossil soils has demonstrated its usefulness,[2] insect faunas are now regularly examined,[3] flotation strategies to extract carbonized seeds form an essential part of excavation programmes, while the processes of alluviation and colluviation in relation to archaeological deposits are being increasingly examined.[4] It can now fairly be said that the study of man's effect on his environment has adopted a truly multidisciplinary approach.

The man–landscape relationship is one dependent upon a number of constraining variables. First and foremost is the geomorphology of the British Isles with its infinite variety in bedrock, soil types, and relief (discussed in Chapter 1). The form of the landscape directly influences the micro-climates of its regions but climate itself, at a more general level, is a major variable as Professor Lamb explains in Chapter 6. The interaction of climate and geomorphology provides the parameters within which the ecosystem—the delicate balance of plants and animals—operates. Focusing in more detail on the ecosystem, its two principal components, of direct concern to this paper, are the biome and man—the living systems and the one dominant animal standing out from them because of his ability to manipulate (Figure 2.1). That animal is itself encapsulated in a series of socio-economic, technological, and biological systems of fascinating complexity, two of which are of direct relevance to the theme here discussed: demography and technology.

Palaeodemography is a subject of utmost importance for the archaeologist but one of extreme obscurity when approached through the archaeological data. At best, before the eleventh century AD population dynamics are in the realms of pure guesswork but there is now some agreement that by the second century AD Britain was experiencing a peak of population expansion, probably in the order of 5 million, which was preceded by a period of rapid growth beginning in the middle of the first millennium BC.[5] Gross changes of this kind, if substantiated, together with minor fluctuations and regional variations, will have had a significant effect on man–landscape relationships.

So too would the related theme of man's technological competence. In what can still be conveniently referred to as the Mesolithic period (roughly 8000–4000/3500 BC) simple chopping tools and fire were the principal means of establishing a degree of control over the environment, but during the fourth millennium food-producing (in other words farming) regimes were introduced which altered the productive capacity of the environment and in doing so caused widespread environmental change. Increasingly sophisticated food-producing strategies and the introduction of metal, particularly iron after about 600 BC, allowed a more intensive mode of farming to be developed, while the nation-wide coercive control which the Roman administration was able to exert in the brief period from AD 43 to about AD 400 gave rise to a minor industrial revolution. Some

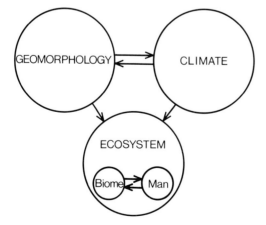

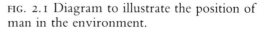

FIG. 2.1 Diagram to illustrate the position of man in the environment.

aspects of these interwoven themes will be examined in more detail in the pages to follow.

The recession of the ice-sheets which covered much of the landmass of Britain during the Pleistocene gave rise to a series of far-reaching changes typifying the post-glacial period. Temperature gradually increased throughout the pre-Boreal period until about 7600 BC when warmer conditions ensued, at which stage the birch-dominated vegetation gave way to a mixed oak forest establishing itself over the entire land mass up to an altitude of between 700 and 800 metres. In parallel with this the thawing of the ice-sheets and the releasing of the ice weight from the land set in motion isostatic readjustments resulting, about 6600 BC, in a sea-level rise sufficient to sever Britain from the Continent.

The study of these changes using fossil data, principally pollen, is a well-developed discipline in its own right. Godwin's pioneering work[6] in establishing pollen zones for the British Isles and in calibrating them when radio-carbon dates became available[7] has formed the essential basis of the study. More recently Hibbert, working at Red Moss in Lancashire, using the principles of biostratigraphic subdivision, has defined six pollen assemblage zones which can be used to characterize successive phases of the Flandrian stage of the Post-Glacial period into chronozones.[8] A collation of the various terminologies in use is offered in Figure 2.2 together with part of the tree pollen diagram produced by Godwin from Hockham Mere, in the Breckland of East Anglia.[9]

The period from roughly 8000 BC to 3500 BC covers the stage when the communities inhabiting Britain were hunters (in the traditional technological terminology this is the Mesolithic period). It is divisible into two broad stages about the date 6600 BC when Britain was finally separated from the Continent. The early stage was one of rapid readjustment following the withdrawal of the ice-sheets; the later was a period of more stability during which time most of the island developed its mantle of deciduous forest and a warm oceanic climate prevailed. It is within this second period that the effects of man first begin to be noticed.

The general view held a few years ago was that human hunting groups had little or no significant effect on the environment. More recent work, however, has shown that localized changes were taking place and that man was the probable instigator.[10] The observations leading to this change of view result from programmes of pollen analysis concentrating on the upland fringes of the forest zone, particularly in the South Pennines, the North Yorkshire Moors, and Dartmoor, where the tree line was found to be consistently below the altitude to which, climatically, it was possible for trees to grow. In these regions it has been shown that successive clearance phases can be recognized which, in some areas, appear immediately to have preceded large-scale forest recession. Associated with the clearances, light-demanding plants like sorrel and ribwort plantain appear and hazel pollen dominates the spectrum. Occasionally flecks of charcoal are found associated with the horizon and inwash strips of silt may occur reflecting a change of conditions, the thinness of the vegetation cover allowing soil to erode into the bogs or lakes from which the pollen samples are taken.

This range of observation is entirely consistent with the deliberate manipulation of the upland forest margin by man using fire to create limited clearances. With the tree cover

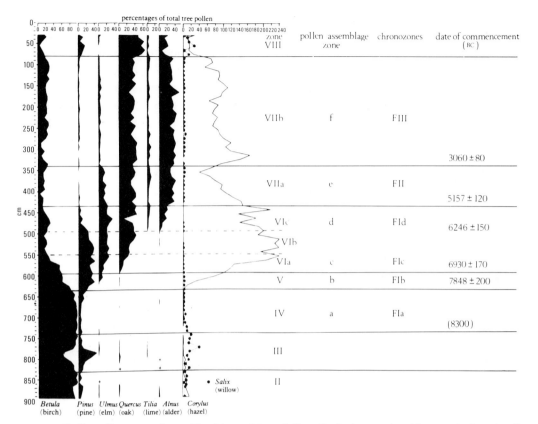

FIG. 2.2 Pollen diagrams from Hockham Mere (after Godwin 1956) with correlation details added.

removed or diminished, the light-demanding plants would flourish. Hazel is not easily destroyed and would quickly sprout from the root stock. Although a direct relationship between the clearance phases and Mesolithic settlement is seldom demonstrable, a survey of the location of Mesolithic sites in the Southern Pennines has shown evidence of a very marked concentration at altitudes approximating to the upper forest fringes.[11] Thus it is reasonable to assume that Mesolithic hunting bands were responsible for the clearances.

Reviewing the evidence, Simmons has convincingly argued that the clearances were the result of specialized subsistence strategies designed to concentrate game, principally the large herbivores such as deer (and any aurochs still remaining), together perhaps with pig.[12] The creation of a clearance in this forest fringe zone would have allowed the browse plants—alder, birch, rowan, and hazel—to flourish, the ash from the clearance fires increasing the fertility of the soil for a brief period. Concentrations of luxuriant browse would undoubtedly have encouraged animals to congregate: at such times they could the more easily be picked off by man in comparative leisure. Such a strategy would, therefore, have considerably lessened the effort necessary for the hunt, not least because red deer tend to scatter in the summer months while roe deer do not normally congregate in large herds at any time. Another advantage of such a system is that it would have encouraged the growth of berries and nuts (particularly hazel) which formed an important component of the human diet.[13]

The simplest way of explaining the annual food-collecting pattern is to assume that groups congregated in winter camp sites in the coastal zone or the river valleys of the forest and that the movement to the upland clearances took place in spring, the hunting groups returning again to their lowland camps in the late autumn. Another aspect of animal manipulation may be reflected in the high concentrations of ivy pollen found at several Mesolithic sites.[14] It is tempting to see this as the result of the creation of ivy fodder dumps to attract animals to the camp in the late autumn and winter, once more to facilitate the kill.

The long-term effects of clearance on the forest margin were frequently accumulative and irreversible (Figure 2.3). Prolonged clearance of poorly drained soils reduces transpiration rates, resulting in the development of waterlogged conditions. In such circumstances soil nutrients migrate downwards, the soil becoming acid, and conditions develop conducive to the growth of peat-forming plants. The end of this process is the creation of blanket bog. A succession of clearances over the centuries, as is witnessed by the pollen diagrams, would naturally lead to a gradual lowering of the tree line to well below the altitude climatically possible, with a consequent extension of upland bog. Thus, the first manipulation of the landscape by man in the period 5500–3500 BC, in some areas, began a process the effects of which are with us today.

A major change in subsistence strategy came about during the fourth millennium BC. It was initiated by the arrival on British shores of immigrants from the Continent bringing with them domesticated sheep and cattle together with supplies of seed corn of cultivated emmer wheat, naked six-row barley, and hulled barley. The exact process by which this remarkable act of colonization was accomplished is the subject of much debate,[15] and the details are for ever likely to remain obscure, but the result was that farming practices were established on British soil and, within the astonishingly short space of 1,000 years, had spread to all parts of the country as far north as Shetland.

The establishment of food-producing regimes in the still predominantly wooded British countryside must have been a hazardous process and there are likely to have been many failures as breeding stock proved unable to sustain the necessary level of fertility or as crop failure or disease undermined the system. Yet the new system of food production held its

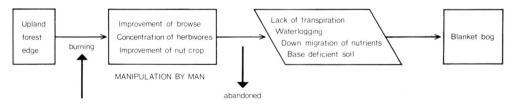

FIG. 2.3 The effects of Mesolithic clearance on upland forest fringes.

own and gradually began to make a permanent mark on the landscape. One prime requisite was for open land in which to grow the crops and run the flocks of sheep. Cattle, essentially woodland browsers, would be content with the existing forest so long as there was a plentiful supply of water readily available. The result of the establishment of a Neolithic food-producing economy was, therefore, to open up the forest canopy. Deliberate acts of deforestation within the deciduous woodland created a mosaic of clearings. In some there is evidence of regeneration as systems failed or communities moved, while elsewhere a permanent open landscape was created.

The chalkland of Wessex provides an interesting insight into the period. The density of monumental earthwork structures, such as causewayed camps, henge monuments, cursuses, and long barrows imply a substantial population sufficiently well established to be able to harness surplus manpower to undertake communal projects. Environmental studies in the area have begun to demonstrate the effects of man on the landscape. The study of the changing molluscan faunas in soil profiles and turf lines buried beneath monumental earthworks gives a clear indication that in many cases the monuments were erected either in large clearings or in extensive open landscapes.[16] At Avebury in Wiltshire the molluscan fauna from the soil profile is strongly suggestive of progressive clearance of the forest cover culminating in open grassland, while beneath the long barrow at Ascott-under-Wychwood the assemblage and soil were together indicative of uncultivated pasture. Such little pollen evidence as there is from Wessex tends to support the view of extensive clearances at this time,[17] though we are reminded that each area should be considered on its own merits. Clearly the extent of the clearances and the rate of change from one area to another are problems which the available coarse-grained evidence cannot be expected to reflect on in any detail. At best all we can hope for from the area are usable generalizations.

In other areas of the country, where conditions favour the survival of pollen sequences covering the relevant period, a closer insight into the effects of early farming on the landscape is possible. The Lake District of Cumbria has been particularly well studied, the lake sediments of both upland and coastal tarns providing long and well-preserved sequences.[18] The diagram from Barfield Tarn serves to display the potential (Figure 2.4). Two distinct clearance phases can be recognized. The first, dating to 3700–3300 BC, is represented by the appearance of light-loving plants such as *Plantago lanceolata* and *Rumex*, and associated with this there is a slight decline in the quantity of beech (*Betula*) and elm (*Ulmus*) suggesting the removal of at least some elements of the deciduous forest. Whether or not these changes were instigated by hunter–gatherer groups or by the activities of Neolithic farmers is difficult to say, but the second clearance phase dating to about 3100 BC can definitely be associated with agricultural practice since cereal pollen appears in some quantity for the first time. The contemporary changes are apparent from the diagram. Weeds of cultivation and other light-loving plants greatly increase while the quantity of oak and elm pollen declines dramatically.

The fall in elm pollen at about this time is a widely recognized phenomenon over much of north-west Europe and as such the elm decline horizon has been widely used to

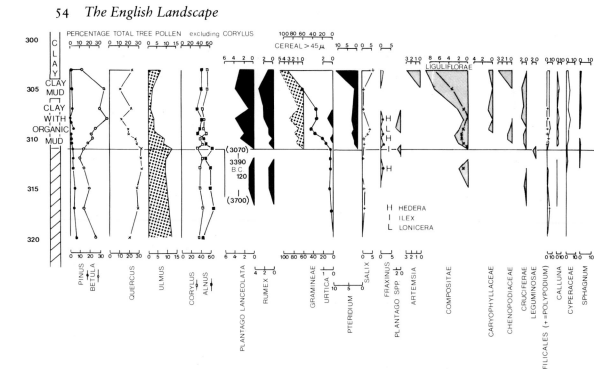

FIG. 2.4 Pollen diagrams from Barfield Tarn, Cumberland, 1965 (redrawn from Simmons and Tooley 1981, *Environment in British Prehistory*, Gerald Duckworth and Co.).

correlate sequences from area to area. A sufficient number of radio-carbon dates have now been obtained to show the broad contemporaneity of the horizon, centring about 3100 BC, but with a comparative wide range resulting, in considerable part, from the limitations of the dating methods.

The elm decline has been the subject of much debate. Some researchers, impressed by its apparent suddenness and geographical extent, consider that disease or climatic change must be the prime cause, while others have put forward anthropogenic explanations of the phenomenon as the result of the cropping of elm to provide leaf fodder for animals stalled throughout the winter. In support of this contention it can be claimed that elm leaves are extremely nutritious and have, indeed, been found trampled on the floor of Neolithic animal stalls in Switzerland.[19]

While the debate is by no means concluded, the evidence at Barfield Tarn demonstrates, quite decisively, that here at any rate interference by man is likely to have been a significant (if contributory) factor since the appearance of cereal pollen cannot be explained in any way other than by deliberate cultivation.

Barfield Tarn reflects a pattern of clearance and cultivation typical of the Cumbrian coast. Inland in the region of Great Langdale, at what would have been the upland fringes of the forest, the pollen evidence shows that the elm decline was accompanied by an absolute fall in pine and birch as well. Evidence of fire suggests deliberate clearance but there is no trace of cereal growing. Between the upland zone and the coastal fringe, in the valleys where samples have been taken, there is no evidence of any decrease in oak.

Taken together, the evidence for Cumbria strongly suggests a complex pattern of land use (Figure 2.5) quite possibly involving a degree of transhumance between coastal home bases, where the crops were grown, and upland pastures, cleared out of the forest fringes, where flocks could be run in summer and early autumn and game caught in much the same way as it had been in the immediately preceding Mesolithic period. An additional attraction of Great Langdale was the ready supply of stone used to make polished axes. These were widely distributed and evidently highly valued as items of exchange. The roughing out of axes is a spare-time activity appropriate to the summer herders.

The pattern which emerges from a study of the Cumbrian evidence, even though still only an outline hypothesis, gives some idea of the potential complexity of the man–environment relationship in an area of diverse resources. No doubt each area of Britain will have developed its own strategies based on the constraints of the local environment. By about 3000 BC man's attack on the landscape was well under way.

Hereafter the pattern of land use becomes even more diverse. Clearance and regeneration seem to be the norm in many areas, with the more delicately balanced ecosystems at high altitudes, or on fragile soils, showing irreversible changes. By about 2000 BC many of the heath and moorland tracts that exist today were already established[20] and in densely utilized areas like the chalklands of Wessex an open agricultural landscape was beginning to become established.

The destructive activities of medieval and later land use have destroyed or at least obscured much of the settlement pattern of the prehistoric lowlands, but around the fringes of upland areas fossil landscapes of the second and first millennia BC can often be traced in considerable detail. One such area is Dartmoor, where programmes of field-work and excavation, combined with intensive environmental analysis, present a very clear picture of land use from about 1600 BC until about 400 BC.

The field-work undertaken by Aileen Fox laid the basis for all further studies.[21] An intensive programme of investigation and mapping defined two distinctive types of

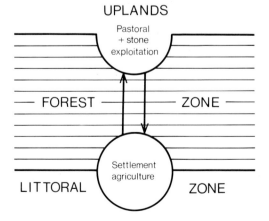

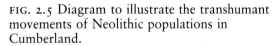

FIG. 2.5 Diagram to illustrate the transhumant movements of Neolithic populations in Cumberland.

settlement: 'pastoral' settlements and 'arable' farms. The former consisted of groups of huts sometimes within enclosures (pounds) or sometimes joined by lengths of walling creating the impression of paddocks, while the latter were typified by a few huts, usually clustered together and surrounded by fields. Since distinction between the two was not always apparent, a third class of 'mixed economy' settlements was allowed. The distribution of the three categories was quite distinct (Figure 2.6), the arable settlements occupying the north-east part of the moor while the pastoral and mixed economy settlements clustered to the south and west. This was explained in terms of the arable sites forming the drier region in the rain shadow of the moor top. In a later reconsideration of the settlement pattern Simmons[22] drew attention to soil surveys undertaken by Clayden and Manley,[23] pointing out that the arable settlements were concentrated on the most productive soils, the brown earths of the Moretonhampstead series. The implication is clearly that the farmers were being highly selective in avoiding the peaty gley podzols and instead clearing forest from the lower sheltered slopes.

The organization of the landscape at this time is a theme of current research,[24] but it is already clear from work undertaken on southern Dartmoor that the land was being divided into parcels by linear boundaries (usually earthworks or stone walls) known locally as reeves. The extent and detail of the system is sufficient to show that exploitation was intense, requiring management of a surprisingly high level of complexity.

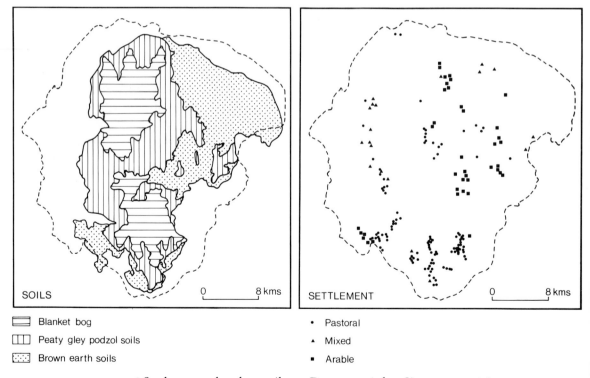

SOILS   0   8 kms

SETTLEMENT   0   8 kms

▭ Blanket bog

⊞ Peaty gley podzol soils

⊡ Brown earth soils

• Pastoral

▲ Mixed

■ Arable

FIG. 2.6 Settlement related to soils on Dartmoor (after Simmons 1969).

Although thorough field survey is an essential preliminary to this kind of study, excavation is required if significant advances are to be made in our understanding of the dynamics of the socio-economic system. The Shaugh Moor project, developed by the Central Excavation Unit of the Department of the Environment to study an ancient landscape on the southern flank of the moor threatened by china clay working, was just such a project, carefully designed to examine the relationships of selected settlement elements against a chronological and economic background.[25]

A major element in the programme was the total excavation of a round containing a number of timber- and stone-built houses. The results showed that the settlement was occupied throughout the period 1600–600 BC and underwent many phases of renovation. The complete enclosure of the settlement and lack of phosphate concentrations within, except in midden deposits around the huts, show that animals were not kept inside the walled area. Comparative lack of occupation debris, in spite of the duration of use, strongly suggests seasonal use by small groups migrating to these upland zones to pasture animals during the spring and summer season. The long reeves and the parcels of pasture into which the landscape was divided are manifestations one might expect of a well-organized system of stock management. A vivid reminder that cattle were involved was shown by the excavation of Saddlesborough reeve where in one phase the hoof-marks of the cattle, driven along the boundary, were clearly distinguishable.

Environmental studies associated with the Shaugh Moor project have failed to distinguish any significant cereal-pollen component in the contemporary pollen spectrum, while the careful flotation of soil samples from the enclosures has confirmed the extreme rarity of cereal grains. The pollen sequence does, however, show that from the mid-second millennium to the mid-first millennium BC the landscape was open—exactly as would be expected if the farming activity of the settlement was based on animal husbandry.

The general impression gained from the new survey and excavation work is of two subsistence strategies: an eastern version, still little known, in which homesteads surrounded by fields occupied the fertile slopes of the moor, and a western- and southern-based version in which some degree of transhumance is implied, the home-based farms presumably occupying the river valleys and lower lands south of the moorland massif. A regime of this kind is not at all unlike that suggested for Cumbria a millennium and a half earlier. A further similarity is that the upland herders on Dartmoor may well have been engaged in collecting tin and copper ores from the mineral-rich superficial deposits of the area, much as the herders of Langdale worked the local stone and manufactured green stone axes. Part-time exploitation of raw materials is likely to have played an important part in prehistoric economies.

Any subsistence strategy which depended upon the exploitation of upland fringe areas was at risk from climatic change. The climatic deterioration of the first half of the first millennium BC, manifest in cooler summers and generally wetter conditions, cannot have failed to have had a dislocating effect on the settlers of the Dartmoor fringe, and indeed in similar environments throughout the British Isles. Lamb's estimate that between 1000 and 750 BC the mean temperature fell by 2° centigrade, shortening the growing season by five weeks,[26] is sufficient to stress the potential of the deterioration to bring about widespread readjustment in food-producing strategies. Some writers have tended to ignore the problem while others have used climatic readjustment to explain every change in the archaeological record. Clearly both extremes are unacceptable.

On Dartmoor the effects are evident: hitherto open landscapes like Shaugh Moor show signs of forest regeneration while the moor-top blanket bogs extend to lower altitudes. In social and economic terms this means that tracts of upland pasture and arable, that had been in intensive use for a thousand years, were now abandoned. How the displaced communities adapted to the new situation is beyond the scope of the present evidence to determine, but several generalizations can be offered. The most likely effect would have been greater pressure on the outer forest margin—areas now difficult to study because of the destruction wrought by medieval settlements. It may, however, be significant that by, or soon after, the middle of the first millennium BC, there developed a new kind of settlement known as the multiple-ditched enclosure. The arrangement of these earth-works, and their location within easy reach of springs, has led to the suggestion that they were designed as cattle-managing settlements[27] (although it must be admitted that not a single site has been adequately excavated). Their general distribution pattern appears to favour the moorland fringe zone, generally avoiding the thick clay-land of the Culm Measures (Figure 2.7).[28] It might therefore be suggested that the multiple-ditched enclosures, established in new clearances in the forest, developed as a response to the socio-economic pressures brought about by climatic change in the region. That they were strongly defended may reflect the increasing social stress inherent in such a readjustment. The hypothesis is undoubtedly an over-simplification of a highly complex process of change taking place over several centuries, but it serves to indicate both the nature of the problems which the archaeologist faces and the way in which, through carefully designed programmes of field-work and excavation, they can be tested.

The climatic deterioration of the early first millennium BC seems to have coincided with a period of population growth in parts of southern Britain, though whether the two

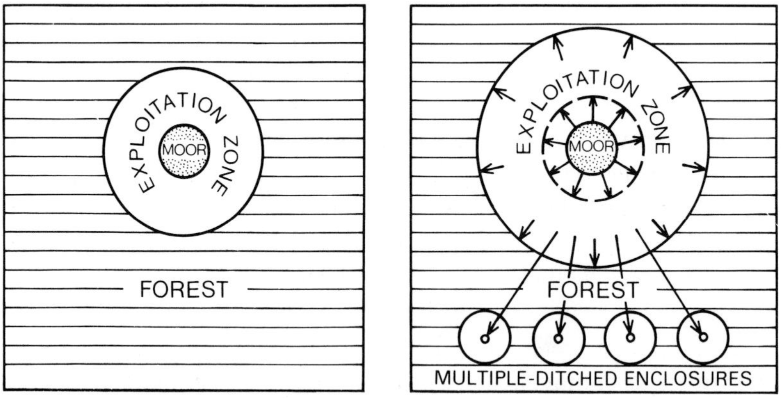

FIG. 2.7 Model to show possible effects of climatic deterioration on the exploitation of a moorland fringe zone.

phenomena were in any way related remains obscure: in all probability they were not. The overall effect, however, even in those lowlands of southern Britain where climatic factors are unlikely to have been of much significance, was of social and economic reorientation. The clearest archaeological manifestation of this was the emergence of strongly defended hill-forts in many parts of the country, which came and went as local conditions changed. By about 400 BC, however, the situation seems to have stabilized with the emergence of a number of strongly defended and intensively occupied forts occupying a wide arc of land spreading from Sussex through the chalklands of Wessex to the Cotswolds and the Welsh Marches. Within this area—the hill-fort-dominated zone—the siting of the forts implies a high degree of territoriality much as would be expected of a society in a state of stress.[29] The increase of population, which manifests itself in a greatly increased number of settlement sites, must mean a more intensively utilized landscape. Of this there is growing evidence.

One particularly informative research programme has been designed to test the effects of man on the chalklands of the South Downs.[30] On the assumption that continuous agricultural use of the Downs has created a downward movement of sediment from the tops and slopes to the bottoms of the dry valleys, the colluvial deposits in the valley floors were sectioned, and artefacts within the soil profiles were carefully collected. These data, together with pedological study of the sediments, molluscan analysis, and, where possible, radio-carbon dating of selected horizons, enable the process of colluviation to be studied. The overall picture obtained for the South Downs is of open, dry conditions with the progressive accumulation of deposits resulting from agricultural activity going back to at least the beginning of the second millennium. In some places in excess of a metre of sediment has collected, representing a considerable denudation of the ancient loess-rich soils of the hilltops. Erosive processes of this magnitude will have dramatically decreased the fertility of the uplands while increasing the fertility in the more restricted areas of the valley bottoms. (This factor no doubt lies behind the selection of valley-bottom locations for late Saxon and medieval villages and farmsteads.)

Whilst the accumulation of colluvial deposits in the area began early, there is some evidence to suggest that an intensification of agriculture, from about the middle of the first millennium BC, caused an increased rate of erosion and hence deposition in the valley bottoms. Much the same picture has come from studies in the lower Severn–Avon valleys[31] where thick deposits of red flood-plain alluvium derived from the rapid erosion of Triassic rocks, mainly Keuper Marl, blanket a variety of other sediments. The process seems to have begun after 650 BC and may well be the result of an increase in arable farming, following a phase of forest clearance. Shotton has tentatively linked this to the introduction of winter-sown crops at about this time: the fields would need to have been fresh ploughed for the winter rains to have carried off the sediment.

Although studies of this kind are still in their infancy, their potential in demonstrating and dating the effects of man on the environment is very considerable. The evidence so far available strongly supports the view that the farming regimes of the south were undergoing modification and intensification in the early first millennium BC.

The farming regimes of Wessex are now comparatively well understood as the result of a series of large excavations producing usable samples of faunal and floral remains.[32] At the hill-fort of Danebury in Hampshire, for example, the animal-bone sample from the first ten seasons of excavations amounts to 150,000 items[33] and covers a period of nearly 500 years of occupation. The random sampling and flotation of soils to provide seeds and related remains adds the floral element to the overall picture of the farming regime. In addition to this the settlements have produced evidence of well-developed storage facilities in underground silos, while field-work, aided by aerial photographic surveys, allows large tracts of the contemporary landscape to be planned. The area around Danebury is particularly well known, as Figure 2.8 will show.

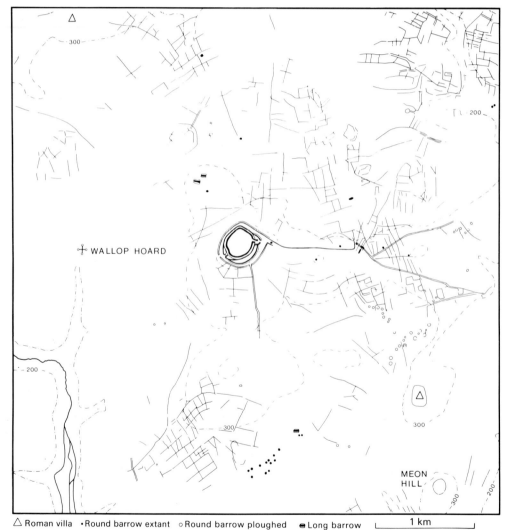

△ Roman villa   ·Round barrow extant   ○Round barrow ploughed   ▪Long barrow |___ 1 km ___|

FIG. 2.8 Field systems and other landscape features around the hill-fort of Danebury, Hampshire (from Cunliffe 1984).

Air photography has also allowed many of the broadly contemporary farmsteads to be planned, and in the area south of Danebury, in the valleys of the River Test and its tributary the Wallop Brook, the settlement pattern revealed is so dense and regular that we may well be viewing an Iron Age landscape in its entirety (Figure 2.9). The individual settlements choose very similar locations on gentle spurs not far from permanent water supply and within easy reach of the open downland above. The farms are regularly spaced in relation to each other, averaging 1.5 km apart. Although it could be argued that the settlement pattern in this area is, for some reason, unusual and may have been dictated by the existence of the nearby hill-fort, a similar magnitude of spacing can be found in many parts of southern Britain wherever field-work has been carried out on an adequate scale. The impression given, therefore, is that on certain favourable soils settlement was dense and the land intensively used.

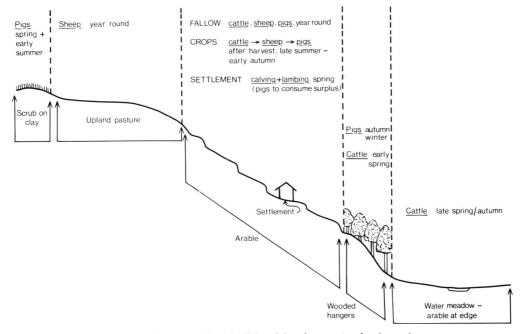

FIG. 2.9 The use of a chalkland landscape in the Iron Age.

Some indication of the economic system can be gained from Table 2.1 which is based on data from Danebury but, as a general model, is probably good for much of the chalkland landscape in the second half of the first millennium BC. The resource potential is divisible into a number of zones: the upland down, far from water, serving as open pasture but broken by patches of clay supporting rough scrub and acid-loving plants; the arable zone, usually on gently sloping hillsides; the hangers too steep to plough but probably covered with trees and scrub; and the well-watered meadow, possibly with arable on the fringes, where colluvial deposits have formed out from the adjacent dry valleys. All of these zones were intensively used.

Table 2.1. Percentages of animals found at the Iron Age hill-fort of Danebury, Hampshire, successively throughout the period from *c.*550–100 BC (data from Annie Grant).

	Early (550–450)	Middle (450–400)	Late (a) (400–250)	Late (b) (250–100)
Sheep/goat	45	57	58	66
Cattle	23	16	16	21
Pig	15	18	14	8
Dog	1	2	6	2
Horse	1	4	3	3
Red deer	x	x	x	x
Roe deer	x	x	x	x
Bird	2	1	3	x
Cat	x	1	x	x
Fox	1	x	x	x
Badger	x	x	x	x
Fish	x	x	x	x

The animal population was dominated by sheep (Table 2.1)—a most useful creature in these circumstances. Sheep needed little care and could spend large parts of the year foraging on the open downs or on fields left fallow, spending the post-harvest season gleaning in the arable fields. Cattle, on the other hand, needed regular watering and so would be kept within easy reach of the meadows. As woodland browsers, herds would have been encouraged to wander in the wooded hangers and would probably have gleaned in the arable fields after harvest. Between them, the two principal farmyard animals, complementary in their needs, used much of those resources which could not have been consumed directly by man, while at the same time contributing their valuable manure to the soil.

Both animals were capable of yielding an exchangeable surplus. The sheep produced wool which was spun and woven in very large quantity, while the cattle produced young— a valuable exchange commodity and source of wealth in comparable Celtic societies for which there is literary evidence. Thus the correct balance of flocks and herds ensured the full use of the landscape (and contributed to its fertility) while yielding a product for exchange. Excess, above breeding and exchange needs, could be eaten.

The pig was an equally valuable member of the economy. Pigs could eat all waste products useless to man, sheep, and cattle, such as acorns and roots from the woodland, rough vegetation from the acid clays, offal, dead carcasses, and surplus milk available at lambing or calving. In a well-run establishment they need in no way have competed with man or the other domesticals for their food. Pigs were therefore a highly efficient means of converting waste to high-quality protein, the living beast acting as a convenient store until his meat was needed.

The late first millennium economy was, therefore, one in which the elements were carefully balanced for a highly efficient level of production. Man seems to have extracted his calories at the base of the food chain, as cereals, supplementing his diet with fat and protein at certain times when the culling of the flocks or herds was called for or when it was time to kill the pig.

The analysis of plant remains and animal bones from Danebury shows that very little change in the pattern of crop or animal management occurred throughout the period of occupation (550–100 BC), and comparable data from other sites in the same type of chalkland environment support the general impression that the economy had reached a level of stability by the middle of the first millennium BC which was maintained for several hundred years. But intensive use of this kind cannot have failed to impose stresses on the landscape. Even extensive flocks of sheep could not have maintained the fertility of the upland soils and over-use must have begun to tell. One hint of stress in the system is provided by a noticeable increase in peridontal disease among sheep in the later period at Danebury. This together with a decline in the number of pigs (resulting, perhaps, from over-use of woodland) are the only hints so far available that the communities may, by now, have begun to feel the effects of over-intensive land use. The potential of the subject, particularly the study of changes in soil quality, has barely been touched.

For much of rural Britain the Roman invasion of AD 43 meant little change in agricultural regime. In Wessex and the South Downs life continued much as before. By the end of the second century arable land, farmed in the traditional way, reached its maximum extent. In the parish of Chalton, in eastern Hampshire close to the border with Sussex, intensive field survey has defined much of the upland limit of agriculture, a boundary everywhere of greater extent than the limit of arable in the late seventeenth century. Indeed, the only significant difference between the two landscapes was that in the Roman period the settlements were scattered while after the eleventh century the population had come together in a village on the site of the present settlement (Figure 2.10). Significantly, the village was optimally sited to be within easy reach of the high-quality soils which had accumulated as colluvial deposits in the bottoms of the dry valleys as the result of intensive ploughing in the prehistoric and Romano-British periods.[34]

The imposition of Roman government on Britain for nearly four centuries, from AD 43– c. 410, inevitably had an effect upon the British landscape. Not only was the population swelled by an army of occupation and a heavy, non-productive, administrative machinery, but the province was forced to contribute in order to support a central bureaucracy in Rome. Put in simple economic terms, in the pre-Roman period surplus was cycled through a complex of social mechanisms such as tithes, gift exchange, conspicuous consumption, patronage, and clientage, but remained within the same overall socio-economic structure. Under Roman rule, while a percentage of the surplus was recycled by investments in private or civic building projects, by pay to the army (who spent their wages in the province) and so on, a percentage was also removed from the provincial economic system and fed into the bureaucratic and military establishments in Rome and around the frontiers. Thus the dual pressures of a greater population and an outgoing tax meant that the province had to be made even more productive than before.

Some level of increased productivity was possible by more intensive management of the

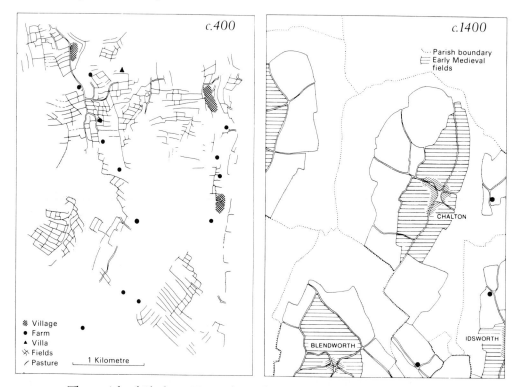

FIG. 2.10 The parish of Chalton, Hampshire, showing the Roman landscape compared with the medieval. The medieval village fields have obliterated all trace of the Roman pattern.

land. Technological advances such as asymmetrical ploughshares and coulters which could turn the soil, scythes and balanced sickles, and the introduction of water mills meant increased efficiency, while improved strains of farmyard animals and, apparently, an extended range of vegetables and fruits, would all have helped to make the province more productive; but the significance of these innovations amounted to little when compared with the great advances brought about by Roman organizational skills and engineering technology.[35]

Land clearance and land drainage were undertaken on a considerable scale. Recent aerial surveys covering the Bunter sandstone outcrop between Nottingham and Doncaster have shown that a vast area of the landscape was parcelled up into rectangular plots divided by regularly laid-out ditches.[36] While the origin of the system is not yet precisely defined, some of the fields were in use in the Roman period and in all probability were laid out as part of a major land-clearance scheme early in the Roman occupation. Further north in the Tyne–Tees region pollen analysis from a number of dispersed locations shows that the agricultural clearances which were appearing in the late pre-Roman Iron Age were fast merging into an open, intensively farmed landscape in the early Roman period.[37] The examples can be multiplied. The clear impression given is of a deliberately organized expansion of arable, out on to soils which might previously have been regarded as marginal or were too heavy or wet to be developed in the late prehistoric period.

The expansion outwards from traditional areas such as the southern chalklands seems to have been accompanied by a slackening of interest in traditional arable regions. The villas which served as focal points for mixed-farming regimes in the south-east of Britain for the most part shunned the light chalk soils and chose instead richer, more mixed soils like the brickearths of the Sussex coastal plain or the greensand bench fringing the Weald. Since the presence of a villa implies a successful farming unit, it could be argued that only on these soils was there sufficient profit to be made to enable the owners to invest in such luxuries as baths, underfloor heating, and mosaics.

By the fourth century there is some evidence to suggest that large tracts of downland ceased to be farmed as arable and were, instead, turned over to sheep rearing. British woollen goods gained an international reputation and an imperial weaving mill was in operation at Venta (most probably Winchester in the heart of the Wessex chalkland). Whether the change was a response to declining fertility or whether it resulted from more complex factors such as a decline in manpower, it is difficult to say.[38] Elsewhere in the country, for example in the north-east, the pollen evidence indicates that agricultural regimes continued to flourish well into the fifth century.

The ability of the Roman administration to alter landscapes considerably is well demonstrated by works carried out in the Fens of eastern Britain. The most notable feature of this work is the artificial waterway known as the Car Dyke which runs from the River Cam to the Trent just beyond Lincoln. For a considerable part of its length, particularly through Lincolnshire, the Car Dyke is wholly artificial; elsewhere it makes use of natural waterways. Until comparatively recently the Car Dyke was considered to be a Roman canal, an idea first put forward by the antiquary William Stukeley in the early eighteenth century. It was argued that it had been constructed in the early Roman period to link the rich cornlands of the Fens to the military supply routes and hence to the garrisons of the North. Part of this argument rested on the recognition of 'field systems' in the Fens, visible on the aerial photographic cover.

More recent work has, however, cast considerable doubt on this interpretation, not least the observation that the Car Dyke was blocked at intervals by causeways of undisturbed natural subsoil[39] and that its separate stretches varied in height. It could not, therefore, have served as a canal for long-distance transport but it could still have functioned for short-haul local journeys. Field-work in Lincolnshire has, however, suggested a totally different function—as a catch-water drain designed to work in combination with another drain, the Midfendic, which in part runs parallel with it some four kilometres to the east. The Midfendic is seen as a drainage dyke in the lee of a discontinuous earth bank serving as a sea wall, the entire system acting in much the same way as a ringvart system.

This reassessment, together with new surveys of the Fen settlements and their environments,[40] is now suggesting that, far from being a great agricultural landscape, the Fens in the Roman period were more like the Camargue. The ditched fields certainly exist but the environment would have been far too saline to have allowed corn-growing on a large scale. It is far more likely, therefore, that the landscape was designed for cattle management. In such an economic system the salt which was abundantly produced in the area would have been particularly useful in salting down meat and in treating hides. Both commodities, particularly the leather, were consumed in quantity by the military establishment in the North. Thus large-scale drainage works in the Fens and around the Fen margins turned a landscape hitherto little used into a productive part of the province.

Another innovation brought about by the Roman presence was industrialization, principally the extraction of metals and stone and the manufacturing of pottery. The eastern Weald provides an interesting and well-studied example from which some idea of scale of production can be obtained. Here, in the hinterland north of Hastings, iron ore was extracted and smelted, very probably under the control of the imperial navy (*classis britannica*). One centre was at Bardown where a smelting works in use throughout the period AD 120–220 has been extensively examined, together with the satellite settlements which sprang up around it at the beginning of the third century.[41] From a consideration of the size of the slag heaps it was possible to arrive at approximate production figures. The estimated annual production of iron from the main Bardown settlement was 40–45 tonnes, with the satellites producing about half that quantity. Estimating the number of such sites in the eastern Weald suggests that the total annual output would have been in the order of 1,000 tonnes.

The implication of these figures, for landscape manipulation, is considerable. In addition to the devastation caused by the quarry pits and the slag heaps, something in the order of 6,000 tonnes of charcoal would have been needed every year. Around Bardown alone this would have meant the use of 13–15 hectares of forest annually and by the middle of the third century, when iron working ceased in the area, it is estimated that 300–500 square kilometres of the Wealden forest must have been felled.[42]

At best the figures provide an order of magnitude rather than an accurate assessment, and it could be argued that careful management, involving pollarding and coppicing, reduced the impact on the landscape. This may well be so, but the overall effect on the hitherto largely untouched 'impenetrable Weald' must have been dramatic. It may well be that the cessation of iron working in the area about AD 250 was as much the result of lack of readily available charcoal as the working out of the ore, or fall in demand. [But see Rackham, p. 73. S.R.J.W.]

The Weald was only one industrial zone: there were many others. The Isle of Purbeck, for example, must have presented something of an industrial landscape. Around the coasts salt was extracted on a large scale; Kimmeridge shale was being worked to make personal ornaments such as bracelets as well as furniture; a wide variety of stone was quarried for building and decorative purposes; and around the shores of Poole harbour a massive pottery industry supplied many parts of the country throughout much of the Roman period. In the height of production Purbeck would have presented a very different face from its present-day appearance of rural charm.

Elsewhere in the country the massive pottery-producing centres in the New Forest, Alice

Holt Forest (near Farnham), the area to the east of Oxford, and the Nene Valley near Water Newton, served large hinterlands and, in the case of the last, the national market. Production on this scale, with massive consumption of clay and fuel, cannot have failed to have had a cumulative effect on the landscape. By the fourth century AD large areas of the British countryside must have looked not unlike the landscape of the seventeenth century on the eve of the Industrial Revolution.

This survey, in attempting to cover a wide chronological span, has necessarily been selective. It began with man's earliest attempts to manipulate his environment by creating clearings in the forest fringe in the sixth millennium BC, setting in train processes which caused, or at least accelerated, the development of upland moors, depressing the tree line well below that climatically possible. The introduction of a food-producing regime in the fourth millennium accelerated these processes and led to the creation of large tracts of open farmland. The man–environment balance was delicate and when there were major changes in climate, as for example in the early first millennium, communities occupying upland areas like Dartmoor were forced to readjust their subsistence strategies.

The intensive farming of some soils would, inevitably, have led to the danger of soil exhaustion by erosion, destruction of texture, and loss of nutrients. Careful management with regular manuring alleviated the problem to some extent but by the end of the first millennium, soils like the chalklands, which had been farmed for three thousand years, were beginning to show signs of stress, and by the late Roman period large tracts seem to have been abandoned in favour of sheep. Elsewhere, however, improved technology and management under Roman administration led to large-scale land clearance and drainage, allowing regions hitherto little used to be brought into productivity. Alongside this agricultural expansion industrial exploitation developed apace, creating devastated landscapes.

The collapse of the Roman world early in the fifth century, and the dramatic decrease in population which seems to have ensued in Britain, gave the over-used landscape a much needed respite to recover, just a little, before a new onslaught began in medieval and more recent times.

3

❦

Ancient woodland and hedges in England

OLIVER RACKHAM

THE study of the English landscape is developing in much the same way as did that of architectural history a hundred years ago. Architectural historians, beginning by comparing written evidence with the buildings themselves, had by 1883 learnt to identify the different periods in the history of churches and castles. Many of the subtler complexities of stone-built architecture were not yet appreciated (and are still an active field of research today); and the vast field of vernacular buildings had hardly been explored at all. By 1983 we have learnt, by similar reasoning, to identify the main features of historic woods and hedges, but there are many questions which we cannot yet answer, and other areas of landscape history are only beginning to be explored: we know as little about the history of roads as our Victorian predecessors knew about barns.

We have to contend, as our predecessors did not, with tenaciously held popular misconceptions about the history of the landscape. The Victorians did not have to devote pages to refuting the notion that Peterborough Cathedral could not be a medieval building because it served the liturgy of the *Book of Common Prayer*. Yet in 1983, after fifteen years of demonstrations to the contrary, people still write articles on the basis that the whole of the rural landscape has always been changing and the hedges, woods, and so on that we have now are no more than the passing effect of fashions in agricultural practice. This doctrine is usually presented either in the form of the 'Enclosure-Act Myth', the belief that our present hedged and walled landscape is merely the result of agricultural reorganization in the eighteenth and nineteenth centuries, or of the 'Capability Brown Myth', the notion that the landscape we have inherited is no more than an extension to the countryside at large of the romantic ideas expressed in landscape parks.

These myths are not merely examples of popular ignorance. No less a scholar than Kenneth Mellanby has recently argued against the conservation of hedges on the grounds that the majority of them have been planted since 1782.[1] The Minister of Agriculture tells us of Suffolk that 'it was in the 19th century during the enclosures that the hedges were built'.[2] Both claims are instantly refuted by innumerable hedges depicted on pre-1782 maps. But assertions of this kind continue to be brought forward to support a theory that existing hedges, woods, and so on are merely a short-lived phase in a constantly changing landscape and therefore do not deserve protection as antiquities. The conservation of the historic landscape, like that of historic buildings, depends on getting the facts right about its dating and development.

The two kinds of English landscape

Why is Essex more like Herefordshire than either is like Cambridgeshire? They illustrate the fundamental difference between what I have called Ancient Countryside and Planned Countryside.[3] Ancient Countryside is the England of hamlets and lonely medieval farmsteads, of winding lanes, dark hollow-ways, and intricate footpaths, of thick mixed hedges and many small woods—a land of surprises and still a land of mystery. Planned Countryside is the England of large regular fields with flimsy hawthorn hedges, of few, often straight, roads, of clumps of trees in the corners of fields, of Georgian farmsteads, and of a large village every two miles—a land of predictability and of straight lines. Not all these features everywhere go together, but in general they do so. The boundary between the Two Landscapes is often sharp and bisects counties and even parishes (Figure 3.1). Examples of Ancient Countryside are most of Essex, Herefordshire, Kent, Devon, and the south-west corner of Wiltshire; examples of Planned Countryside are Cambridgeshire, Lincolnshire, most of Wiltshire, and the north-west corner of Essex.

   The distinction is not superficial or recent, nor as we shall see is it confined to England. Thirty years ago it was more prominent than now, and the further back we go the more prominent it becomes. In general, as anyone will know who studies early maps, Planned Countryside is the landscape of which the Enclosure-Act Myth is true. In the main, it

FIG. 3.1 Ancient countryside (AC) and Planned Countryside (PC).

results from the sudden reorganization, in the draughtsmen's offices of the eighteenth and nineteenth centuries, of what had previously been a landscape of villages set amid the strip cultivation of open-fields; only here and there do woods and other features survive from earlier periods (Figures 3.2, 3.3). Ancient Countryside is in general the piecemeal growth and development of centuries. Its history is complex and in some areas shows the effects of earlier periods of rural planning. Most of it was recognizably the same in 1700 as in 1945 (Figures 3.4, 3.5); in many areas even individual features are of unknown but certainly pre-1500 date. To pursue the architectural analogy, the difference between the Two Landscapes is that between Liverpool or Swindon on the one hand and York or Lavenham on the other.

Trees and their management

Wildwood

After the end of the last glaciation England was successively colonized by different trees, which, in the course of millennia, came to form prehistoric forests, the *wildwood*, covering the whole country. Recent studies in pollen analysis have shown that wildwoods were not the uniform 'mixed oak forest' of earlier authors but a complex mosaic of different kinds such as limewoods, oakwoods, hazel-woods, ashwoods, elmwoods, and pinewoods.[4] In general, oakwoods and hazel-woods predominated in north and west England, limewoods in the Midlands, east, and south.

Although some kind of woodland management may have been practised by Mesolithic peoples, the first clear evidence of systematic human interference with wildwood comes with the arrival of Neolithic settlers in about 4000 BC. These peoples introduced the non-woodland arts of agriculture from the Mediterranean countries to north-west Europe. They began the process of destroying the wildwood, which, continued and expanded in later millennia, has created our present farmland and moorland. They also introduced woodland management and began to convert parts of the remaining wildwood into woods as we know them in the historic period.

Woodland, wood-pasture, and non-woodland trees

In England wildwood is no longer remembered. Throughout history, trees have been involved in the subtle interactions between natural processes and human affairs that have shaped the cultural landscape. Apart from orchards and garden and street trees, there are four separate and independent systems of land-use concerning trees (Table 3.1, p. 73).

1. *Woods,* which are the result of *woodmanship,* that is of management applied to trees that form the natural vegetation. A wood traditionally yields a regular supply of *timber* and *underwood.* Underwood makes use of the property that most native trees have of *coppicing*: when cut down, a tree grows again from the stump, or sometimes from the root system, to form a *stool* which produces an endless succession of poles or rods. Every five to thirty years the wood is cut down—the poles being its main and regular product—

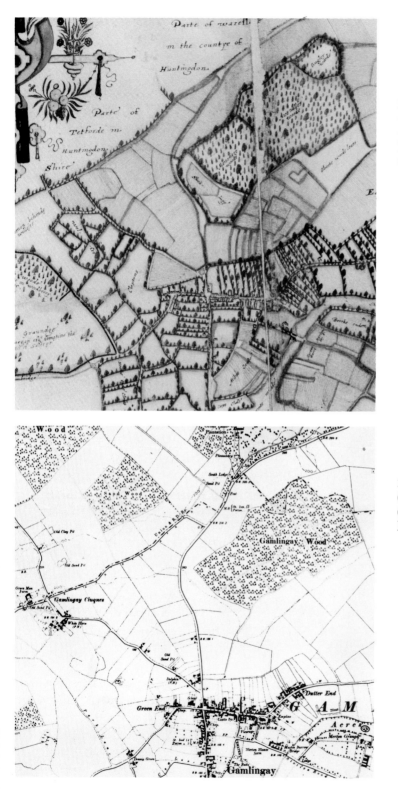

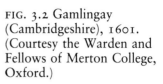

FIG. 3.2 Gamlingay
(Cambridgeshire), 1601.
(Courtesy the Warden and
Fellows of Merton College,
Oxford.)

FIG. 3.3 Gamlingay
(Cambridgeshire), 1900.
(Courtesy the Bodleian
Library, Oxford.)

FIG. 3.4 Lawshall (Suffolk), 1611.
(Courtesy the Suffolk Record Office,
Ipswich Branch.)

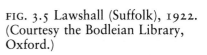

FIG. 3.5 Lawshall (Suffolk), 1922.
(Courtesy the Bodleian Library,
Oxford.)

and allowed to grow again. Scattered among the stools are *standard* trees, usually oaks, which are allowed to stand for several rotations of the underwood and are then felled to yield timber suitable for beams and planks. It must be emphasized that woods are not destroyed by being felled, but by people grubbing out the stools and using the land for something else. The Bradfield Woods, Suffolk (Figures 3.6–8), have been felled at least seventy times and are not diminished. Nor is planting trees a normal part of woodmanship.

2. *Wood-pastures*, land used both for trees and for grazing sheep, cattle, or deer. The two uses are opposed: the shade of the trees is bad for the pasture, and the livestock are liable to eat the regrowth of the trees. Various methods have been devised for reconciling them. A characteristic wood-pasture practice is *pollarding* (Figure 3.9): the trees are cut like coppice stools but at seven to fourteen feet above ground, which is more difficult and laborious but prevents the animals from getting at the regrowth. There are three variants of wood-pasture:

(*a*) *Wooded commons*, where the grazing and sometimes the trees belong to persons having common-rights.

(*b*) *Parks*, private wood-pastures in which the owner keeps deer, confined by a special fence called a *park pale*.

(*c*) *Wooded Forests*, a kind of wood-pasture in which the king (or some other magnate) has the right to keep deer and to protect them by a special set of by-laws. In the Middle Ages a Forest was a place of deer, not of trees; some Forests were wooded (such as Epping Forest), others not (such as Dartmoor Forest). I spell Forest with a capital F to distinguish it from *forests* and *forestry* in the modern sense.

Table 3.1. Systems of land-use involving trees

System	Land-use	Date of adoption in England	Type of tree		
			Timber	Under-wood	Pollard
1. Woodmanship	Woods	Neolithic	++	++	Only on boundaries
2. Wood-pasture	(*a*) Wooded commons	Before AD 700	+	+	++
	(*b*) Parks	*c.* AD 1040	++	+	++
	(*c*) Wooded Forests	*c.* AD 1070	++	+	++
3. Hedgerow and field trees	Farmland	Before AD 700	++	++	++
4. Modern forestry	Plantations	*c.* AD 1600	++	—	—

FIG. 3.6 Ancient wood after coppicing. The underwood of hazel, ash, and other trees has just been felled; most of the produce has been taken away but some of the rods await collection. The timber trees, oaks, have been left standing and a few more promoted. *Bradfield Woods (Suffolk), March 1971; photograph by W. H. Palmer.*

FIG. 3.7 Ancient wood one year after coppicing, showing regrowth of hazel, sallow, and other underwood. Small timber trees of ash, birch, and oak. *Bradfield Woods (Suffolk), April 1982.*

FIG. 3.8 Ancient wood in second year after coppicing, showing regrowth of ash, hazel, and other underwood. Young timber trees of oak. *Bradfield Woods (Suffolk), July 1976.*

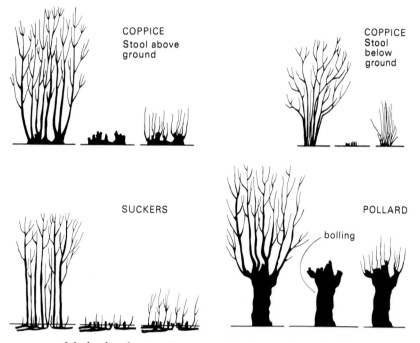

FIG. 3.9 Methods of managing trees. (Redrawn from Rackham 1976, *Trees and Woodland in the British Landscape*, J. M. Dent and Sons.)

3. *Non-woodland trees* in hedges and standing in fields (Figure 3.10). These may be timber trees or pollards, as well as the underwood stools of hedges themselves.

4. *Plantations*, which differ from woods in that the trees are established by planting and are intended to die after felling. Plantations are the silvicultural equivalent of arable farming and bear no relation to the natural vegetation of the area.

Woodland and wood-pasture are separately recorded by Domesday Book (1086) for some counties (such as Lincolnshire) and are mentioned as distinct in some pre-Conquest charters.[5] The charters also show that hedges and non-woodland trees were familiar objects at least as early as the eighth century AD. Plantations, with rare and unimportant exceptions, did not become part of the scene until the seventeenth century and are outside the scope of this paper.

Secondary woodland

Not all woods are ultimately derived from primeval wildwood. Any piece of land automatically turns into woodland unless actively prevented from doing so (Figure 3.11). Hampstead Heath is no longer a heath; it is rapidly becoming a wood, as did the heaths which covered a sixth of Surrey when they ceased to be grazed and cut a century ago.[6] The same has happened down the centuries whenever a heath, field, fen, or industrial site has ceased to be used.

FIG. 3.10 Field with many ancient pollard oaks. Fields full of non-woodland trees are characteristic of the fringes of the Breckland and date from at least the sixteenth century. *Risby (Suffolk), April 1980.*

Secondary woods exist from all periods since Roman times. They are still being formed as railways, commons, road verges, meadows, and industrial premises fall into disuse. But new woods are not a replacement for ancient woods destroyed. They are of trees which colonize easily, such as oak, birch, and hawthorn, rather than of lime, hornbeam, and so on, which do not spread. New woods have often, even after several centuries, not acquired the whole range of characteristic woodland plants.

Woods and woodmanship

Woods in the Middle Ages

The origin of woodmanship goes back in the archaeological record to the Neolithic period.[7] Anglo-Saxon documents tell us that woods already had definite names, ownerships, and boundaries, and were managed in particular ways.[8] The detailed and continuous recording of the histories of particular woods begins with the more abundant documentation of the thirteenth century.

Medieval England was one of the least wooded countries in Europe. As we shall see, woodland in Domesday Book (including wood-pasture) adds up to only 15 per cent of the

FIG. 3.11 Secondary woodland, about fifty years old. The ridge-and-furrow (shown partly flooded) proves that the land has been ploughed at one time. The trees, oak, and hawthorn, and the lack of coppice structure are typical of recent woodland. *Hayley Wood (Cambridgeshire), May 1969.*

land area, a smaller proportion than France has now. Woods were a small, important, and permanent part of the landscape. For instance the *Ely Coucher Book,* a survey of 1251, says of the parish of Little Gransden (Cambridgeshire):

The Wood. There is one wood which is called Heyle which contains fourscore acres. Item, there is one other wood which is called Litlelund, which contains thirty-two acres. The total of all the wood is fivescore and twelve acres . . . [9]

Hayley Wood still exists, and now belongs to the Cambridgeshire and Isle of Ely Naturalists' Trust; the many records from intervening centuries prove that it is indeed the same wood, almost unchanged in area apart from the effect of making a railway.[10] Other pages of the *Ely Coucher Book* record Hardwick Wood, which after a more chequered history[11] is now also a Cambridgeshire Naturalists' Trust reserve; Oxenholt Wood (Glemsford, Suffolk), only 7½ acres, which survived until, tragically, it was replanted in 1972; and the five woods of Barking (Suffolk), from 5 to 130 acres in area, all of which are still there.[12] The records mention coppicing and other management. Sometimes there is evidence, such as the Old Norse wood-name Litlelund, that the woods were already ancient by 1251. Other sources tell us of the woods of Bury St Edmund's Abbey, two of which, Felsham Hall Wood and Monks' Park (in the Bradfields, Suffolk), are still coppiced more than 700 years later.[13] Wayland Wood, which still exists in Watton, Norfolk, was already a notable wood in Anglo-Saxon times, for a hundred was named after it.

Management is recorded in surveys, estate accounts, etc. from this time onwards. A wood normally consisted of underwood stools with a scatter of timber trees. Underwood was cut on a rotation of 4 to 9, less often of 12 to 20, years;[14] this is shown by actual samples of the produce as well as by records. The actual area cut varied widely from year to year.[15] Underwood had many specialized uses, especially for fencing and thatching wood and for wattle-and-daub (the form in which it is often preserved); but its chief use was for domestic and industrial fuel. Underwood was of whatever species of tree happened to constitute the wood.

Timber trees were usually oak. Oaks were scattered through almost all kinds of woodland and, unless very abundant, were not cut with the underwood but allowed to grow to timber size. The timbers in medieval buildings show that the carpenter chose and felled the smallest oak that would make the beam required; he did not, unless he had to, waste time and money on felling big trees and sawing them lengthwise (Figure 3.12). In most woods there was a rapid turnover of small oaks, often less than one foot in diameter, which were felled at between thirty and seventy years of age and easily replaced.[16] There was much transporting of timber, as shown by the existence of timber-framing in places such as Cambridge and Thetford which had no local woodland. Large oaks for special purposes, such as the roofs of castles and cathedrals but also the humble mill-post, were rare and expensive and were brought long distances, often from parks and Forests rather than from woods. Boards, most of the value of which was in the cost of sawing, were normally imported from the Continent.[17]

Woods were a scarce and renewable source of energy, and trouble was taken with their conservation, especially with maintaining the boundaries. There were also minor products such as nuts and edible fruits, acorns for fattening pigs, and so on, which by the Middle Ages had become useful but unimportant by-products; some of them were more prevalent in wood-pasture.

Later history

Woodmanship, thus described, continued with remarkably little change. After 1600, coppice rotations tended to lengthen; timber trees were allowed to grow larger and were sawn lengthwise when felled. It is a popular fallacy that woodmanship was transformed by legislation, such as the Statute of Woods in 1543, or by the growth of book-learning, as exemplified by Evelyn's *Sylva* of 1664. Hayley Wood, Hardwick Wood, and countless others all went on as though the laws had never been passed and the books never written. As late as 1900 many woods differed only in detail from what they had been in 1250.

In the seventeenth, eighteenth, and nineteenth centuries there were successive waves of agricultural expansion, each of which destroyed some woods (such as Litlelund) but left others intact.

FIG. 3.12 A fifteenth-century timber building. The posts, rafters, and other structural timbers are of various sizes, each squared from the trunk of a single small oak tree. The vertical planks in the walls came from an entirely different source, probably from continental manufacturers. (The building is now to be seen at Wandlebury near Cambridge.) *Tadlow Granary (Cambridgeshire), July 1971.*

In the nineteenth century woodmanship fell into decline, the chief cause being probably the railways bringing cheap coal to the countryside and allowing renewable sources of energy to be neglected.[18] Nevertheless, most ancient woods remained in existence until 1945. There then followed three decades of unprecedented destruction, in which woods were treated as mere vacant land to be converted either to plantations or to farmland; between a third and a half of the remaining ancient woodland was destroyed.[19]

Since 1973 there has been a new interest in the conservation of ancient woods. Woods are not isolated relics of antiquity, but belong to an unbroken tradition which goes back to the beginnings of civilization and which is our last remaining link with the prehistoric landscape. They have also come to be valued as places of public resort, nature reserves, and once again as sources of timber and energy. For all these reasons (and for lack of funds) there has been less destruction in the last ten years. Coppicing has been revived, especially in Essex and Suffolk.

Ancient woods as they are now

The study of ancient woods begins on the map. It is a peculiarity of England that many woods are not merely named after villages or farms but have their own names, often as old as those of the settlements themselves (such as the Viking wood-names Litlelund and Wayland). Some wood-names are from long-forgotten local families (such as Peverel's Wood in Debden, Essex; the Peverels are there last heard of in Domesday Book) or religious houses (such as the three Prior's Woods in Takeley, Widdington, and Birchanger, Essex, which belonged to Takeley Priory, suppressed in the fourteenth century).

Ancient woods have sharply-defined edges which are bounded not by straight lines but by sinuous or zigzag perimeters. The earliest detailed maps (Figure 3.2) show many wood outlines exactly the same as they are now. A medieval woodbank is typically a rounded bank with an outer ditch, some 25–40 feet in total width (Figure 3.13). A wood with a complex history may have many woodbanks indicating changes of boundary and divisions of ownership. Banks are often set with ancient pollard trees and remains of hedges, which further define the boundary. Woodbanks are recorded as existing structures in twelfth- and thirteenth-century documents, and may be mentioned in pre-Conquest charters.[20] Such banks continued to be made down to the nineteenth century,

FIG. 3.13 A great woodbank with external ditch, exposed by felling the underwood. *Bradfield Woods, April 1973.*

but the later ones are progressively less massive and are usually straight or regularly curved.

Medieval woods often preserve minor features of the natural land surface—ponds, dells, minor stream courses, and so on—that elsewhere are destroyed or confused by cultivation. Secondary woodland, in contrast, may contain evidence of a previous land-use, such as barrows (meant to be seen from a distance), moats, or the ridge-and-furrow of cultivation.[21] (Industrial remains do not always prove a wood to be secondary: some industries such as coal-mining could go on within a wood.)

Ancient woods are of many kinds. Woods are characterized not by their standard trees but by their underwood. Standard trees come and go, and are of species (usually oak) arbitrarily chosen by woodmen to become timber. Underwood stools are long-lived and give a wood its character and historical continuity. We thus have ash–maple–hazel-woods (in various combinations), limewoods, different kinds of elmwood and hornbeam-wood, alder-woods, chestnut-woods (of sweet-chestnut, a Roman introduction from Southern Europe), oakwoods (in which the underwood is oak as well as the timber trees).[22] Rarely does an ancient wood consist entirely of one tree community. In parts of Essex a twelve-acre wood may contain five different types of woodland. With few exceptions, these are not the direct result of management; the tree communities have been given the same management for centuries and are still distinct. Their boundaries are irregular and are not related to management boundaries; often there is some relation to soils. Every medieval wood is uniquely different from every other in much the same way as is every medieval church.

Many tree communities are known to be of ancient origin. Limewoods still predominate in certain very limited areas (such as around Sudbury, Suffolk); they have a good historical record and there can be no doubt that they are relics of lime-dominated wildwood. Hazel-woods, now much less rare than limewoods, can similarly be traced back to hazel-dominated wildwood. Other kinds of wildwood appear to have given rise to our ancient oakwoods, alder-woods, ashwoods, and some types of elmwood. These all have their own independent histories, and some of them can be traced back at least to the Middle Ages on the very sites which they now occupy. In Essex, for instance, there is a medieval wood-name of pre-Conquest form, *Lindris*, from Old English *linde* 'lime' and *hris* 'underwood'; a thousand years later, this wood still has lime underwood.[23] Not all types of woodland can yet be explained: hornbeam-woods and maple-woods are known to be ancient but their origin is uncertain.

Woods often contain some of the actual stools which grew in the Middle Ages. Coppicing prolongs the life of a tree, and the stool gets bigger after each felling (Figure 3.14). Stools of ash occasionally reach 18 feet in diameter and are estimated to be 1,000 years old.[24] Similar giant stools are to be found in lime, maple, alder, oak, elm, and chestnut.

Ancient woods have characteristic plant species. When a new wood is formed it does not suddenly acquire all the woodland plants and animals. Birch and oak appear at the start; hornbeam and hazel later; lime, although it may have been the original wildwood

FIG. 3.14 Giant stool of ash, estimated to be 400 years old; last felled *c.* 1920. *Hayley Wood (Cambridgeshire) March 1967.*

tree, will not now recolonize at all. The lime-tree is one of many plants which rarely appear in secondary woodland, even after centuries have elapsed. Others include the service-tree, the unusual hawthorn *Crataegus laevigata*, oxlip (*Primula elatior*), and Herb Paris (Figure 3.15). A list of fifty such species has been compiled for Lincolnshire alone.[25]

FIG. 3.15 Herb Paris, a characteristic plant of ancient woodland. *Buff Wood (Cambridgeshire), May 1982.*

The wood-pasture tradition

Wooded commons

These are probably of prehistoric origin and were the only wood-pasture known to the Anglo-Saxons. In its simplest form, wood-pasture might be little more than the turning loose of cattle or sheep to make a precarious living on whatever grass, brambles, or low branches grew within their reach. Large native mammals were already much reduced by millennia of dense settlement, but in some areas there were red deer, roe deer, and, rarely, wild swine. These beasts were hunted for meat or for sport, but appear not have been the object of special land management.

Parks and wooded Forests

Wood-pasture was given a new lease of life by the interest of the Normans in deer husbandry as an alternative to conventional agriculture on poor-quality land. The earliest known park, Ongar Great Park (Essex), is just pre-Conquest, but parks and Forests are otherwise the introduction of William the Conqueror. By 1086 there were about 35 parks and 25 Forests, presumably for native deer. Shortly after this the fallow deer, a Near Eastern species, was introduced; it proved especially suitable for parks and Forests and became the characteristic deer of England, as it still is. By 1200 there were about 140 Forests and by 1300 about 3,200 parks in England. Parks were a source of fresh meat and also a status symbol, belonging to the nobility, gentry, bishops, and religious houses. Forests were much more complex in organization than parks and were the supreme status symbol, more than half being the king's. The distribution of parks is strongly correlated with that of woodland, but there was no connection (other than by chance) between Forests and wooded areas.[26]

Forests were usually adapted out of pre-existing commons. The king's deer were added to, but did not replace, earlier grazing and woodcutting rights, and the king did not necessarily own the land. Forests, although much less efficient producers of venison than parks, were not just a hobby of kings and earls. They produced a small but much-needed income from fines for breaches of Forest Law, and their over-staffed bureaucracy gave the king opportunities for rewarding those who served him well (such as Chaucer) with honorific sinecures.

It is often stated that medieval Forests were of vast extent. This is a fallacy based on the fact that the legal boundaries of Forest administration were drawn to include much wider areas than the actual Forests in which the deer lived.

Wood-pasture management

Parks, being expensive to fence, tended to be more compact in shape than woods, often rectangular with rounded corners (Figure 3.16). Many early parks have a boundary bank with an *internal* ditch, designed to keep animals in, the reverse of a woodbank designed to keep them out.[27]

Commons and Forests have a quite different shape, less compact than that of woods,

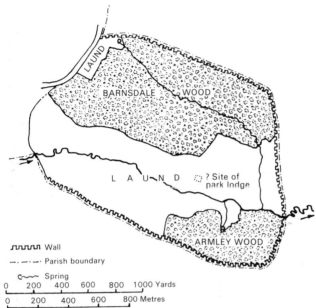

FIG. 3.16 Barnsdale Park, Rutland. Large early deer park (first heard of in 1269) with 'economical' outline, woods, launds, and site of lodge. Shown as in 1850. (From Rackham 1976, *Trees and Woodland in the British Landscape*, J. M. Dent and Sons.)

with concave outlines funnelling out into roads and often with enclaves of private land in the interior (Figure 3.17). This is the shape to be expected of land which it is no one person's duty to fence.

Arrangements for lessening the conflict between grazing and trees were of two kinds:

1. *Uncompartmented* commons, parks, and Forests. The whole area was accessible to livestock at all times. Trees were cut as pollards, not coppiced, in order to protect the regrowth. Timber trees were usually allowed to grow larger than in woods to reduce the problem of replacement. New trees often arose in the shelter of spiny thickets of thorn or holly.

2. *Compartmented* commons, parks, and Forests. Each wood-pasture was divided into a number of *coppices,* enclosed by woodbanks, which were felled like ordinary woods and were then fenced to keep out livestock until the underwood had grown sufficiently not to be harmed. Usually there were also permanent grassy areas (*plains* or *launds*) accessible to animals at all times and often containing pollard trees.

Wood-pastures as they are now

Wooded Forests and commons are more stable than might be expected from the apparently conflicting uses. They have declined since 1350, but usually because of interference from outside rather than by imbalance between woodcutting and grazing. Epping Forest, which is uncompartmented, was heavily grazed for more than 700 years, yet its tree-lands and plains were much the same in 1880 as they had been in 1180.[28] The Enclosure-Act movement was particularly hostile to Forests and commons, and destroyed Enfield Chase (Middlesex) in 1777, Hainault Forest (Essex) in 1851, Wychwood Forest

FIG. 3.17 'Waltham' and 'Henhault', i.e. Epping and Hainault, Forests as surveyed in 1772–4 by Chapman and André. The map differentiates the Forests and other wood-pasture from nearby or adjacent woodland. Within the Forests there were no coppices and no demarcated woods, but the map distinguishes accurately between treeless plains and tracts of pollards. Note the concave perimeters, which dated from the Middle Ages, with hundreds of boundary houses. The southern tip of Waltham Forest is omitted. The outline of Epping Forest north of Chingford is still almost unchanged, but only small parts of Hainault survive. (From Rackham 1980, *Ancient Woodland*, Edward Arnold (Publishers) Ltd.)

(Oxfordshire) in 1858, and many others. Much of what escaped this period still survives, though usually in a disused and fragmentary state.

Parks were a troublesome and precarious enterprise and many of them were short-lived, either reverting to ordinary woodland or becoming farmland. But the tradition of deer-parks continued and in later centuries merged with that of the landscape parks of country mansions. The medieval royal park of Woodstock (Oxfordshire), with its great oaks, is still preserved within the eighteenth-century Blenheim Park.

The small compartmented Forest of Hatfield (Essex) still survives in working order, with almost all the complex structure and land-uses of the coppices and plains.[29] Epping Forest retained most of its original boundaries and structure until the Epping Forest Act of 1878. The pollarding rights were then suppressed (in the belief that they were a malpractice) and the grazing has since declined, with the result that the historic character of the Forest's pollards, grassland, heaths, and bogs is now melting away to ordinary secondary woodland. Burnham Beeches (Buckinghamshire) and The Mens (West Sussex) are wood-pasture commons which still have some pollards and other historic trees; the plains have survived worse than the wooded areas. Staverton Park (East Suffolk), which is private, is a miraculous survival of a little-altered medieval park; it has 4,000 ancient pollard oaks (Figure 3.18).[30]

Wood-pastures do not preserve the wildwood tree composition as do woods. Elm,

FIG. 3.18 Ancient pollard oaks in a medieval deer-park; last pollarded in the eighteenth century. *Staverton Park (Suffolk), May 1982.*

hazel, ash, and lime, the more palatable trees, are replaced (especially if there is no compartmentation) by oak, beech, and hornbeam, which are less easily destroyed by browsing.[31] Herbaceous plants are often those of grassland or heath rather than of woodland.

Ancient trees, especially pollards, are the distinctive feature of wood-pastures; they are better represented in England than almost anywhere in Europe. Examples are the many 500-year-old oaks of Sherwood Forest (Nottinghamshire); the oak pollards, up to 900 years old, of Windsor Forest; and the ancient beeches of Frithsden (Buckinghamshire) and Felbrigg (Norfolk) (Figure 3.19). The eighteenth century appreciated the special beauty of ancient trees and incorporated them into such landscape parks as Ickworth and Heveningham (Suffolk).[32] Old trees are the specific habitat of many lichens and of beetles and other animals, some of which are believed to be relics of wildwood as are the special flowering plants of ancient woodland.[33]

Hedges

Hedges are an essential but not a peculiar part of the English landscape. We leave the boat at Calais for the hedgeless monotony of northern France; but a little beyond Rouen we suddenly enter the *bocage* of Normandy, a land of winding lanes, hamlets, and innumer-

FIG. 3.19 Ancient pollard beeches in a former wood-pasture common; last pollarded in the early eighteenth century. *Felbrigg Beeches (Norfolk), February 1970.*

able hedges full of pollard trees, like Essex of old. The distinction between hedgeless *champagne* regions and *bocage* regions is to be found all over Europe: I have seen it in the Alps and Italy, and have found small areas of ancient hedges in Greece[34] and even Crete. It is not easy to generalize this deep-seated distinction, except that *champagne* tends to go with villages and level terrain and *bocage* with smaller settlements and often with mountainous country. Hedged country is equally typical of North America, where 'fence-rows' extend for at least a thousand miles across the eastern United States.

Origin of hedges

It is popularly believed that all hedges are mere artefacts, the effect of people planting them. In England this is true of nearly all the more recent hedges but not necessarily of the older ones. There are two other ways of getting a hedge.

Some hedges are the *ghosts* of woods that have been grubbed out leaving the edge of the wood as a field boundary. The marginal trees (often already made into a hedge to protect the wood's interior) may be left as a hedge having woodland, rather than hedgerow, characteristics. At Shelley (Suffolk) I have been shown a remarkable roadside hedge 600 yards long composed almost entirely of the wild lime-tree with occasional services. Both are woodland, not hedgerow, trees; lime is the commonest tree of ancient woods in the area but is unheard-of growing by hundreds in a hedge. The mystery is resolved by an eighteenth-century map showing a 'Withers Wood' adjoining just that length of road where the lime hedge now stands.[35] This exception reminds us that most hedges are not just strips of woodland but have their own identity.

Hedges can also arise by default. Close to Hayley Wood there was a railway from 1862 to 1969, separated from the adjoining field by the usual wire fence and shallow ditch. Along the fence there is now a row of hazels, hawthorns, ashes, briars, blackthorns, and maples, which will shortly be managed as a hedge. The railwaymen used to mow the grass verges each year, to prevent them from becoming woodland, but were evidently unable to reach a narrow strip at the base of the fence. The presence of hazel suggests that the new hedge began to develop before 1930, when grey squirrels (which annihilate hazel-nuts) arrived in the area. A hedge arises in this clandestine way whenever a ditch, bank, a lynchet between two ploughed fields on a slope, or an earthen wall is neglected for a few years not too far from a source of tree seed. Fences turn into hedges by birds sitting on the fence and dropping seeds; the fence protects the incipient hedge against grazing and persons tidying up. North Americans are convinced that all their hedges (which are similarly of a variety of trees and shrubs) arose thus by default.

History of hedges

The Enclosure-Act Myth, as a generalization, has been untenable since 1911, when E. C. K. Gonner showed that such Acts covered less than a fifth of England.[36] At a reasonable estimate, allowing for Acts overlooked by Gonner, for processes other than Act of Parliament, and for lands still unenclosed, no more than half the hedged and walled landscape of England dates from after 1700. (The landscape-emparking movement involved a much smaller area.) The Enclosure-Act movement, in effect, filled the middle of England with hedges and made it superficially like the peripheral counties which were already full of hedges. It is unfortunate that much of the early study of the history of hedges was done in Huntingdonshire and Northamptonshire which are Planned Countryside at its most extreme; a quite different story would have been told by Herefordshire or Essex.

Before 1700 England had been divided, like the rest of Europe, into areas of *champagne* and of *bocage*. Thomas Tusser, for instance, in 1573 contrasted the 'Champion countrie' of Cambridgeshire and Leicestershire with the 'seuerall' of Suffolk and Essex; being an Essex man, he preferred the latter, partly because of the 'plentie of fewell and fruit' which grew in 'euerie hedge'.[37] Other writers of the period call the hedged country the Woodland, meaning not land *possessing woods* but land *producing wood* from hedgerows.

The hedged country in 1700 had arisen in many ways. Some of it was the product of earlier, more or less systematic, enclosures; for instance the Sussex coastal plain had once had open-field, which disappeared between 1450 and 1650.[38] In other areas (such as much of Essex) hedged fields have existed since time immemorial and there is no record of anything else.

Large-scale maps tell us much about hedges between 1580 and 1700. In the future Ancient Countryside, hedges were much commoner than fences; they were usually set with hedgerow trees, often at remarkably close intervals. Although there have been many piecemeal alterations—adding a hedge here, grubbing out one there—the great majority of individual hedges now surviving in Ancient Countryside parishes were already there in 1700 if not long before.

It is sometimes said that even in Ancient Countryside the early fields were large and most of the present hedges result from subdividing them. This sometimes happened, but should not be exaggerated: to halve the average size of a set of fields requires only 40 per cent more length of hedge. Nor is it a true generalization. At Lawshall (Suffolk) the average field size in 1612 was less than four acres, and was doubled in the next 230 years by grubbing out some of the hedges (Figure 3.20); a similar story is told by Earl's Colne in Essex (Table 3.2).

Table 3.2. Average sizes of fields in two Ancient Countryside parishes.

	Date	Acres
Lawshall (Suffolk)	1612	3.9
	1922	8.6
Earl's Colne (Essex)	1598	5.4
	1922	8.2

In open-field parishes hedges were less common but were rarely absent altogether. The map of Gamlingay (Cambridgeshire) in 1601 shows many miles of hedges in the closes

(a)

(b)

Hedges added since previous map ++++++++++
Hedges destroyed since previous map ··········

Woods ///   Plantations ///

0 ———————————— ½ ———————————— 1 Mile

0 ——— 1 Km

FIG. 3.20 Hedges in Lawshall (Suffolk): (a) 1611; (b) 1842; (c) 1884; (d) 1927; (e) 1980.

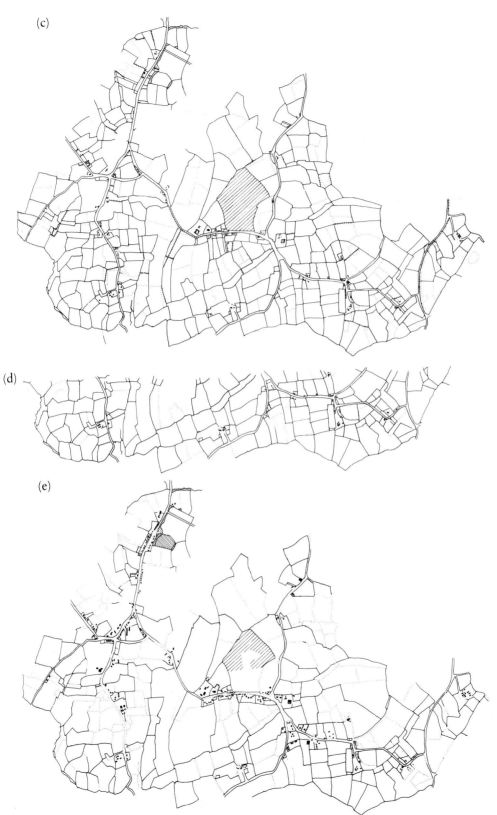

(c)

(d)

(e)

around the little town;[39] some of them still exist (Figures 3.2 and 3.3). The next parish, Little Gransden, was likewise open-field but had what were already in 1649 'auncient quick hedges' in the vicinity of Hayley Wood.[40] Grantchester (Cambridgeshire) had several miles of hedges (some of which still exist) among the strips of the open-field.[41] Soham (Cambridgeshire) has never had an Enclosure Act; massive ancient hedges still separate the parish meadows from the strip-cultivation.

But hedges and hedgerow trees were a familiar part of the landscape long before the earliest large-scale maps. They were valued as legal boundaries, for confining livestock, and as sources of fuel, timber, and thorns for repairing other hedges. They were coppiced, pollarded, grubbed out, planted, stolen, allowed to grow and obstruct the highway, disputed between neighbours and between landlord and tenant, and studied by naturalists. Here are a few examples from the great wealth of early documents:

> . . . upon a fair bough
> that was well covered in blossom
> In a thick neglected hedge
> mixed with reed and green sedge
>
> *   *   *   *   *   *
>
> There stood an old stock nearby
> where the Owl sang in her turn.
> It was all overgrown with ivy;
> It was the Owl's dwelling-place.
>
> *The Owl and the Nightingale*
> (12th-century poem; my translation)

The Abbot and Convent shall, at their own expense, cause a hedge to be planted lengthwise from the first gate up to the second, so that the place may become a lane (*venella*) between the two gates . . . taking branches from the trees growing in the said hedge to maintain the hedge.
Colchester Cartulary, 1272[42]

Ralph Cheseman cut down and took away thorns growing in [the plaintiff's] hedges to the value of ½ mark.   *Court roll, Newton Longville (Buckinghamshire), 1283*[43]

One man making a certain ditch and planting a live hedge . . . 18 perches [99 yards] long and 7 feet wide . . . 6s. at 4d. the perch.   *Estate accounts, Gamlingay, 1330*[44]

James Mede complains that John Palmer senior in the month of March [1443] cut down to the ground, took and carried away divers Trees . . . viz. oak, ash, Maples, white thorn & black, lately growing in a certain hedge . . . between heighfeld and hegfeld, and had been repeating this trespass from time to time for 7 years [previously] . . . by which the said James . . . has suffered damage to the value of 20s.   *Court roll, Hatfield Broad-oak (Essex), 1443*[45]

Richard Bunhall has 7 perches of hedge overhanging the King's highway with branches and thorns in the lane called Wodnenlane . . . penalty 40d.   *Court roll, Great Canfield (Essex), 1512*[46]

Vitis sylvestris [wild clematis] . . . groweth plentuously between ware and Barckway [Hertford-shire] in the hedges, whiche in summer are in many places al whyte wyth the downe of thys vine.

William Turner, 1548[47]

Every hedgebreaker taken in breaking of hedges and carrying of suchlike wood shall pay . . . 16*d.* and 3 hours punishment in the stocks . . . 4*d.* to the lord, to the owners of such wood 4*d.*, to the bailiff 4*d.*, and to him that shall take an offender 4*d.*   *By-laws, Saffron Walden, 1561*[48]

Pollard Trees which this Estate is very much incumbered with & if a great deal more was cut down it would be much better for the land. [There were 6,058 pollard trees in the hedges of a 187-acre farm!]   *Thorndon (Suffolk), c. 1742*[49]

Dating hedges

Until about 1970 people supposed that the trees and shrubs in a hedge were determined either by the whim of the planter or in some vague way by soil, climate, or management. Dr Max Hooper noticed that all these factors were of less importance than the age of the hedge. He counted the tree and shrub species in 227 hedges whose ages, varying from 75 to 1,100 years, were known from written records, and found that species were correlated with age.[50] Hence the celebrated rule of thumb, often miscalled 'Hooper's Hypothesis' (it is not a hypothesis), that the number of species of tree and shrub is approximately equal to the age of the hedge in centuries. (The number has to be counted in a standardized way, in a 30-yard-long sample of hedge, and observing certain conventions as to what constitutes a 'species' and a 'shrub'.)

In the last few years there have been many local studies, for instance that of A. Willmot on the hedges of Derbyshire[51] and that of S. Addington on south Norfolk.[52] Hooper's Rule works in many parts of the country: it picks out the occasional ancient hedge among the modern hedges of Cambridgeshire and the occasional modern hedge among the ancient hedges of Essex. But there are areas in which hedges have too many, or too few, species, for their age. Such exceptions do not of course discredit the rule, but warn us to apply it intelligently.

There are three hypotheses as to why older hedges should have more species:

1. A hedge acquires further species by colonization as it gets older.

2. In earlier times it was the custom to plant hedges with more species than was customary later. Although hedging plants were already articles of commerce by 1316,[53] the process became more commercialized, and therefore simpler, in later centuries. Medieval hedge-planters commonly dug up saplings from woods or existing hedges, and did not think the species mattered much:

Item, in pulling plants of thorns and ashes to put along 1 ditch on the east of the manor-house to the churchyard.   *Forncett (Norfolk), 1376–8*[54]

In Enclosure-Act times, some 200,000 miles of hedge were planted in a century, and the thousand million or so plants could be supplied only by big business in the form of commercial nurserymen. Georgian hedges were usually of hawthorn with timber trees at intervals; the latter have by now been cut down and the regrowth of their stumps has provided a second species. Victorian hedgers often omitted the oak or ash and planted pure hawthorn.

3. Most recent hedges were planted, but the older ones are more likely to have been of natural origin—either the ghosts of woods, or developing out of fences etc.—and therefore mixed from the start. (The Hayley Wood railway hedge ought by Hooper's Rule to be 700–800 years old.)

These processes have normally combined in various ways to produce more species in the older hedges, but sometimes they fail to do so. Small areas of Enclosure-Act hedging among Ancient Countryside, as in the Neroche area of Somerset, may have escaped commercialization and thus be of a mixture of species, though not necessarily the same species as in the surrounding medieval hedges. Conversely, an ancient hedge (like an ancient wood[55]) invaded by suckering elm may lose other species through competition and come to be of pure elm.

The number of species in a hedge, like the shape of the arches in a stone building, is an important piece of evidence about its age, but other evidence should be considered also. There are late survivals of medieval techniques in hedges, as in buildings. There are Victorian imitations of medieval hedges as there are of medieval churches. Genuinely ancient hedges have other peculiarities. They are rarely quite straight—straight lines in the landscape are usually post-1700. They are often on massive banks with lynchets, and contain giant coppice stools or ancient pollards. Maple is rarely found in post-1700 hedges, nor hazel or spindle in hedges more recent than 1500. None of these characteristics, other than the pollards and giant stools, is conclusive in itself, but taken together they enable nearly all ancient hedges to be recognized.

Were there Two Landscapes in Anglo-Saxon England?

Domesday Book

Domesday Book gives particulars of some 7,800 woods. Elsewhere I have analysed the statistics and compared them with other sources, and have compiled maps of the distribution of places that had or had not access to woodland (Figure 3.21) and of the proportion of the land area that was wooded (Figure 3.22).[56]

The England of 1086 was certainly not in general a well-wooded land even by twentieth-century standards. The average proportion was 15 per cent of woodland including wood-pasture. But there was much local variation: small areas were more than half woodland; larger areas had no woodland at all. Little remains of this distribution, for it was to be eaten away by the land-hunger of the next 250 years: by 1350 the well-wooded areas of Domesday, except for the Weald and Chilterns, had become no more than averagely wooded. With rare exceptions, the Hayley Woods of the later Middle Ages and of today were the middle-sized and small woods of 1086; the bigger woods do not survive.

But the woodland distribution of 900 years ago has left a ghost of its former existence. It

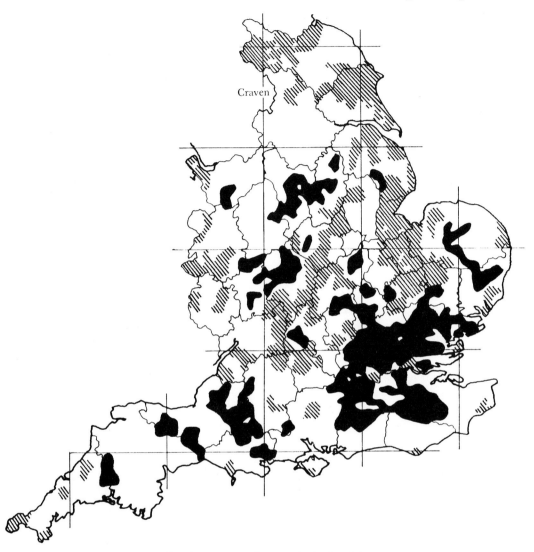

Craven

FIG. 3.21 Presence of woodland in Domesday Book England in 1086.
Hatched areas: no woodland recorded at all. *White areas*: woodland possessed by some settlements but not others. *Black areas*: woodland possessed by every settlement.

No account is taken of the amount of woodland. There are no usable returns for counties north of Cheshire and Yorkshire, nor for Craven. (From Rackham 1980, *Ancient Woodland*, Edward Arnold (Publishers) Ltd.)

corresponds very closely to the later distinction between Ancient and Planned Countryside. All the big concentrations of woodland in Norman England were in what is now Ancient Countryside. In future Planned Countryside there were only middle-sized and small concentrations and scattered individual woods, and well over half the villages had no woodland at all. Where the frontier of the Two Landscapes divides a county, as in

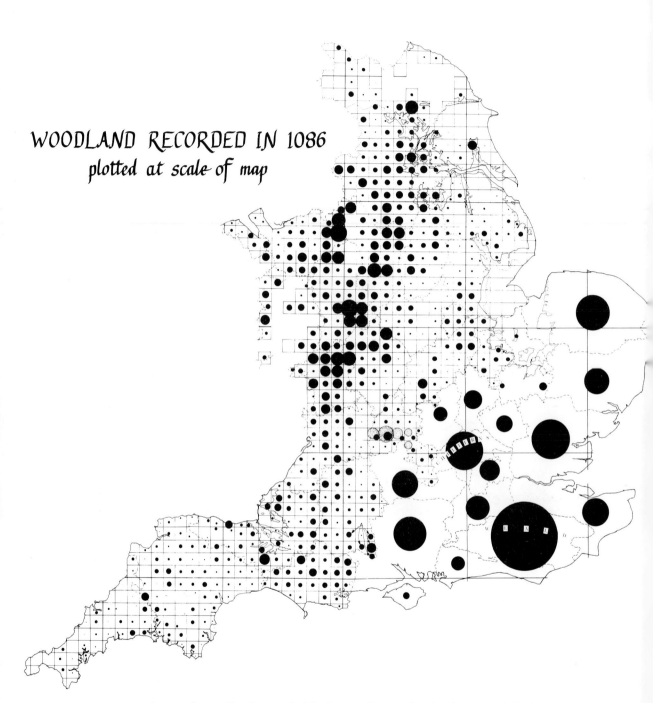

WOODLAND RECORDED IN 1086
plotted at scale of map

FIG. 3.22 Areas of woodland recorded in Domesday England. The size of the black circles represents the estimated area covered by woodland in 1086 at the scale of the map. In area counties woodland is mapped by 10 km National Grid squares: each black circle represents the total woodland area assigned to places located within the square. In swine- and swine-rent

Warwickshire, Worcestershire, and Buckinghamshire, it corresponds faithfully to the wooded and woodless parts of the county in Domesday Book.

Every county that was later champion—that is open-field—and is now Planned Countryside had in 1086 less than, or slightly more than, the national average of 15 per cent of woodland and wood-pasture; only a small part of Somerset had as much as 18 per cent. Counties that are now Ancient Countryside covered a wider range; they included all those with well above the national average, such as Worcestershire except its south-east corner (43 per cent), the north-west half of Warwickshire (35 per cent), and Staffordshire (32 per cent); but also Devon (3.8 per cent) and Cornwall (3.2 per cent). Future Ancient Countryside was more than twice as wooded in 1086 as future Planned Countryside (Table 3.3); the latter covered a third of England as recorded in Domesday Book but had only one-sixth of the woodland.

Table 3.3. Area of woodland (including wood-pasture) in Domesday Book

	Wood, millions of acres	Total land area, millions of acres	Percentage of wood
Lands now Ancient Countryside	3.28	17.6	18.7
Lands now Planned Countryside	0.79	9.7	8.2
All England as recorded in Domesday Book	4.08	27.3	14.9

(Derived from the county statistics published in my *Ancient Woodland*, subdividing counties where necessary.)

Place-names

Was the landscape of 1086 created, as we used to be told, by centuries of Anglo-Saxons laboriously hewing open-field strips out of the universal wildwood? If so, we ought to find the wildwood commemorated by place-names. Everywhere in England we should find names ending in -ley (Old English *leah*, a clearing in woodland), -hurst (*hyrst*, a settlement in a clearing), or -field (*feld*, a 'field' in the sense of an open space close to woodland with which to contrast it). This is not so (Figure 3.23). Such names are thick on the ground in Ancient Countryside (such as Essex, Staffordshire, Derbyshire) but are rare in Planned Countryside (such as Lincolnshire, Leicestershire, Breckland). Where the frontier of the Two Landscapes divides a county it is faithfully reflected by the place-names.

Anglo-Saxon documents establish that these names, in general, already existed some centuries before Domesday Book. The eleventh-century distribution of woodland was

---

counties woodland is mapped county by county, the Weald and Chilterns being treated separately. No distinction is made between kinds of woodland. Stippled circles in Oxfordshire represent Forests. (From Rackham 1980, *Ancient Woodland*, Edward Arnold (Publishers) Ltd.)

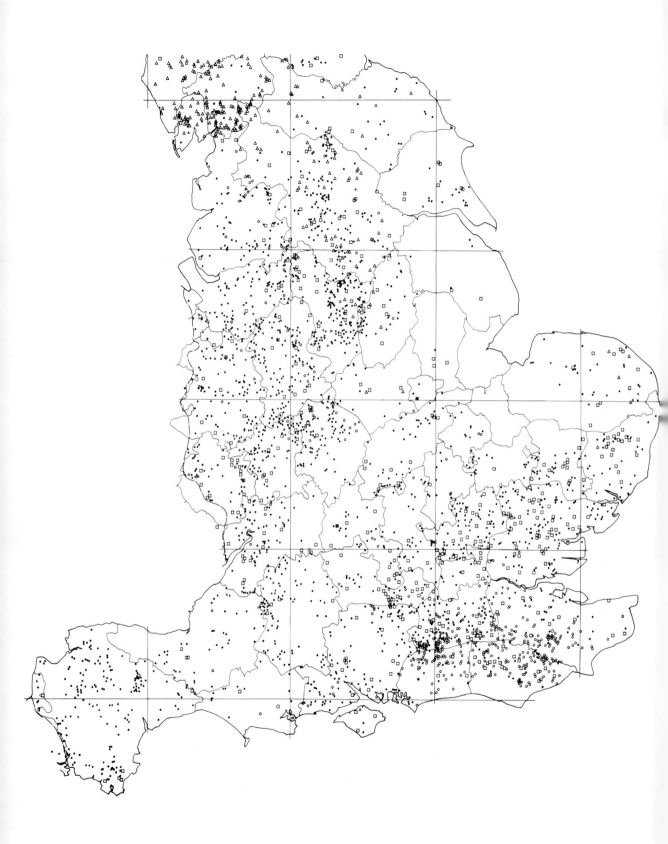

therefore not of recent origin. There are some exceptions: for example, there is a group of -ley villages around Hayley Wood, indicating that a local tract of wildwood survived into Anglo-Saxon times but was reduced to scattered woods by 1086. But the place-names show that the division between the Two Landscapes, as expressed by the woodland, was not in the main the work of the Anglo-Saxons. In Ancient Countryside the Anglo-Saxons acquired a landscape with abundant woodland in which they made clearings (or renamed Roman clearings) and called them leys and fields. In what was to become Planned Countryside they took over a land in which woodland already had scarcity value and there was little opportunity to give names to clearings.

Anglo-Saxon charters

This analysis is clothed with vivid detail by the charters, dating mostly from between AD 700 and 1050, which are the title-deeds of pieces of land defined by descriptions of their boundaries. Charters show that the England of a thousand years ago was not so very different from what it is now. There were woods with names, boundaries (probably with woodbanks), definite ownerships and management; wood-pastures differentiated from woodland; hedges and hedgerow trees; stiles and gates; many kinds of watercourse; and major and minor roads.

Old English had at least four words for hedge: *hege* (our 'hedge'), *haga*, *hegeræwe* ('hedgerow'), *ræwe* ('row'), among others. *Haga* is probably no more than a south-country dialect form of *hege,* but the other words may distinguish different kinds of hedge. Usually they appear to mean hedges in the modern sense; for instance the charters mention hazel-rows, thorn-rows, and willow-rows. An eighth-century charter of Beasfield (Kent) specifies a live hedge (*cwichege*).[57] Many hedges were already old; there was for instance an 'old hedge' at North Wootton (Somerset) in 816.[58] At Kington Langley (Wiltshire) in 940 there was 'the hedge row that Ælfric made', probably the earliest record of anyone planting a hedge.[59] At Grimley (Worcestershire) in *c.* 966 there was an 'old hedge-place' (*ealdan hegestowe*), which may be the earliest allusion to a destroyed hedge.[60] There are many references to hedgerow and other non-woodland trees; for instance:

along the road to the pollard oak; from there along the road from where it adjoins the wood . . . by the little hedge along the spinney . . . along the hedge to the old maple-tree . . . from there to the hoar [lichen-covered] apple tree . . .   *Boundary of Hurstbourne Priors (Hampshire), 901*[61]

There have been many regional studies of charters, but no national analysis has been attempted before because of the amount of material and its very uneven distribution. There are about 820 charter-bounds, which mention 14,226 objects or features. (I exclude

FIG. 3.23 Distribution of names of towns, villages, and hamlets involving 'ley' (●), 'hurst' (○), or 'thwaite' (△), and of towns and villages involving 'field' (□). Broken lines along the Welsh and Cornish borders indicate the westward limit of predominantly Anglo-Saxon place names. (From Rackham 1980, *Ancient Woodland*, Edward Arnold (Publishers) Ltd.)

charters that are Welsh, or have no bounds, or are of unidentified places.) They belong mainly to the southern half of England; there are many for Warwickshire and Berkshire but few for Yorkshire or Suffolk and none for Cheshire or Norfolk. I have divided England into 31 disricts (Figure 3.24a), each district chosen, as far as possible, to be uniform in topography and to contain enough charters to provide between 400 and 500 boundary features. Fifteen districts, with 6,664 features, are in what is now Planned Countryside; sixteen districts, with 7,562 features, are in Ancient Countryside.

The charters mention the word *wudu*, 'wood', 106 times, that is 0.75 per cent of the 14,226 features; there are in addition 59 place-names of which *wudu* is an element (such as Woodley). Including other words for woodland, the 820 bounds mention a total of 383 woods, 2.69 per cent of the total features. Taken district by district, the charters usually agree well with the distribution of woodland in Domesday Book (Figure 3.24b). The two districts comprising the greater part of Worcestershire have 36 woods mentioned among their 1,325 boundary objects; the south-east corner of Worcestershire and adjacent south-east Warwickshire, almost woodless in Domesday, have six woods among 665 points. The western Cotswolds from Cheltenham to Mells have 22 woods among 575 points; the eastern Cotswolds, the Bibury–Burford country, have only one wood among 319 points. This distinction between the wooded and woodless Cotswolds, though seemingly illogical, is still with us today. There are a few anomalies: the small group of charters for the Fens has abnormally many woods, which suggests that there were still a few woods left in the Fens and that these were specially useful as boundary markers in terrain that had few other identifiable landmarks.

The charters are another independent source which corroborates the accuracy of the distribution of woodland in Domesday Book and indicates that in general it had not been rapidly changing. They confirm that there was a definite distinction between the Two Landscapes in respect of woodland. Woods, even though their scarcity might have made them more useful landmarks, are mentioned distinctly less often in what was later to be Planned Countryside (Table 3.4).

What of the ancient hedges by which we now recognize Ancient Countryside? The charters mention 372 hedges, 2.6 per cent of all boundary features, plus 48 places named after hedges. The proportion ranges from 33 hedges in north-west Dorset—one feature in 16 was a hedge—to none at all in the Berkshire claylands or the Fens.

Charters for what is now Ancient Countryside mention 253 hedges, 3.4 per cent of all boundary features; those for what is now Planned Countryside mention 119 hedges, a proportion of 1.8 per cent. There is nearly a twofold difference in the frequency of hedges, but some districts are anomalous. No hedge is mentioned in Cornwall, even though it is a land of prehistoric field-systems; probably Cornwall, then as now, was so full of hedges and walls that they were of no use as landmarks. Conversely, there are more hedges than we should expect in north-west Hampshire and mid- and north Wiltshire: unless there was some local reason why hedges should be specially chosen as landmarks for their rarity, we have to suppose that that part of England was more richly hedged than it later became.

Other distinctions between the Two Landscapes are shown in Table 3.4. There is

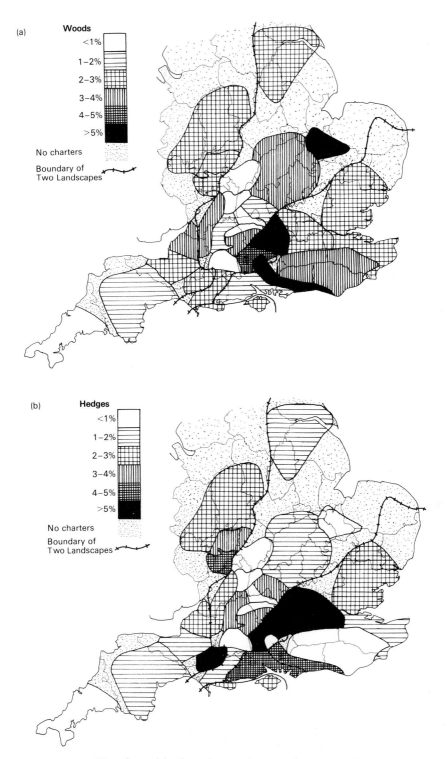

FIG. 3.24 Woods and hedges featured in Anglo-Saxon charters.

Table 3.4. The two landscapes in Anglo-Saxon charters.

	Lands now Ancient Countryside		Lands now Planned Countryside	
	Number of records	Percentage	Number of records	Percentage
Woods (Anglo-Saxon *wudu, graf, holt,* etc.)	224	3.0	159	2.4
Hedges (Anglo-Saxon *hege, ræwe,* etc.)	253	3.4	119	1.8
Trees: all species	389	5.1	368	5.5
oaks	64	0.85	21	0.32
thorns	87	1.15	162	2.43
Heaths and places named after heaths	37	0.48	10	0.15
All features	7,562	100.0	6,664	100.0

little difference in respect of the total number of trees mentioned, but the species are different: oaks, limes, and birches were mainly in future Ancient Countryside, but future Planned Countryside had many more thorns and elders. An unexpected difference is that Ancient Countryside has nearly four times as many mentions of heath as does Planned Countryside.

Origins of the Two Landscapes

Three independent types of evidence have shown that the distinction between the Two Landscapes was well established by Anglo-Saxon times. Their characteristics have altered down the centuries, but the geography has changed very little. A thousand years ago there was the peripheral England of wood and heath, hedges and hedgerow oaks; and there was the central England of few hedges, few heaths, less woodland, and downland thorns and elders. (The documents controvert any rationalization that hedges might have been conceived as a substitute for woodland.)

Did the hedged part of the Anglo-Saxon landscape result from the enclosure of an earlier landscape that had lacked field boundaries? Open-field strips were not the aboriginal land-divisions of England; they may not have existed at all before the middle Anglo-Saxon period. Bronze and Iron Age, 'Celtic', and Roman field-systems all have well-marked boundaries. Such field-systems are most easily, and most often, recognized when disused; but many pre-Anglo-Saxon field boundaries may still be in use. Wide areas of mid- and south Essex, which as far as we know never had any open-field, are still covered with semi-regular rectangular patterns of fields and roads (Figure 3.25). These are the remains of rural planning on a gigantic scale, wholly at variance with the chaotic manorial organization of the area in the last thousand years. As P. J. Drury and W.

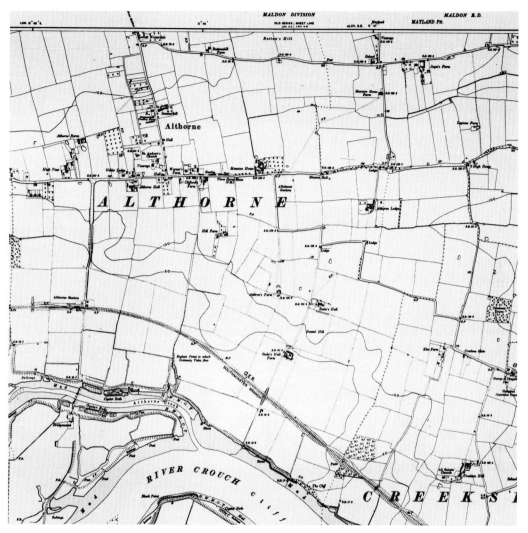

FIG. 3.25 Regular field patterns (Essex). (Courtesy the Bodleian Library, Oxford.)

Rodwell have shown, they cannot be later than Roman; some of them are intersected by Roman roads as they might be by railways or motorways.[62]

Were early field boundaries hedged? It is arguable that the hedges they now have are not original. But the Romans were familiar with hedges (Latin *vepres*) in Italy; the writers Columella and Palladius Rutilius describe how to make a hedge by a technique more elaborate than we have today;[63] and Siculus Flaccus distinguishes planted and natural hedges.[64] Julius Caesar mentions hedges as near as Belgium.[65] We are not told whether the Romans had hedges in Britain, but there is a little archaeological evidence that they did.[66]

The Romans and their predecessors had scores of thousands of miles of field boundary, and we can hardly suppose that they would have had the time, even if they had the inclination, to prevent many of them from becoming hedges.

In all probability the Anglo-Saxons took over England as an at least partly hedged landscape, out of which the open-fields were made. We know much about the abolition of the open-fields, but the story has yet to be told of the earlier agricultural revolution which created them. Beginning in the Dark Ages, a 'De-Enclosure Movement' flooded Europe like a tide from Russia to Ireland. It flowed for a long period, and a ripple of it even reached America: seventeenth-century Sudbury (Massachusetts) set up an open-field system after Sudbury (Suffolk) had abolished its open-fields.[67] The tide of de-enclosure did not reach everywhere: it covered most of the English Midlands for so long that little now remains of the pre-open-field landscape. The peripheral counties of England, on the whole, were reached only here and there; the open-field tradition was weak and soon disappeared; and large areas, such as South Essex, were not reached at all. In a few places, such as Tadlow (Cambridgeshire), open-fields lasted only a short time and did not efface an earlier geometric field system.[68]

The making of the open-fields corresponded, and was perhaps connected, with a great reorganization of rural life, a 'collectivization' of agriculture involving also the development of communal cultivation and the regrouping of settlements to form villages.[69] It is not clear from Anglo-Saxon charters or even from Domesday Book how much of this had been accomplished. The many hedges in the charters of parts of Hampshire and Wiltshire, if representative, may be the survival of a Romano-British hedged landscape later to be reduced to open-field.

Why was the open-field movement more successful in some parts of England than in others? It was more successful where it reorganized existing farmland that had already been made by somebody else. Where men had to make their fields before they could till them, they usually remained individualists with scattered farmsteads and private fields. Hence the association in the charters of hedges with the vicinity of woodland or heath. Open-field agriculture was strongest in districts with little or no woodland; one of the motives may well have been to use existing farmland more efficiently where there was no room for expansion.

The Two Landscapes thus reflect a division of England that goes back at least to the late Roman period. The Romans and their predecessors had reduced well over half of England to farmland and moorland. The remaining woodland, though probably greater in area than it is found to be in Domesday Book, was not very different in distribution. The present Planned Countryside and Ancient Countryside correspond, in the main, to areas that had little or much woodland at the end of the Roman period.

In the typical Midland counties, most of the great woods disappeared before English became the language, and no memory of them remains. The land was already mainly farmland in Anglo-Saxon times, and was suitable for the agricultural revolution that created the open-fields and for the later agricultural revolution that abolished them to make the present Planned Countryside. Little now remains of the Roman landscape save crop-marks, possible parish and estate boundaries, a few roads, and maybe some of the ancient woods.

In the typical peripheral counties the Romans left much woodland, though penetrated everywhere by clearings and often densely populated—the towns included Colchester and St. Albans. Their successors took over the clearings and made new ones to such an extent that by 1350 most of the great woods themselves were remembered only by place-names. In such terrain the open-field movement spread only locally and soon receded. The landscape that we now have, or still had in 1945, is not the product of agricultural revolution but of two thousand years of growth, decline, and piecemeal alteration.

When I coined the term Ancient Countryside in 1975, I did not know how ancient it was: there seemed to be no way of dating the origin of features that were earlier than 1500. The last eight years have begun to reveal its true complexity. The 'classic English landscape' of hedges and woods does indeed involve the whole of our history since Classical times; it deserves to be treated with more understanding and respect than it has been given in recent decades.

4

Mapping the medieval landscape: forty years in the field

M. W. BERESFORD

THE medieval landscape is perhaps the most tantalizing of all: not quite superseded, remote and yet recoverable. The technology of surveying and cartography had not then progressed far enough for there to be more than a few scattered records of how that landscape appeared to contemporaries, and while late-medieval landscapes of Italy and the Low Countries were painted as background to many Nativities and Calvaries, there was as yet no school of English landscape painting. In another sense, however, the medieval landscape is not far from our doorstep, with many elements remaining into modern times, sometimes unchanged and sometimes half-submerged in later development. The topography of its agricultural systems has been transformed by the process of their enclosure into hedged and walled fields, but its network of paths and lanes is still the basis of our rural communications and of many suburban streets; yet the submergence of medieval field systems and even of industrial remains had gone far enough for their recovery to have to await the development of landscape history with its researches based on field-observation, aerial photography, pre-enclosure maps and surveys from the post-medieval period, and conventional archaeological examination.

The widespread physical remains from pre-enclosure agriculture were the first elements to command attention, but their field-study led to a recognition of the visible evidence at the sites of deserted medieval villages and then of an even larger number of 'shrunken' or 'migration' sites in the surrounds of existing villages. These two phenomena, now counted in thousands, draw attention to massive economic changes, some connected with great decreases in the total rural population and others with more deliberate changes in land-use from arable to pasture. Additionally, the discovery of deserted sites has put many new items on the agenda of medieval archaeology, itself a young discipline with its journal less than thirty years old. At deserted village sites, house structures can be investigated from periods earlier than any surviving above ground, and the antiquity of the minor topographical elements in the village can be investigated with a hope of reaching back into pre-medieval influences and survivals. At surviving villages, houses and gardens not only cover evidence of this sort but also make it unlikely that it could ever be available for uncovering. The deserted sites, on the other hand, provided that the plough and the bulldozer are not allowed to destroy them, will afford future generations the opportunity to exercise skills and techniques as yet unimagined in the exploration both of the medieval landscape and of earlier settlement.

FIG. 4.1 Village houses, crofts, and open fields: Laxton (Nottinghamshire). Ploughing, sowing, and harrowing two selions; windmill erected in adjoining furlong: plan of 1635 (from Orwin and Orwin 1938).

When this lecture was advertised it was given the single title 'Forty Years in the Field' as a warning that the approach would be predominantly autobiographical: the study of the medieval landscape has been an academic development almost confined to my own lifetime although of course many others, particularly William Hoskins,[1] have made significant contributions to the subject.

The select reading list (p. 127) and the particular works mentioned in the Notes and References should dispel any fear that the autobiographical is to be equated with the egocentric. Indeed no bibliography can do justice to the help and companionship of others, usually non-historians, in so many journeys into the countryside; and the subject at large has been fortunate, in our age of increasing leisure and increasing ease of access to the countryside, not only to find a readership to patronize its published work, but a small army of amateur observers and explorers eager to assist in field-work or excavation. Indeed, largely thanks to courses and conferences organized by extramural departments (and I think particularly of Trevor Rowley's work from Oxford) more adult students possess an awareness of this subject than do undergraduates in the history schools of universities, ancient and modern.

The lecture therefore attempts in the first place to explain the tardy interest of the profession in landscape features of the medieval period and then, with necessary autobiographical bias, to recapture the particular combination of circumstances and personalities which took the subject rapidly forward. If chance factors seem to be stressed

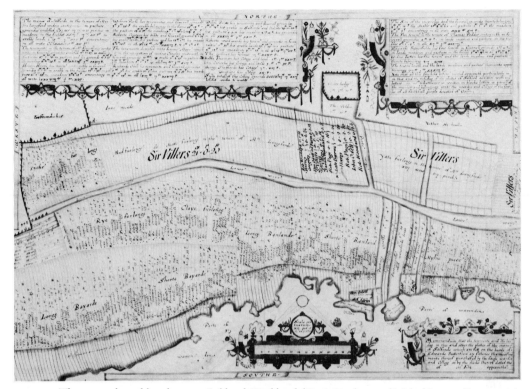

FIG. 4.2 The unenclosed landscape: Salford (Bedfordshire). Furlongs divided into selions, with access tracks. Surveyed in 1590 for All Souls College with tenants' names indicated. (Courtesy the Warden and Fellows of All Souls College, Oxford.)

in this association, then that would seem to me, looking back over forty years in the field, to be a proper acknowledgement of the way in which one's research interests can be born and develop, how others complement, and how piles of bricks one has built up can be then knocked down and rebuilt in another meaning.

I do not claim landscape history as a subject in its own right *pace* the Landscape History Society and its *Journal*. It is a servant of subjects and in itself (like geography or education) a conglomeration of academic disciplines. The first public proclamation of its existence as a named multi-discipline could be counted W. G. Hoskins's *The Making of the English Landscape* in 1955, its scope extending before and after the medieval period, but in fact the subject had been opened up a decade earlier not only by Hoskins's own surveys of the landscape of Leicestershire[2] and Midland England[3] but by other first forays into the history of fields and villages. By a coincidence he and I, unknown to each other, took landscape history into the virgin pages of the *Economic History Review* in the same volume, dated 1943, he writing of the improvement of the wastes of Exmoor and I of the north Warwickshire Coldfield;[4] while our papers on the deserted medieval villages of our respective counties came close on each other's heels. My Warwickshire paper was read in

Birmingham in December 1947; the Leicestershire society's *Transactions* do not record the date of the meeting when Hoskins's paper[5] was read but I believe it was 1946.

To turn to personal testimony, and to Cambridge in 1939. Members of Smiley's university will be aware of some features of that pre-war cultural landscape lately revealed: mine are less dramatic. I was an undergraduate in a history school where, as far as I recall, no one in any lecture said anything that could be construed as a comment on the historical landscape or drew upon it as a part of historical exposition. Had I been interested in military history I suppose I might have had to consider landscape aspects of battlefields, although later acquaintance with the agricultural landscape of Bosworth Field (where Richard III called for a horse to carry him across the pastures of a deserted village site) and Naseby (which was unenclosed at the time of the battle) made me wonder whether the military historians envisaged their pawns moving over a land surface as timeless and featureless as a chess-board, independent of the variety of the farmland and the farming seasons involved. And had I been interested in architectural history at that

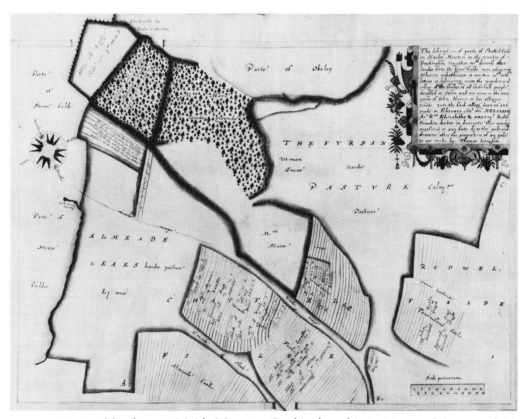

FIG. 4.3 A mixed landscape: Maids Moreton (Buckinghamshire). Fringes of the open fields near the parish boundary. Also 51 acres of meadow (Almeade); woodland; 144 acres of rough pasture (Fursan); 5½ acres of a 'gorsey' close. Surveyed in 1592 for All Souls College. (Courtesy the Warden and Fellows of All Souls College, Oxford.)

time I could—although it formed part of no syllabus—have found in the libraries a solid accumulation of studies of manor houses, castles, churches, and abbeys. Of the much larger number of buildings that housed the ordinary rural population I could have read virtually nothing since their standing remains were so few.

It is not too difficult to see why the subject of landscape history was postponed so long. The very subjects it first served—the chronology of settlement, fluctuations in population, together with changes in agricultural techniques, crops, and land-use—were themselves a late development in medieval economic history, which was itself a late development within academic history. Seen as part of the history of history, field research into historical landscapes needed an input also from other disciplines, particularly archaeology and geography, but from my recollection academic apartheid was the rule in 1939: the tribes were separated by the triposes but, my spies tell me, even if historians had then knocked on doors labelled 'archaeologist', they would have had difficulty in finding a medievalist and, having found one, would probably have found him at work on an abbey or a castle site, treating architectural history, as it were, to a day out on the Underground.

As early as 1908 Hadrian Allcroft had presented a conspectus, *Earthwork of England*, with a suggestive but small medieval portion; and the pre-medieval bias of the earthworks included in the pre-war county surveys of the Royal Commission on Historical Monuments or delineated on large-scale Ordnance Survey maps make up the visual equivalent of a deafening silence.

In the mid-nineteenth century a field surveyor working in part of the East Riding of Yorkshire was alert to earthworks surviving from deserted medieval villages but his example was not followed elsewhere.[6] Indeed, the earthworks of the streets and property boundaries within the deserted site of East Lilling (North Riding) were labelled 'moats' even though gravity would have had to be defied in order to fill them with water. An early Stuart survey now in the British Library identifies the site as a former village, and it is so acknowledged on the current Ordnance Survey map.

The Ordnance Survey's early indifference is the more surprising since its first Archaeological Officer, O. G. S. Crawford, published not only the first air photograph of a deserted medieval village site (Gainsthorpe, Lincolnshire, 1925)[7] but in 1928 printed part of a pre-enclosure field map (Calstone, Wiltshire), in *Wessex from the Air*, alongside an air photograph of the area. In justice to Crawford's memory I must acknowledge that towards the end of his life, as editor of *Antiquity*, he gave space to an exposition of researches under a title that I have adapted for this lecture.[8] In retrospect that paper is significant for its inbuilt assumption that there was *one* unchanging medieval landscape to be mapped, waiting only to be charted by the right combination of field-work and documentary study. Its over-ambitious project for charting the landscape of all England was less reprehensible: it was simply the exuberance of inexperience and relative youth.

In 1939 Cambridge certainly knew the phrase 'historical geography' and indeed my tutor Bernard Manning once taught that subject in the Geography faculty.[9] His pupil and friend, the absurdly young Clifford Darby, had already prefigured a later career by editing and contributing to the *Historical Geography of England and Wales* published in 1936;

but Manning's historical geography was nearer to the content of a conventional historical atlas of the day, the geography of past political frontiers. Darby's *Historical Geography* invoked past landscapes, but always in the aggregate, with maps in plenty but all small-scale distribution maps: the topography, past or present, of particular places did not enter in; nor were medieval and sixteenth-century maps and surveys adduced to illustrate surviving landscape features.

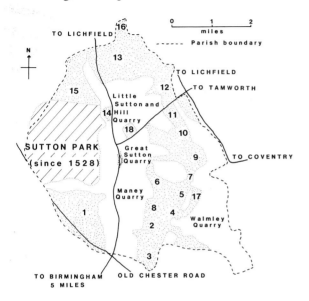

FIG. 4.4 An unenclosed landscape: Sutton Coldfield (Warwickshire). An infield–outfield system of cropping, commons lying fallow for long intervals in a rotation: characteristic of poor soils. The numbers represent different fields. The author's first published essay in landscape history (redrawn from Beresford 1941–2).

It is interesting in retrospect to see how easily the identification of relict features from medieval landscape might have been achieved long before 1939: so near and yet so far. In 1883 Seebohm had published a plan of the thousands of constituent strips or selions by which the fields of medieval Hitchin were farmed, and Hitchin was a stone's throw from Cambridge.[10] In 1939 some Cambridge dons must have had on their walls framed originals of David Loggan's vivid late seventeenth-century views of the unenclosed fields of Cambridge at harvest time; or, if not, the reproductions in F. W. Maitland's *Township and Borough*; and Maitland's Oxford audience at the Ford lectures of 1897 would have heard him use the vestigial grass commons of Cambridge as part of his evidence for the town's origins. From Oxford also, antedating the continental examples of Meitzen (1895), J. L. G. Mowat had published in 1888 a portfolio of plans drawn from college archives, mainly of unenclosed parishes;[11] while between 1928 and 1936 G. H. Fowler had made maps of pre-enclosure Bedfordshire available in print.[12] No one, however, seems to have taken any of these volumes from the study to the field for comparison, although students living in these days of cheap photocopying devices should not forget how expensive a photograph of a large map then was, and how laborious the alternative of tracing by hand.

*   *   *

R. H. Tawney's remark, 'History needs not more books but more boots,' has been often quoted (although the source not identified). In 1912 he transcribed not only sections of the fine portfolio of large-scale Elizabethan field-maps made for All Souls College[13] but also the Elizabethan map of depopulated Whatborough (Leicestershire), marking 'the place where the towne of Whateboroughe stoode' and the surveyor's explicit identification of visible ridge-and-furrow in the sheep pastures with the strips (selions, ridges) of the abandoned medieval arable fields.[14]

As an undergraduate writing essays about the Tudor agrarian problem I must have

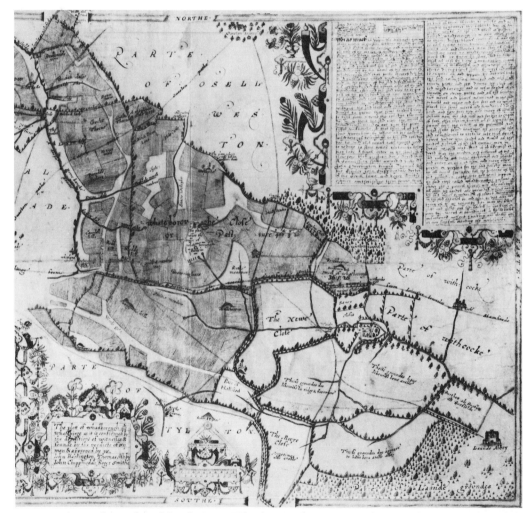

FIG. 4.5 An early enclosed landscape: Whatborough (Leicestershire). 'The Place where the town of Whatborough stood' and the remains of its former open fields after conversion to pasture and depopulation of the village. Survey of 1620 for All Souls College. (Courtesy the Warden and Fellows of All Souls College, Oxford.)

looked at these map evidences with particular interest, for although I had not taken geography at A level I had brought with me from school, thanks to an inspired teacher of that subject (W. H. Sutton), a keen interest in anything that could be mapped. But lecture-room history and the Midland landscape, through which the train took me twice each term, were in such separate mental compartments that ridge-and-furrow from the train window seemed some modern farming routine. Nor did I conceive that a former village could leave earthworks, for surely, had it done so, would not Archaeology (such was my simple faith) have long made it a place of pilgrimage?

FIG. 4.6 The hedged fields of Whatborough. The view, taken in 1955, is from the south-west.

As Tawney himself said ruefully to me more than once, had he actually walked in Bedfordshire and Leicestershire (rather than in the Cotswolds) he would have deprived Beresford and Hoskins of the chance of making a reputation and a livelihood. I suspect that Tawney's exhortation to leave the study for boots and the countryside was intended less as a directive towards the quasi-archaeological aspects of past landscapes than towards their surviving buildings such as he knew in Cotswold wool-market towns and cloth-making villages, perhaps influenced also by his colleague Eileen Power whose *Medieval People* (1924) was illustrated with photographs of relevant buildings.

Asa Briggs has recently dated his own (and my) initiation into historical landscapes from our attendance at Professor Power's lectures when she and Tawney were in wartime exile at Cambridge.[15] My own recollection puts the initiation on a different occasion when he and I were members of a small seminar group whom John Saltmarsh packed into his open coupé and drove to a riverside field at Grantchester, armed with typewritten extracts from a fifteenth-century survey of the component selions of a King's College holding which he had encountered in the college archives. From the edge of the meadow we progressed westwards, stepping out the distances corresponding to the perches by which the fifteenth-century surveys had measured the widths of the selions. And there they were, faintly, in the grass: so faintly that the recent Royal Commission plan hesitates to mark them except as 'cultivation remains'.[16]

The seed which John Saltmarsh sowed that afternoon did not immediately take root. I might have responded to a map but it was a written survey, transcribed and translated, which he had used; and although his insistence on us each doing some local study in the vacation did drive me into the past landscape of my home town, Sutton Coldfield, there was no temptation to do field-work there since its fields were covered with bricks and mortar,[17] and when I did become first involved with documents, in time stolen from examination revision, they concerned the administrative history of enclosure rather than its topography.[18]

I did know of pre-enclosure maps through browsing in the map room of the University Library; and ever since my first tutorial meeting as a freshman, when Charles Wilson pushed into my hands as essay material a brand new copy, I had known the Orwins' *Open Fields* and the map of Laxton in 1635 which they reproduced there.[19] The book also had an air photograph of a tangle of selions where several furlongs jostled each other at Crimscote (Warwickshire).[20] Although they enormously illuminated the subject by demonstrating the practical agricultural explanation for the physical form of ridge-and-furrow, the Orwins seem not to have looked for ridge-and-furrow on the ground, even at Laxton. Perhaps they were deterred by knowing that selions there had been amalgamated into groups, although still unenclosed: but in fact the ridge-and-furrow (as I later showed from air photographs)[21] does corrugate the Laxton landscape. Until their deaths the Orwins always remained sceptical of the ridge-and-furrow identity.[22]

Neither the Orwins' map of Laxton nor Saltmarsh's exercise with the written survey of Grantchester sent me immediately to make ground/map comparisons. Laxton was quite inaccessible from either Cambridge or my home for a lad obliged to count his scholarship pennies and I had no access to medieval surveys of fields near home; nor would I have been able to read the medieval script. It was not until I was living at Rugby, surrounded by a corrugated countryside of almost endless grassy ridge-and-furrow, that I had the opportunity to return to testing its identity with former selions by putting together the Saltmarsh introduction to the ground and the memory of the Orwins and Laxton, and using the leisure of weekend walks to take with me tracings of local pre-enclosure maps. Kinwarton (Warwickshire) was the first parish where I peered into field after field, ticking off the correlations;[23] Ilmington (Warwickshire) was made raw material for practice exercises at a local history summer school held at Barford House;[24] and Braybrooke (Northamptonshire) was my first exercise over the county boundary, taking me also (although I did not then recognize them) over the earthworks of streets and houses from an abandoned portion of that village.[25]

In itself the identity of ridges with selions on some pre-enclosure map was an antiquarian triviality. What could it add to knowledge of a medieval landscape that the map did not itself already provide?—at best the opportunity to observe the rise and fall of the ground which uncontoured plans could not show and to speculate upon the influence of soil and relief upon selion length, width, and direction.[26]

FIG. 4.7 The dissolution of the medieval landscape: Leicestershire. Townships in black had their open fields enclosed and villages depopulated before 1600; shaded areas were enclosed by agreement between proprietors, 1600–1750; the remainder by Act of Parliament after *c.* 1750. (Redrawn from Beresford in Hoskins 1949b.)

My enthusiasm for extending the scope from particular identities to a general identity arose from its possible use in progressing from the small number of townships where pre-enclosure maps were made and survive to those without maps but with ridge-and-furrow. Hence, I hoped, the extent of open-field farming might be determined, for it was still regarded in the 1940s as a feature of the Midlands and southern lowlands. If indeed the lynchets of the Pennine dales or the ridges under Cheviot heather were the mark of the medieval plough, then they could be added to the other evidences which Professor Postan was then adducing to argue for the intensity of medieval population pressure upon marginal lands. Thus came weekend after weekend in which sheets of the six-inch OS, covered with my pencil lines wherever ridges were visible, began to re-create open-field landscapes unrecorded in any surviving map. In one exercise, even now unpublished, I went back to a terrier of the type which Saltmarsh used at Grantchester,[27] fitted the descriptions together like a jigsaw, and then walked the path from Stratford-upon-Avon to Anne Hathaway's cottage at Shottery counting out the ridge-and-furrow which Shakespeare must have known as open-field selions (locally called 'acres') where he saw on amorous summer evenings how 'Between the acres of the rye, The pretty country folk do lie.' The right of way has not been blocked by recent building, and ridges still survive in a school playing-field, as they do a few miles away in the parkland of Welcombe where Shakespeare's butcher father helped to convert arable to permanent pasture by contentious enclosure.[28]

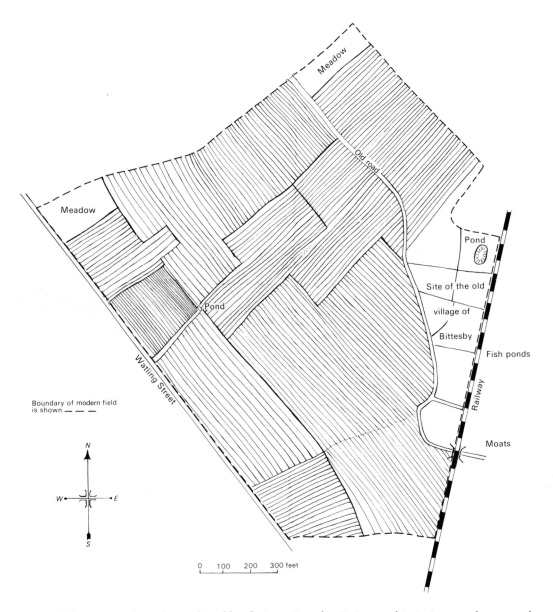

FIG. 4.8 Reconstruction of a medieval landscape: Bittesby (Leicestershire). A ground survey of ridge and furrow. (From an original drawing by Peter Ransom, 1947.)

It was the transfer of selion patterns to an Ordnance Survey map at Bittesby in 1947 (Leicestershire) which first thrust me into that other major element from former medieval landscapes, the earthworks of village sites. I took time to accept that the earthwork at the centre of that township, while certainly not ridge-and-furrow, could be the remains of a village. In extenuation, the earthworks did not include clearly defined houses since (as in so much of the clay Midlands) there was no local stone easily available for peasant house-building, and the earthworks from abandoned wooden and wattle-walled houses are usually shapeless, quite unlike those in the chalk Wolds which had proclaimed themselves to the Captain of Engineers as house earthworks a century earlier (above, p. 110). It soon became apparent from published and unpublished documents that Warwickshire had very many Bittesbys—eventually some 128 in all—and field-work quickly produced earthworks of the Bittesby type.

At that moment the RAF made available the thousands of vertical air photographs taken in the course of wartime sorties and post-war Ordnance Survey revision. The archive was then housed in Nissen huts in the grounds of Medmenham House near Henley-on-Thames, and the freedom to browse there enabled one to wander over the Midlands infinitely faster than on foot or by public transport. Although not all the photographs were taken under optimal conditions for identifying earthworks, and fields still had to be tramped, the investigation of former landscapes was immensely accelerated especially as the air photograph revealed soil marks and crop marks rarely discernible—and even more rarely decipherable—to an observer on the ground.[29] My major attempt to convince my fellow historians of the ridge-and-furrow identity was illustrated by setting air photographs[30] and corresponding sections of pre-enclosure maps side by side, and all subsequent work on deserted village sites drew heavily on the RAF collection.

It was an exhibition in Rugby public library of these comparisons and the search for Warwickshire deserted villages which first brought me into contact with William Hoskins, whose patient exploration of the Leicestershire landscape had already taken him to its proliferation of deserted village sites.[31] He was hospitable and generous to someone who was not a university teacher or research student, and it was an immense pleasure to obtain a copy of the Whatborough air photograph, to match it with a photocopy of the 1586 plan from All Souls,[32] and to meet Hoskins with it to walk over 'the place where the towne of Whateboroughe stoode' on a hill-top no more than 455 feet above sea level but a Snowdon in the Leicestershire pastures that windy morning. It was the first of many happy meetings. He accepted an article from me when he edited *Studies in Leicestershire Agrarian History*[33] and did me a longer-term service when he acted as referee for applications I was then making for university lectureships.

In that lottery I drew Leeds (failing Nottingham, Glasgow, and London) and left the Midlands for ever in April 1948. My treks through Warwickshire had been in the leisure time of an adult education lecturer and organizer working mainly the night shift: now I had the leisure appropriate to whatever research was expected of a university lecturer, and was set in a strange country. As it proved, Leeds was an excellent base in every sense. It was convenient for further pursuit of ridge-and-furrow in the landscape of the northern uplands and it also extended the horizon of the deserted village study.

Even that was unexpected. In the period from which contemporary evidence has best survived it was generally assumed that desertion and depopulation were Midland phenomena: from the Midland counties came the complaints to Tudor councils and to the Midlands went the official commissions of inquiry. Yet within a few weeks I was counting up those Yorkshire parishes which seemed from the six-inch Ordnance Survey maps in the library to have no villages, and in a search for early Yorkshire maps in the manuscript room of the (then) British Museum was fortunate enough to encounter John Norden's 1625 survey of Sheriff Hutton parish, noting of East Lilling that 'it hath been a hamlet of some capacity though now utterly demolished'.[34]

In late June after the examinations I went with Philip and Eric Lawton to stay in Malton Youth Hostel for two nights as the base for my first entry into the Yorkshire Wolds, where the empty parishes seemed the most numerous and the most accessible. We pushed our way through crops which obstructed the footpaths that the Ordnance Survey map alleged existed, aiming for the suspiciously isolated church at Wharram Percy. It proved to stand in a romantically isolated valley surrounded not by crops but by three or four pasture fields, and in those fields were earthworks more clearly like house foundations than anything I had seen in the Midlands, and akin to those in Crawford's 1925 air photograph of Gainsthorpe (Lincolnshire). We lingered long and paid the penalty of missing the last bus from Wharram le Street crossroads but, even after counting the blisters from the hot tarmac on our forced march down to Malton, counted the day well spent.

Earlier that June I had been invited by Professor Postan to join the Danish archaeologist Axel Steensberg, Hoskins, and a number of others in a visit to Leicestershire sites including Knaptoft, and to Hamilton,[35] where Hoskins had just organized some trial excavations rather like those that I had essayed at Stretton Baskerville (Warwickshire) on the eve of my departure for Leeds. Neither of us had archaeological training, and the sites were not straightforward, having no firmly delineated house foundations. Even after seeing the clearer evidences at Wharram Percy I certainly had no thoughts of excavating: the site was remote from Leeds; I have never been a car owner; and I was not well enough acquainted with either colleagues or students to inveigle them into becoming chauffeurs or labourers. Within the next twelve months I did manage short expeditions with borrowed tools, crude surveying equipment, and little but enthusiasm for a guide, but always to sites near main roads and bus routes. Neither of the sites selected for their accessibility (Steeton, West Riding and East Lilling, North Riding) had houses with stone foundations, and work went on for no more than a few weekends. It must be emphasized that the object of excavation at that stage, both by Hoskins and myself, was very limited. Above all we were seeking two things: firstly to prove that these earthworks at the centre of empty parishes were indeed of medieval houses, not from one of the then better-known types of prehistoric or Roman occupation; secondly to obtain dating evidence for the latest period of occupation before desertion.

There were still sceptics abroad: even in 1954, when I had completed *The Lost Villages of England,* pre-publication excitement was heightened by the receipt of a postcard from another historian, bringing this advice: 'I feel impelled to advise you to consider whether or not you should really go ahead with such a book, and to weigh it very carefully as I myself have no desire to be drawn into further controversy but my hand would be forced if the book maintained the argument I suspect'; and had not J. H. Clapham, Professor Emeritus of Economic History in the University of Cambridge, written in 1946: 'deserted villages are singularly rare'?[36]

FIG. 4.9 The recovery of a landscape: Wharram Percy (Yorkshire). A long-house of the late fifteenth century lying just beneath the turf; the blackened stones of the central hearth lie near the upper measuring rod. Domestic and animal quarters lay under the single roof.

It was indeed naïve of us to believe that dating evidence could be obtained in amateurish excavations, but the house-shaped earthworks at Wharram Percy gave some hope of meeting the first of the two objectives mentioned above. In 1949 the BBC North Region invited me to give a radio talk to celebrate the 600th anniversary of the Black Death, and in the course of it I mentioned that the plague had often been wrongly accused of permanently depopulating villages: although there were plenty of deserted villages, I said, instancing Wharram Percy, it was not difficult to cite documents from late fourteenth-century tax collections to show that such villages still had plenty of taxpayers thirty years after the Black Death. This talk happened to be heard by the headmaster of Settrington village school, near Wharram, who told me that he would act as advocate to Lord

Middleton, who was chairman of his school managers and owner of the village site, if we wished to come and excavate at Wharram Percy.

We came for weekends in 1950 and 1951, we saw, but it can hardly be said that we began to conquer until 1952. John Hurst was then beginning post-graduate study at Cambridge in medieval archaeology. He and Jack (now Professor) Golson had been encouraged by Professor Grahame Clark and Professor Postan to join forces and apply to some deserted village site the techniques which Professor Steensberg had developed in Denmark. Golson came to see me in Leeds as their ambassador, and in June 1952 Hurst paid his first visit to our site. As ever, he immediately envisaged the long-term potential and offered to supervise the excavations if I could raise the volunteers. It seemed an admirable division of labour, and excavation has continued on that basis each July ever since, broadening into a research project covering all aspects of the historical landscape in the two parishes of Wharram Percy and Wharram le Street. From Wharram Percy Hurst conceived the idea of an inter-disciplinary (Deserted) Medieval Village Research Group (1952) and many of its members were active in the foundation of the Society for Medieval Archaeology in 1957.

Archaeologists do now refer to Wharram Percy as a classic site and it certainly occurs in examination papers, but for myself I prefer the fame of the following anecdote. I was shown by the chief examiner for a certain O level examination in social history the answer which a confused candidate (with perhaps a confused teacher behind it all) had given to a question on deserted villages. 'There were once thought to be 2,263 deserted village sites in England but that is now known to be a Tudor exaggeration. There are only two, and their names are Beresford and Hurst.' Our partnership has been described more accurately by a reviewer as one between the prolix professor and the taciturn Man from the Ministry.[37]

After 1952 the charting of deserted villages proceeded apace and the dots accumulated on the distribution maps.[38] Many of the additions were due to the explorations of members of the Research Group, amateur and professional, historians, geographers, and field archaeologists. Between 1954 and 1968, 1,110 were added, so that when a map of the Isle of Wight's 32 sites was exhibited at a Royal Archaeological Institute lecture Sir Mortimer Wheeler was heard to exclaim, looking at the pock-marked plan, 'My God, they've sunk the Isle of Wight'. In fact the island has on average one deserted village site every five square miles: using a different index of intensity, Oxfordshire had one-third more villages at the beginning of the fourteenth century than in 1981, and Northamptonshire one fifth more.[39] If we take into account the complementary phenomenon of earthworks which indicate shrinkage in the number of houses rather than a total desertion, it is clear that in many parts of the country the landscape has never been so populous as at the height of the Middle Ages.

This accumulation of information from many different sources is more than an antiquarian collection. The sheer number of deserted sites demands a real adjustment of vision if we are to turn from the landscape of the modern countryside to that of the Middle

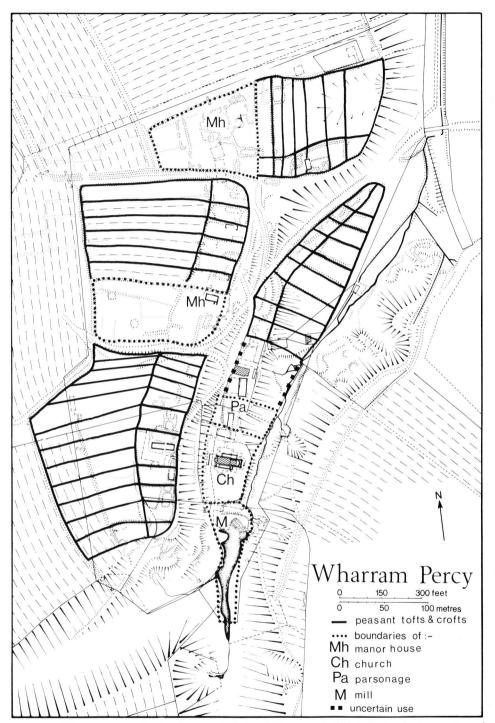

FIG. 4.10 The recovery of a landscape: Wharram Percy (Yorkshire). A reconstruction of the village plan, *c.* 1200. Based on excavation of one manor house, two crofts, and on ground survey and air photographs. This may be the result of a planned layout (p. 126, below).

Ages: perhaps more than when a study of ridge-and-furrow is invoked to bring arable farming back to remote parts of the Pennine dales and the Cheviots. The restoration of so many sites to the landscape does more, however, than point to former high densities of rural population: a retreat of settlement on this scale—paralleled of course in other parts of Western Europe—makes it necessary to consider its causation or causations in even the most elementary treatment of our history. Field-study has established the intensity of desertion but documentary study has not yet firmly assigned causes. In 1954 the assumption was that although desertion occurred a little earlier than the period when complaints about the man-eating sheep reached their peak, it was undoubtedly associated with the desire to increase pastoral husbandry at the expense of arable.[40] Thanks to Dr Christopher Dyer's recent studies of the West Midlands it seems that villagers could drift away over a long period, propelled (if I understand him rightly) by something akin to a rent strike.[41]

Before the archaeological examination of deserted village sites very little was known about the standards of living represented by the ordinary village houses. Few remained above ground, thanks to the transformation which Hoskins christened the 'Great Rebuilding' of the Tudor and early Stuart period,[42] and it was all too easy to treat a picturesque two-storey half-timbered or yeoman house of that period as indicative of the medieval shape and size of the medieval peasant house.

A remarkable amount of archaeological effort was directed to peasant houses on deserted sites after 1952. By 1968 there had been nearly 300 excavations of various sorts,[43] and the annual entries in the 'Medieval Britain' section of *Medieval Archaeology* show that the interest continues. As a result it is now known that from the fourteenth to the sixteenth century the typical peasant house, whether of stone, timber, or of both, was a 'long-house'—so named from its high ratio of length to width—and within its length the same roof covered both the domestic and the animal quarters. Their flimsiness caused such houses to be frequently repaired and rebuilt but without grubbing up their foundations, so that excavators have been able to recover successive periods of house-building, earlier and earlier as they trowelled deeper and deeper until they reached the post-holes and sleeper-trenches of simpler timber buildings.

The alignment of these houses in relation to the adjacent village street proved to be capable of changing, and indeed the total number of houses in a village street could change if more than one house was built in a single toft or if toft boundaries were themselves changed to match pressure on building space. Quite early in the excavations at Wharram Percy the fluidity and flux within the village plan was emphasized by discovering underneath one such succession of foundations and hearth-floors not an early peasant house but the abandoned lower storey of a twelfth-century manor house which had once occupied that part of the village site.[44] The more elaborate complex of rooms and outbuildings from another manor house at the north end of the village had already been recognized from its earthworks, and the distinction between this complex and the earthworks of long-houses was already apparent in Captain Bayly's survey of 1851.

The fluidity of plan seen in the relocation of peasant houses and a manor house has some parallels with changes in the fabric of the parish church of Wharram Percy which served five townships, four of them now deserted. The period of population contraction is marked by successive contractions in the area of the church, pulling down two aisles and shortening the chancel. The aisles and a side chapel had been added at an earlier period when population was still growing, and the nave of the Norman church was much larger than that of its Saxon predecessor. These changes in plan were recoverable only by excavation, which is rarely possible in a village church.[45]

I have used Wharram Percy to illustrate the progress of archaeological enquiry in the 1950s and 1960s. During that time John Hurst's responsibility for the direction of the work became absolute and my own contribution was willingly confined to that of recruiting officer, catering manager, and public-relations man. This coincided with a diversion of my own research interests towards urban history, first of medieval towns and then of the process of house-building in Leeds during the Industrial Revolution. From this detached position I was perhaps better able to appreciate the progress of excavation at other deserted village sites, particularly West Whelpington (Northumberland), Goltho (Lincolnshire), Barton Blount (Derbyshire), Faxton (Northamptonshire), Upton (Gloucestershire), and Hound Tor (Devon).[46]

There comes a stage in any line of research where, as in the *Golden Bough,* the older generation awaits the arrival of the young princes who will greet them, stab them, and reign in their place. Or, in a kinder metaphor, the middle-aged await the Young Turks whose role is constructive in its destruction: criticizing, elaborating, and showing where one has had blinkers, made positive mistakes, or simply stopped dead in one's tracks when a few steps further would have turned a corner. It is useful and sobering, however, after this brief chronicle, which could not easily avoid patting my generation of landscape historians on the back, to turn to whatever body movements are appropriate for guilt and repentance in the light of the Young Turks' researches, the more important of which are included in the Select Reading List at the end of this chapter.

It was right, though no doubt over-ambitious, to believe in the 1940s that it would be useful and informative if the whole array of open-field evidence could eventually be assembled on one map, particularly when air photographs became available to locate selions as crop marks and soil marks where the ground itself had lost the familiar corrugation of ridge-and-furrow.

It was certainly possible to show some of the margins where the plough teams had once penetrated but, as Professor Mead's survey of Buckinghamshire showed,[47] there were areas of light and dry soils which were not capable of preserving the marks of selion boundaries and therefore left open the question of whether they had ever had open fields.

Woodland areas, as another chapter indicates, have their own potential for revealing aspects of past landscapes, but they make a veil which air photographs cannot penetrate and very little foot-slogging field-work has been carried out in woodlands in this country, so that we do not know the extent to which they conceal former fields and villages (as they certainly have been shown to do elsewhere in Europe).

While there now seem to be these awkward limits to the reconstruction of the full range of open-field landscapes, there are also doubts about the interpretation of what reconstruction has revealed. The Orwins' hypothesis had been that the 'furlongs', that is the blocks into which selions of the same axis (or 'grain') were gathered, were the visible consequence of step-by-step reclamation of land for ploughing. This hypothesis was most boldly challenged when Dr Thirsk argued that we must not expect England to have been so different from Europe as to escape the massive relocation of villages and reallocation of field land which could be documented in parts of France and Germany from the twelfth century onwards.[48] Dr Titow made an effective defence of the accepted view,[49] especially by pointing out the unlikelihood that such a massive disturbance of property boundaries could have occurred without leaving some documentary traces, and it was always difficult to envisage the chequerboard of open-field furlongs, seen in so many pre-enclosure maps and in even more blocks of ridge-and-furrow, as the product of some reorganization: surely they embodied the very essence of the piecemeal?

It was the patient field-work of David Hall[50] and Christopher Taylor,[51] looking carefully at the course of many individual selions, which began to show that the apparently separate furlongs were in some instances the result of subdivision of larger units with the same selion 'grain',[52] making the original selions thus very much longer. From another direction Mary Harvey and June Sheppard drew attention to pre-enclosure maps and surveys of Yorkshire villages whose open fields, even in the immediately pre-enclosure period, did have exceptionally long selions and large areas with similar selion grain, such as one might expect if the division of the whole township's fields into selions had been made on one single occasion—a Great Realignment indeed.[53]

Rather like deserted villages in the forties which sprang to the eye once attention had been drawn to them, blocks of long selions have proliferated in the literature of the early eighties. Ever in the van of progress, the research team of field-walkers at Wharram Percy, headed by David Hall and Colin Hayfield, has shown that in all five townships of the parish most selions were very long and a 'piecemeal' furlong rare. Other Yorkshire Wolds townships have similar patterns, and it now remains to be seen where else the long selions will emerge. The piecemeal patterns certainly predominate in other parts of England, particularly in the Midlands, and for these to conceal an earlier, more regular, planned alignment is intrinsically unlikely.

A related question has hardly received attention yet: if there was a period when selions were laid out in such regularity, what did they replace? And can field-survey and a re-examination of air photographs show any signs of other and older field divisions beneath, and would these also be Saxon, but earlier, or Romano-British?

Although documentary references to the process of laying out the open fields of a village in one grand design have not yet been encountered, there are not infrequent indications in later documents within the pre-enclosure period that in open fields a regular pattern of ownership once prevailed whereby in each furlong the occupants held their selions in the same succession: A always next to B, B to C, and so on. This was certainly the case in the Wharram townships but it is extensively documented elsewhere in England.[54] Such regularity cannot be an accident and it suggests an ordered and deliberate assignment. In some villages the order A, B, C, D . . . in the furlongs was the order A, B, C, D . . . of houses along the village street, the pattern of the Scandinavian *solskift*.

Its widespread occurrence even where selions are gathered in piecemeal furlongs does not pose insuperable difficulties of interpretation: the habit could first have arisen in assigning selions in situations of piecemeal colonization, become an accepted part of practice, and then been adopted if a Great Realignment occurred. Indeed the large area which a single selion comprised in the new alignment might have helped to preserve the regularity—A, B, C, D—within the furlongs, right up to the time of their enclosure; whereas in the smaller piecemeal furlongs there is plenty of evidence that B often sought to

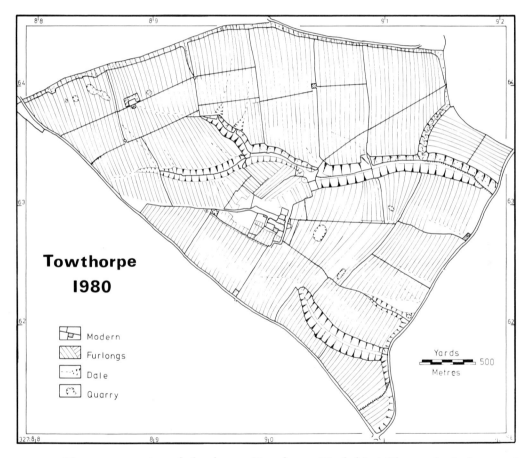

FIG. 4.11 The reconstruction of a landscape: Towthorpe (Yorkshire). The regular furlongs and long selions of a Great Realignment, period unknown. Towthorpe was finally depopulated, *c.* 1690, when holdings were amalgamated. Ridge-and-furrow, crop-mark, and soil-mark survey by David Hall. Ridge-and-furrow is intact under the belt of woodland on the northern parish boundary.

acquire selions from his neighbour, A or C (or from both), as a first stage in that agglomeration of holdings which was so often a prelude to full enclosure and sometimes a substitute for it.

While therefore one can hope for further progress in elucidating the chronology of open-field development through a yet closer examination of evidence from our present landscape, research has so far been less rewarding in attaching particular visible features to the different varieties of agricultural and tenurial systems which are known to have operated in England. There is a book on the subject, as eye-catching for its bulk as a long selion in a conventional landscape.[55] Its very length emphasizes the number of field systems which maps and surveys record, but the absence of photographs among its illustrations proclaim that its editors failed to marry the study of field systems and study in the field.

Recent studies of the medieval village and the medieval field have another linking element beyond the revelation of fluidity and flux in each. If planned furlongs, made up of long selions, then why not planned villages? And if (as happens) there are plenty of the latter to be found once one looks for them,[56] was a replanned village and replanned fields a single act of reorganization? Logic would suggest so, since the physical disturbance of the latter would be less of a problem if the whole landscape was being replanned. The magnitude of either operation, presupposing a social organization capable of imposing a common will, is remarkable enough in itself, but to find both operations together is as remarkable a comment on the capacity for social engineering as it is on surveying skill, opening our eyes to operations as significant in their way as those that brought stones for the henges of prehistoric England.

If Great Realignments took place before the period when documents became available, can archaeology help? It would need excavation on a massive scale for archaeology to determine the date of a single planned village, and even the extensive work at Wharram Percy is far from that goal. Yet although excavation is not likely to give a quick answer to the question of when the furlongs were first laid out, there is an approach which can suggest limiting dates: that is, by field-walking over currently ploughed fields, the collection of pottery from the surface, and an analysis of its distribution to indicate clusters of human occupation.

From the results of this work, of which the principal exponents have been Christopher Taylor and David Hall in Northamptonshire,[57] has arisen the concept of original polyfocal settlement in the Saxon period, with these smaller settlements coming together later to sites familiar to us as medieval villages. These older and smaller sites, another variety of deserted village, leave their scatters of pottery to be recovered now on ground where we know that selions and furlongs later ran.

It is from evidence of this sort that archaeologists are now suggesting an eighth- or ninth-century date for the laying out of open fields with long selions and also for unitary, nucleated villages accompanying them, rejecting earlier conjectures that the most obviously regular and planned features were a result of resettlement after devastation at the Norman Conquest.

'Everyone shall have prizes', said Alice, and the Old Guard and the Young Turks may therefore both be correct. It was worth while forty years ago to seek traces of the medieval landscape by matching maps, documents, and visible elements in the modern landscape, but it was imprudent to assume that there lay awaiting discovery a single, centuries-long canvas devoid of change, *the* medieval landscape. It is now as impossible to envisage a static medieval landscape as it would be to envisage a uniform one of identical villages and fields in such a variegated terrain as England.

Envoi

The lecture confined itself to the rural landscape and within it to the landscape of field and village. Even within the rural landscape this omits those medieval industrial activities which have left their mark on the present landscape (mining, quarrying, and peat extraction, for example); the many moated sites, the investigation of which has produced its own Research Group; and—less studied so far—the thousands of paths and roads which intermeshed with the natural waterways to form the transport system. The town, the castle, the monastery, and the rural market-place are also missing: not because they fell outside the ambit of the title of the lecture series but simply through limitation of time. Techniques of field-observation, aerial photography, and dirt archaeology have been as profitably applied in the last forty years to these landscape elements as to villages and fields, and sometimes by the same researchers.

   Finally it may seem impolite to have spoken of the medieval landscape in a college whose crest includes the porch of a medieval church and to have said so little about churches, except those in ruins, or about other surviving medieval buildings. It was the impoliteness that afflicts those who know they have a train to catch or—to use a more accurate metaphor for this occasion—the impoliteness of a man who can hear that he holds back the movement of furniture and the conversion of the room from a landscape of teaching into a landscape of eating.[58]

Select reading list

The systematic exposition of the historical elements for whole parishes is limited to those in recent volumes from the Royal Commission on Historical Monuments (1968–   ).

   Following his general survey (Hoskins 1955) came the still incomplete series of county volumes in the *Landscape* series which Hoskins initiated (for instance Allison 1976, *Yorkshire East Riding;* Steane 1974, *Northamptonshire;* Palliser 1976, *Staffordshire;* Taylor 1973, *Cambridgeshire*). Something of the flavour of his TV voyages into the landscape is caught in Hoskins 1973. Cantor 1982 comprises a group of essays with less weight than the title suggests: the editor's chapter on parks and that of Hindle on roads are pioneer works.

   On the landscape in general see Beresford 1957 (paperback edn, 1984) together with Baker and Harley 1973. On fields Taylor 1974 can be supplemented by the essays in Rowley 1981, where there is a very full bibliography. Of works still in print on deserted villages the best are Rowley and Wood

1982 and Muir 1982. Progress of archaeological work to 1968 was brought together in Beresford and Hurst 1971. The recent contribution of archaeology to medieval studies is surveyed in Hinton 1983. On settlement in general see Sawyer 1976 and Taylor 1983. On air photography Beresford and St. Joseph 1958, 2nd edn. 1979; Wilson 1982, and works in its very full bibliography.

5

The agricultural landscape: fads and fashions

JOAN THIRSK

I DO not regard agriculture as a fashion industry, despite the title of my essay. But views on the best way to farm land and the best crops to grow are constantly changing; so my title is chosen as a shorthand term to draw attention to that fact. The current view on the most efficient farming regimes and the most rewarding crops will not dominate the scene for ever. Opinion and practice will change, as they have changed many times before.

Historians are not asked to prophesy the future. It is their business to describe and explain changes in the past. But *that* is a broadening experience, because it gives a glimpse of the alternatives between which our future choices are likely to be made. And so I have chosen as my theme those changes in the agricultural landscape of the past which, in my view, point most directly to changes through which we are passing now, and which are likely to become more conspicuous in the decades to come. In other words, I am concentrating on developments in the landscape that did not take centuries to complete, but could be observed in the course of decades.

Some of you will have expected me to set enclosures at the centre of my remarks. They wrought a more thoroughgoing transformation of our landscape than anything else in the past, but they took six hundred years to work to a conclusion. The system of farming arable land in scattered strips and allowing common rights over almost all land (arable, meadow, pasture, and woodland) at different seasons, was one regime; hedged fields and consolidated units of land, individually farmed, were another. For a long time the two systems existed alongside each other. Both economic systems had their merits, and as external circumstances, economic and social, changed, so the arguments in favour of each were weighted differently. But in the end enclosure triumphed and common-field systems were swept away. The English landscape acquired many more hedges, trees in hedges, and stone walls, and developed that intimacy which contrasts so strongly with prairie landscapes, the closest parallel we can find nowadays to the scenery of common fields. But no changes in the landscape occur without reflecting changing human relationships as well, and as a historian I cannot talk about landscape without introducing people into the scene. The intimacy of the English village community was dealt a severe blow when the common fields disappeared. It put an end to common labour; daily meetings of villagers in common toil. Social intimacy did not die, of course, for man is a social animal, but it shrivelled. It survives in villages, but it reminds me of a house plant snatched from its ideal environment, adjusting to an atmosphere that is less congenial though not intolerable.

Enclosure effected a revolutionary change in the agricultural landscape, both visually and socially. The changes which I shall describe effected a more modest transformation of its appearance. But behind the visible scene some powerful economic and social forces were again at work, exerting the pressure for change. These are so reminiscent of the circumstances emerging now in the later twentieth century, and the solutions being offered are so similar, that my theme is virtually chosen for me. Past and present can meet in sympathetic discussion of the same issues. More constructively, past experience should broaden our perspective on the present choices.

The agricultural landscape in the Middle Ages did not exhibit a conspicuously wide range of crops. The chief arable crops were cereals—wheat, barley, oats, and rye—and some legumes, though not in great quantity—mostly beans, peas, and some vetches for stock feed. Small crops of flax and hemp yielded the fibres for the making of linen and canvas, but much more cloth, of course, was made from sheep's wool. Occasionally the records show an unusual crop like woad or teasels being grown for the cloth industry. And all classes, churchmen and noblemen, farmers and cottagers, paid some attention to vegetable and herb gardens, though we only know a little about the best-cultivated examples that belonged to monastic houses.

Much new variety was introduced into this rather limited cropping pattern in the sixteenth and seventeenth centuries. The first stimulus came from a rapid rise in population which called for far more food than ever before. Grain was the first necessity, but since the rise in numbers went hand in hand with inflation, those who were successful in grasping the new economic opportunities had more money to spend on better living standards, and wanted more meat, more dairy produce, and more variety in food in general. By the end of the sixteenth century the grain supply was virtually sufficient to feed everyone in all but the worst years of harvest failure. Grain prices started to fall, and worsened sharply after the mid-seventeenth century. Farmers had difficulty in selling all the grain and wool that they produced; even meat and dairy produce threatened a surplus unless food was allowed to be exported. In consequence, some farmers started early, some started late, but all in the end were driven to seek other activities which would yield a better reward. An alternative agriculture began to emerge.

Today we contemplate grain mountains, butter mountains, and cheese mountains, and again we see enterprising individuals looking for an alternative agriculture. One man in West Sussex is specializing in the growing of garlic, another in Oxfordshire is setting up a rabbit farm (selling his rabbits in Belgium and France, where the price is a good deal better than in England), others are keeping goats and ewes for the production of goats' and ewes' milk cheeses. But few memories go back to the seventeenth century, and who remembers that we have been through this search for variety, for a new diversity, before? The best illustration of the parallels between past and present is the sight of fields of flowering yellow rapeseed that we now see around us in May in southern England. Rogue plants are already colonizing the verges of the motorway. An agricultural journalist fulminated in 1980 against this unpleasant crop, matched, he said, by its unpleasant name. 'It does not fit in with the soft greys and greens of our traditional English landscape,' he wrote; 'it was made for Van Gogh, not for Turner; for oils, not watercolours. It looks wrong and it smells wrong; like a great sheet of nasty new linoleum. It is quite new here. Ten years ago we grew 10,000 acres in the entire country . . . this year it is almost a quarter of a million acres. Still, the farmers like it, it is easy to grow, yields well, cleans the soil and gets rid of weeds. It also makes an awful lot of margarine. All the same, I'll be grateful when we are back to wheat and barley again. Rape is one of these new-fangled ideas from France; that's what's wrong with it.'[1]

But rapeseed is not new in England in the twentieth century. In the sixteenth century it was warmly welcomed as a crop that would yield oil, in place of olive oil which was becoming increasingly expensive. In 1549 olive oil was costing one-third more than in 1542.[2] Oil was needed for treating woollen cloth in the last finishing processes, for making paints and soap, and for burning in lamps. Rapeseed had established itself in the Netherlands much earlier—certainly by the mid-fourteenth century, whence it spread into Germany and France. When English contacts with continental Europe flourished at a new level of intensity, under the Tudors in the sixteenth century, the consequences for agriculture and horticulture were far-reaching. English landowners, merchants, and cloth manufacturers recognized the possibilities of rapeseed oil; and by 1551 some rapeseed was being grown around King's Lynn in Norfolk. In the 1570s men were galvanized into fresh activity by another sharp rise in the price of olive oil; and Parliament passed a Bill to encourage the making of oil in England. By 1576 oil imports from Spain were dwindling; its price was alarmingly high, and some of the blame was laid on the fact that so much was now being sent to the West Indies. Then in 1577 the French imposed heavy new tariffs on some of their exports, and a year later French oil was also said to be 'extreme dear'. Many different schemes for making oil from seeds were mooted in England at this time: more oil from linseed was one possibility; turnips were thought to be another possible source.

In fact, success was to be achieved with rapeseed. But at this early stage people hardly knew where best to grow the crop. An English clothier who saw its possibilities for the textile industry made a start by sowing 550 acres in the Forest of Dean in the 1620s. But it had already found its first niche in eastern England, as we have seen, and this turned out to be its most congenial home. It was evidently flourishing in the fens around the Wash by 1579, since Sir Thomas Gresham, from his home in Osterley, in Middlesex, commissioned his son-in-law, Nathaniel Bacon, living on the Norfolk coast at Stiffkey, to buy seed from there, so that his newly erected oil mill could get busy. He wanted to contract for 400 or 500 quarters a year from growers in parts of Holland in Lincolnshire. Here rapeseed established itself most successfully in its early days. Its success was partly due to the fact that the farmers who were the most willing to take up newly drained fenland around the Wash were foreigners, Dutch and French. Local Englishmen were deeply prejudiced against fen drainage and would not take up the land, whereas the Dutch and French did, and they were already thoroughly familiar with rapeseed in their native countries.[3]

In the course of the seventeenth century rapeseed became a commonplace crop throughout the eastern half of England from the East Riding to Essex. One of its great advantages was soon recognized in the work it provided for four to six weeks before the grain harvest, at a time when other jobs were lacking. By the end of the seventeenth century rapeseed was also at home in the western half of England: from Monmouthshire and Herefordshire ships passed down the river Wye carrying rape oil for dispatch through Bristol; and in 1698 someone was growing it at Whitwell, near Worksop, in Derbyshire. But the best soils were considered to be marshland, fen, or other moist soils. Along the coasts of eastern England one of the market towns which benefited most was Wisbech, which positively bristled with oil mills in the early eighteenth century. Consequently, it boasted street lighting in 1700, some sixty years before Midland towns like Leicester enjoyed this amenity.[4]

Rapeseed continued to flower in English fields into the early nineteenth century. It grew in the Pickering area of north Yorkshire in the 1780s, for example, and in the East Fen of Lincolnshire around 1830. But its decline set in with the import of cheaper oilseed from abroad, and in the course of the last hundred years its former history in England has been forgotten. Thus rapeseed came and went between about 1530 and 1830. It was introduced in a period when French and Dutch agricultural influences were at their height, and it is here again under not very different circumstances. It is here because it is the policy of the EEC to encourage the production of cheap vegetable oil for the food industry. Because of this, an agricultural journalist in 1978 considered that 'the future for oilseed rape is undoubtedly assured'. But if any mischance clouds the future of rapeseed in England, we may find its place taken by another oil-bearing plant, jojoba, which produces an oil with much the same chemical properties as sperm-whale oil. This is now on trial on the edge of the Somerset Levels.[5]

The news of trials with jojoba on the edge of the Somerset Levels has a curious parallel with the past in another respect. When Englishmen wanted to cultivate new plants in the sixteenth and seventeenth centuries, the only land that they could lay their hands on easily was either run down, totally derelict, barren, or ill-favoured in one way or another. Thus rapeseed was first tried in the fens and the Forest of Dean. If jojoba had been on trial in the sixteenth century, the ill-drained Somerset Levels would have been an entirely appropriate place. And because the worst lands were chosen, the chances of success for new crops, in the first instance, were not of the best. But in a congested countryside, waste land, on the neglected fringes of parishes where no one wanted to live, was the place to look for cheap land, where prejudices against new crops had the weakest influence. It was in this unpropitious countryside that hopes for a more diversified agriculture in the future were nurtured. Yet diversification was to be the saviour of depressed seventeenth-century agriculture, just as some would agree with that recipe now.

Another group of plants that entered the fields in the sixteenth century, some with more, and some with less, success, were dye plants for the textile industry. They were not entirely new in England; they grew without much attention in certain districts in the Middle Ages. But they were launched on a new lease of life when foreign supplies could no longer be relied upon, and became expensive. Wars and foreign embargoes on export disrupted trade links, and home-grown dye plants seemed to be the answer. We are unusually fortunate in having the letters of one of the young men involved in the first experiments with the growing of the red dye, madder (*Rubia tinctoria*). The expert growers of madder were found in Zeeland in Holland, and one rotation used there (the practicalities of which I still do not fully understand) was rapeseed, madder, rapeseed, madder, wheat. The government actively encouraged madder-growing in the 1620s, bidding the Commission on Trade in 1622 to 'enquire into the causes how dyeing stuffs have become dear'. A London dyer engaged a young Salisbury man, George Bedford, whose family had been engaged in cloth-making and dyeing for at least two generations, to go to Holland and learn how to cultivate madder. When we think of the discomforts and delays of cross-Channel journeys in those days, we might expect Bedford to have stayed in Holland for a long period—say a whole year; but no, he made seven journeys from Harwich to Holland between July 1622 and October 1623, spending between two weeks and two months there on each occasion. Thus he watched cultivation at different seasons, arranged to buy plants, and brought them back. Finally, he persuaded a Dutchman to come to England in April 1624 to take charge of a plantation in Appledore, on the edge of Romney Marsh. It was almost certainly one of those pieces of half-derelict land that no one else wanted. A

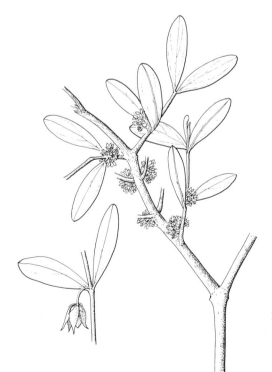

FIG. 5.1 Jojoba. (Drawn by Rosemary Wise.)

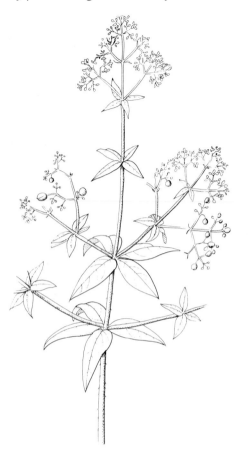

FIG. 5.2 Madder. (Drawn by Rosemary Wise.)

parson at Ivychurch, not far away in Romney Marsh, in 1641 described the area as a whole as 'an unhealthful place' where one lived among 'rude and ill-nurtured people for the most part'.[6]

Bedford's madder plantation at Appledore was planned in conjunction with coleseed, so he was evidently intending to follow the Dutch rotation, but it was not a great success. Bedford had trouble with other people's pigs rooting among the madder, and he had abandoned the enterprise sometime before 1630. But his was not the only plantation in existence at this time, and others had a longer life. Charles I had a gardener of Dutch origin, William Shipman, who had a plantation at Barn Elms outside London; and in 1630 Malvern Chase was marked out as the site of another trial with madder. The government continued to encourage experiments, and although the Civil War put madder out of mind, in 1660 Sir Nicholas Crisp had a plantation at Deptford, along the Thames, which he claimed was then employing 1,000 people, cultivating, drying, and preparing the roots for the dyer.[7]

Madder-growing was still only a fragile enterprise. It could interest only those who could afford to wait three years for some return on their money, since the roots take time

to grow to a reasonable size. Some gardeners got round this problem by growing vegetables between the rows. Commercially, it was not unsuccessful, though evidently Dutch prices were keen, and Dutch quality high. But it was also much valued as a labour-intensive crop, offering work in weeding three or four times in the summer, in banking up the plants, and again from harvest until spring when the roots were dug up and dried.[8]

In the end, madder followed rapeseed into the fens. Cornelius Vermuyden, the Dutchman who had been involved in the scheme of land improvement in Malvern Chase, where he had made an undertaking to grow madder, shifted his interests to the drainage of the fens round the Wash. It is very likely that the drainers and farmers in his circle interested themselves in madder because of the Vermuyden connection. From about 1661 we find madder well established in the Isle of Ely, around Wisbech, this particular enterprise being initiated by a man who leased small parcels of land here and there, $2\frac{1}{2}$ acres, $4\frac{1}{2}$ acres, 7 acres, but in some cases larger units of 20 acres, 25 acres, even 75 acres. The price of madder fluctuated greatly from year to year, according to the yield of madder in Holland. In the 1670s prices were low, and Dutch competition may have killed the crop in Ely altogether by 1698. But plants do not disappear as readily as does public interest,

FIG. 5.3 Safflower. (Drawn by Rosemary Wise.)

and we have to be careful before dismissing madder from Ely, just because our documents fall silent.

The plant returned to favour in the 1760s and 1770s, when it was growing at Barn Elms, the very place where lay the earlier plantation of William Shipman in the 1620s, almost 150 years before, perhaps on the very same land. One of the obstacles to success with madder had centred on the payment of tithe, but this was removed by legislation in 1757 which fixed on a money payment per acre in place of payment in kind. Faversham in Kent became a successful centre of madder growing at this time, and its grower, John Crow, won a premium for his crop from the Royal Society of Arts in 1772. The Society was offering a subsidy to madder growers in these years, and in five years some seventy-eight claims, representing 300 acres, were received, including applications, in 1765 and 1767, from Arthur Young, the well-known writer on agriculture and Secretary of the Board of Agriculture. High prices for Dutch madder had revived English interest, but by 1774 the Dutch price was falling again and the English crop was not expected to survive. Nevertheless, it had been a good crop while it lasted, giving much work to the poor.[9] Now that handicraftsmen appreciate the soft colours produced by vegetable dyes on wool and cloth, is there not a living for a madder grower or two in these islands?

A less familiar dye plant that was tried in Oxfordshire, but did not spread further, was safflower (*Carthamus tinctorius*) or bastard saffron, a thistle-like plant, valued for its scarlet, pink, and rose colours, much used for dyeing ribbons and silk cloth. It was successfully grown around Strasbourg, and Englishmen thought it should grow equally well in England. In the search for more profitable crops in the 1660s, one pioneer had two or three hundred acres of it growing by 1673 (though he did not say where), but it was growing at the same period (or perhaps this was the same plantation) at North Aston (south of Banbury). It was said to be still growing there in 1707, as well as at Chipping Norton. But it faded out in the early eighteenth century, its failure being explained by labour problems, because it ripened at the same time as wheat, because English seed was not as good as the German, and because imported seed was so expensive that the English crop could not compete with its continental rival.[10] Will no one take an interest in safflower nowadays? It makes a good vegetable oil, having a higher content of linoleic acid than any other oil, yet the only safflower oil that reaches our shops comes from America, and is expensive.

A highly successful dye plant, on the other hand, was woad (*Isatis tinctoria*), the source of the blue colour that was also used in dyeing blacks and greens, and which was indispensable before the arrival of indigo in the later sixteenth century. Even afterwards, indigo and woad were used alongside each other or together, until the coming of aniline dyes in the nineteenth century. Woad had flowered modestly and uncared for in certain parts of England in the Middle Ages, but again it was the French who taught the English the best techniques of commercial cultivation in the sixteenth century. Is there not room for a few woad growers nowadays, so that we can dye our handicraft wools and cloths in woad? Admittedly, it has a disgusting smell when the leaves are fermenting, before being made into woad balls. Queen Elizabeth begged her loyal subjects not to grow it alongside

FIG. 5.4 Woad. (Drawn by Rosemary Wise.)

the roads on which she processed through her kingdom. But it gives a beautiful colour. A small piece of wool cloth dyed in woad lies in the County Archives Office of Hampshire, sent by a Salisbury dyer to his prospective client in the early seventeenth century, and the colour is as fresh as the day it was dispatched. But perhaps woad *is* a commercial crop somewhere in England, since in January 1979, when snow lay thick on the ground, we were told that Oxford United was so determined to play its football match against Watford, regardless of the weather, that the pitch was marked out in the snow with woad.[11]

If you do not know the woad plant I can describe it, because I have grown it in my garden. It grows to a height of three or four feet, has longish narrow leaves that turn a bluish-green colour as they ripen; its yellow flowers appear in May. Commercial woad growing started—or restarted—in England in the early 1540s when supplies from the Azores and France, particularly from the basin of the Garonne in the Toulouse area, were interrupted. Frenchmen came to England to teach its cultivation, and starting from the Hampshire, Sussex, and Dorset coasts, it spread out along the moist river valleys of southern England, using old pasture land. This was, in fact, its most congenial habitat.

More than one place called Wickham in the kingdom grew woad, a fact that is not surprising when one realizes that 'wick' is an old English place-name element meaning, among other things, 'a dairy farm', and dairies are well situated when they lie amid river meadows. So woad was growing in the seventeenth century at High Wycombe in Buckinghamshire, at Wickham in the parish of Spalding in Lincolnshire, and next door to Wickham in north Oxfordshire at Broughton, south-west of Banbury.[12]

The virtues of woad were that it absorbed some of the excessive fertility of old pasture land before it was sown with grain, and so was a good first crop when breaking up ancient grassland for a few years under arable. English woad fetched such a good price in the early 1580s, when grain prices slumped badly, that a great many people in southern England turned to woad, saying it was the only way they could pay their rent. The profit from one acre was equal to the profit from six acres of grain. The government genuinely feared that grain supplies would run short, and banned woad growing altogether in 1585. However, it allowed a restricted acreage in 1587, and freed the plant from all controls in 1601. Woad settled in, and remained, a thoroughly respectable and serviceable crop throughout the seventeenth and eighteenth centuries. It was much valued for the work it gave to the poor, and we can measure the truth of this statement in a detailed account of woad growing at Milcote in Warwickshire, where forty-one acres in 1626 employed on average 224 people a day in May, 249 in June, 145 in July, and 105 in August. When I visited Milcote, on the banks of the Avon, some 350 years afer this date, the scene was different but not altogether

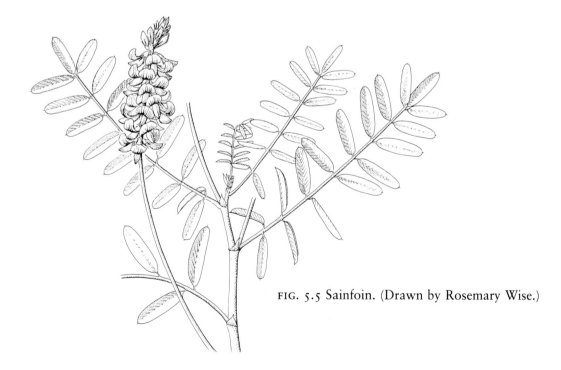

FIG. 5.5 Sainfoin. (Drawn by Rosemary Wise.)

unrecognizable. I watched a smaller group of men and women engaged in another labour-intensive activity, planting cabbages.[13]

English woad never quite achieved the reputation of foreign woad. It found its markets in the second-rate, rather than the first-rate textile centres, places like Newbury, Andover, Evesham, Mansfield, Chesterfield, and Grantham. It was almost certainly used to dye cheaper cloth, like butchers' aprons, and perhaps covers for carriers' carts. By the eighteenth century the criticism that was levelled at the crop was that it could attract too many poor into a parish. Woad fields did indeed attract the migrant poor; not a few poor itinerants working in the woad fields left a sad record in parish registers, dying far from home without a name.[14]

Another plant that has adorned our landscape at different periods, and is now creeping back again, is the vine. It was grown in the Roman period; vineyards are mentioned in 1086 in Domesday Book, usually associated with the head manors of great lords, and in the Middle Ages monastic houses tended vineyards carefully. In the sixteenth century vines excited fresh interest on a new scale. Some of that interest was fanned by disgust at the £100,000 of fine gold 'at the least', it was said, which was carried to France every year to pay for French wine. 'No country robbeth England so much as France', said the politicians. But the challenge in growing something about which the classical writers wrote so enthusiastically was another stimulus. And Englishmen at that time could still see

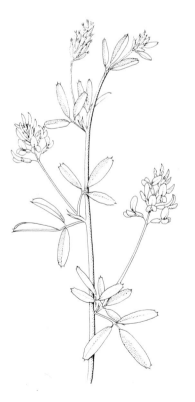

FIG. 5.6 Lucerne. (Drawn by Rosemary Wise.)

in the countryside degraded vine terraces, and knew 'Vineyards' as a field name. It became a gentleman's hobby to make new vineyards, and we have documentary evidence of their continuing existence—they were not a nine days' wonder—and the satisfaction of their owners, continuing through the seventeenth and into the eighteenth century. Robert Plot described in 1686 a vineyard of Sir Henry Littleton at Over Arley in Staffordshire which produced wine which he said was indistinguishable from French. But Plot was sceptical about the possibilities of doing this every year: 'this I suppose was done only in some favourable over-hot summer', he wrote. But one of Plot's readers, who annotated the copy which is now in the Bodleian Library, added in the margin: 'I have made most years a considerable quantity of good wine of my grapes at Derby'.[15]

In Elizabeth's reign Lord Cobham and Lord Williams of Thame were singled out for the excellent reputations of their vineyards, and in 1750 Lord Cobham's vineyard at Painshill in Surrey was still thriving, producing wine that sold in local inns at 7s. 6d. a bottle, a very fancy price. Vines were still listed in seedsmen's catalogues in the late eighteenth century. Now they are enjoying a new vogue, often on old monastic or other sites known to have been vineyards in earlier centuries. At Pilton in Somerset a new vineyard now occupies the site of an old vineyard of Glastonbury Abbey; in the 1960s Margaret Gore-Browne laid out her vineyard at Beaulieu in Hampshire opposite a monastic vineyard and on the site of an eighteenth-century one. At the last count in 1981 there were 800 owners of vineyards in England and Wales, the most northerly in Derbyshire. All have come into existence since 1945, most since 1960, and the number is steadily rising.[16]

A great number of new plants were the subject of experiment in England in the sixteenth and seventeenth centuries, not all of which became routine field crops. Clover, sainfoin, lucerne were successfully established as green crops for livestock. But similar interest was shown, and experiments tried, with spurrey, melilot, burnet, and parsley, but hopes for those plants flagged and died. A booklet on *Flowers of the Cornfield* says of spurrey nowadays that in parts of Europe it is 'cultivated for use as a fodder, but here [i.e. in England] it is looked upon as a weed to be got rid of'. I wonder why.[17]

The most significant of all new plants in altering the agricultural landscape in more than one way were vegetables, and I cannot introduce them without some general remarks, explaining the circumstances behind this invasion. The discovery of the American continent, and travels to Arabia and the Far East, resulted in the introduction of many new plants into Europe in the sixteenth century. But that is not the whole explanation of what happened. The plants to which I have so far drawn attention, rapeseed, madder, safflower, woad, and vines, did not have to travel far to reach England. They were long familiar on the continent of Europe. What brought them to England at this particular time was a fundamental change of attitude towards the economic and social possibilities waiting to be exploited in agriculture. Closer contact with the Continent helped to spread many fresh ideas. So did all the printed literature of the Renaissance. Classical works on agriculture and estate management opened to their gentlemen readers a totally new view of the way they might manage their estates, develop them, put their land to better use, and grow unfamiliar crops. On visits abroad they tasted fruit and vegetables that were either totally unknown to them or known only by name from the pages of writers such as Columella or Varro. Columella, for example, arrested attention by devoting considerable space to horticulture. He made it clear that he regarded gardening as the poor man's concern, but he also said that horticulture had been formerly neglected, yet was now 'quite a popular pursuit'.[18] A remark like that struck a sympathetic chord for an English reader around 1530, because much the same words could have been used to describe the state of horticulture in England at that date. The basic vegetables in the Middle Ages had been onions, garlic, and leeks, with some green leaves added, particularly lettuce and cabbage. But green stuff seems to have been associated with peasant poverty and was suspect; it was certainly not valued as a fine-flavoured or nourishing food.[19]

The reading of the classical literature on vegetables and herbs started a new fad or fashion in the early sixteenth century, that caused old prejudices to be laid aside and established instead the conviction that vegetables and fruit were positively beneficial foodstuffs. The German humanist, Konrad Heresbach, published in 1570 a description of agricultural practices as he knew them on the lower Rhine around Cleves, and his book exerted considerable influence in England in translation after 1577. In it Heresbach made

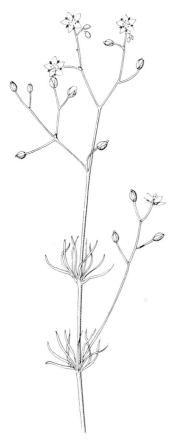

FIG. 5.7 Spurrey. (Drawn by Rosemary Wise.)

an intellectual leap forward that was profoundly significant for the future history of horticulture. He had absorbed the theories of Columella that fruit and vegetables were the food of the poor, but he went beyond this to express the view that theirs was a far more nourishing diet than the costly fare eaten by the rich. The poor, in relying on the food of gardens and orchards, he said, enjoyed 'a great deal more commendable and hurtless diet'. Moreover, these things needed no fire to cook them and were easy of digestion. Some could be preserved at home, 'not driving men to seek pepper as far as India'.[20]

The eating of vegetables and fruits was now the rich man's fad, and the first consequence was that gentlemen's vegetables and orchards were given fastidious attention, and no expense was spared. No better illustration of the zest, indeed the positive excitement, that rich men felt for their new hobby could one find than in a little scene enacted in Whitehall Palace in 1604, some seventy years or so after the horticultural revolution had begun, when the Spanish Constable of Castile was entertained by James I at a banquet, in the course of negotiating a peace treaty between England and Spain. Seated at table, the King's first act was to pass to the Constable a melon and half a dozen oranges on a very green branch, telling him they were the fruit of Spain transferred to England. And the Constable proceeded ceremoniously to share the precious melon between himself, James I, and his Queen.[21]

Fads and fashions are not inappropriate terms to use for this vegetable- and fruit-eating revolution when it first started. The fashion took hold in court circles, captivating kings, nobles, and then gentlemen. When they travelled abroad they brought back new plants and foreign gardeners to work their miracles in growing melons and oranges, asparagus and new kinds of cabbage on their estates. Fruit and vegetable eating became a new gastronomic experience, starting among the rich and working its way down through the middle classes. It created a new branch of agriculture.

The personal interest of Henry VIII in all this is well known. Richard Harris, the Irishman who became his gardener, planted a garden of cherry trees of something over one hundred acres at Teynham, near Sittingbourne in Kent, in about 1533, getting his trees from the Low Countries. This became 'the chief mother' of many other Kentish orchards, and others further afield.[22] But Henry's compulsive enthusiasms went further than this: he became a gluttonous eater of globe artichokes. He may first have encountered them through his Spanish connections, when Catherine of Aragon was his Queen. The very word 'artichoke' is derived from the Spanish *alcachofa* which is a corruption of the Arabic name for this plant. But perhaps he met them for the first time in France at the court of Francis I. The fads and fashions prevailing at the French court greatly influenced Henry. Francis I paid salaries and sums of money to travellers who would bring back to France new plants, herbs, and trees. A similar scheme in England seems to lie behind some enigmatic phrases in a letter from one Edmond Boner to Thomas Cromwell in 1533, as he crossed the Channel from Dover to Calais. He wrote anxiously to enquire whether some seeds he had collected from Rome, Bologna, and Lombardy, which he had dispatched via the Duke of Norfolk to Cromwell, had arrived. Plant hunting was almost becoming a part of government policy, a direct copy of procedures in France.[23]

Globe artichokes were introduced into the English garden by Henry VIII's fancy for them. As Heresbach rightly described them in 1570, they were 'a kind of thistle'. Such a description did not make them sound immediately attractive. But one of Henry VIII's household account books itemizes artichokes in 1531, which were specially brought to the King's grace; and in 1534 when Lord and Lady Lisle were at Calais, expecting a visit from Henry VIII, they received a letter bidding them procure all the artichokes they could find in the vicinity and keep them for the King's pleasure. This was at his 'special commandment'. So when Heresbach described artichokes as a kind of thistle in 1570, he added that they were, nevertheless, 'in great estimation at noblemen's tables'. The craze spread until gentlemen devoted whole gardens to them, like Henry Oxinden of Great Maydeacon in Kent, who in 1640 gave great care to the laying out of a flower garden and an artichoke garden. By the later seventeenth century they were thoroughly commonplace, in private and in market gardens. Having cost crowns apiece in the sixteenth century, they were bought at Althorp in Northamptonshire for fourpence each in 1634, and were a glut on the market of London by the end of the seventeenth century.[24]

Many other vegetables that were cosseted and mollycoddled in gentlemen's vegetable gardens in the sixteenth century had moved out into the fields by the end of the seventeenth century. Demand from gentlemen's households encouraged this; so did the great cosmo-

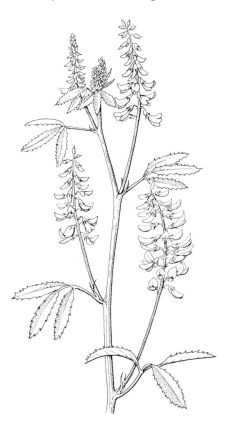

FIG. 5.8 Melilot. (Drawn by Rosemary Wise.)

politan population of London; so did the many French, Dutch, and German refugees in England who brought their own taste for vegetables with them, together with high skills in cultivating them. They used hot beds, bell glasses, and cloches, and their gardens in England were a picture of order and system. But another important element in the process of expanding vegetable cultivation was the recognition that it gave much valuable work, and produced more food per acre of land than conventional agriculture. And, of course, the poor man's familiarity with the rough-and-ready vegetable gardening of the past equipped him to take advantage of the new opportunities when gentlemen began to eat vegetables with such zest.[25]

For a long time in the sixteenth century fastidious Englishmen insisted on getting their onions and cabbages from Holland, presumably because their quality was considered better than the home grown. We find these vegetables in ships' cargoes in the 1590s. But Dutch and French refugees set up their own market gardens near large towns after about 1560, around London, Norwich, and Canterbury. At Sandwich in Kent a notable group established themselves on its ideal, light, sandy soils, and the Sandwich carrot became famous. But the specialist market gardener was joined by farmer-gardeners; they had a hand in both agriculture and horticulture, and were adventurous innovators. Many were prominent in politics in the 1650s, after the republican Commonwealth was established in 1649, and a new spirit of enterprise and hope was abroad. They entered into experiments in agriculture with relish, some taking up newly drained fens around the Wash, where they grew 'garden stuff', as it was called, among the wheat, oats, and rapeseed. A fine crop of onions was visible in Ewell Fen, for example, in 1657; even though home-produced onion seed never seemed to be successful, and the seeds continued to be got from abroad, onions were now a field crop. The favoured varieties were the Strasbourg onion with a red skin, and the St Omer onion. Around this time, or perhaps a decade later, cabbages and carrots were also grown in fields. Great plantations of cabbages were seen in Dorset by 1684, and carrots grew abundantly at Beckington in Somerset at the same date.[26]

By comparison potatoes were slow to establish themselves; it is plain from contemporary comments that English growers encountered difficulties. Spanish potatoes seemed to rot, rather than multiply, in English soil. Yet they flourished in Ireland, having been introduced there in the early years of the seventeenth century. By the 1650s, when Cromwellian soldiers went to Ireland, they saw them growing abundantly in the fields; in fact, soldiers reported seeing whole fields overrun with them. This news revived interest in the crop in England, and by the 1660s people were trying them again in Wales and north-west England, especially in Lancashire. It is from this time that our documents show potatoes spreading successfully as a field crop. But at this stage they were still not expected to be eaten as a vegetable but rather turned into flour for bread and pastry, and ideally you were recommended to mix the potato with wheat and barley flour.[27]

As vegetable growing came to be treated more seriously, its merits as a source of food and an economy in the use of land, were more carefully argued. A public-spirited citizen of Shrewsbury, Richard Gardiner, had urged the growing of vegetables to feed the poor in 1599, recalling the disastrous failures of the grain harvest in the earlier 1590s when he had

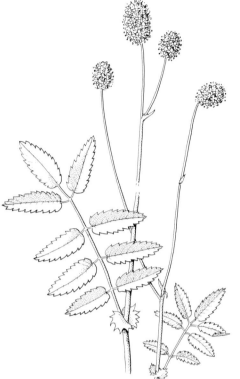

FIG. 5.9 Great burnet. (Drawn by Rosemary Wise.)

managed to grow 700 cabbages and carrots on four acres of land, and had fed many hundreds of people for twenty days. Vegetables not only fed many people, using land with great economy; they also provided a great deal of work, and this helped to solve one of the principal problems of seventeenth-century England, the problem of finding more work for the poor. The pamphleteers argued with increasing vehemence the case for more land to be used for vegetables for the two purposes—to provide more work and more food—and it became an axiom that the same quantities of food could be got from one acre of vegetables as from four acres under grain.[28]

So the fads and fashions of the upper classes of the sixteenth century ultimately set up a new branch of agricultural enterprise, namely horticulture, which has entirely transformed the landscape in some parts of the country, in the fens, in parts of Kent, in Hertfordshire, in the Evesham area of Worcestershire, and elsewhere. But horticulture also changed cultivation procedures in agriculture. Depressed farmers in the seventeenth century noticed the productivity of land when cultivated with the spade. They noticed how carefully soils were dug and redug; indeed, some people at first were positively prejudiced against the spade, arguing that soils would be ruined by so much digging. They noticed how seeds which the gardeners carefully set by hand in prepared rows, and then thinned and weeded, yielded larger plants and a heavier harvest. So they began experiments in the fields imitating the gardeners' techniques. In the beginning the methods were primitive indeed. On the Isle of Thanet canary seed was sown in prepared rows in the 1720s by letting it drop through the spout of a teapot. When Jethro Tull at much the same time decided to grow sainfoin as a more profitable crop than grain, he calculated that this expensive seed, when sown at seven bushels to the acre, dropped 140 seeds on a square foot of land whereas the crop was heaviest when only one plant occupied a square foot. So drilling and hoeing with horse-drawn machines began in earnest in the 1720s and 1730s, starting a revolution in cultivation that has truly altered our agricultural landscape. It has now brought an orderliness into our fields which in spring makes them look as if they had been marked out with a rule.[29]

Thus horticulture taught lessons to agriculture. But when population began to increase rapidly again after about 1750, and the demand for grain surged ahead once more, horticulture tended to retreat somewhat into the background. However, when the great agricultural depression of the 1880s and 1890s struck, attention turned once again to vegetable production—one of the few branches of farming that was prospering—and it was in this period that great strides forward were made in the grading and marketing of fruit and vegetables.

It is possible that we are now living at the beginning of another substantial horticultural advance, which may take decades to work itself through and whose full consequences we cannot yet assess. We have a more appreciative taste for vegetables, which some might now call a middle-class, no longer just a gentlemen's, fad. The argument that vegetables offer a healthier diet is an intellectual conviction with some. It is recognized (as in the seventeenth century) as a more economical way of using land to feed our growing world population. And it is commended, as in the seventeenth century, as a source of work. Nor is that work to be dismissed as all drudgery. In 1723 vegetable gardening was commended 'for the support, profit, or *pleasure* of human life'.[30] Those three virtues are recognized still. Since we now look towards an age with insufficient work for all, vegetable growing certainly offers 'food for thought in a jobless age', the headline given to a letter in *The Times* in January 1983, advocating the provision of more land for allotments for those who are unemployed and dispirited by that condition, and who would find 'interesting and rewarding work in the open air'.[31] As for the intellectual pleasure of vegetable growing (and for sixteenth-century gentlemen that was one of its justifications), nothing could be more satisfying than to appreciate the sophistication of the most professional vegetable gardening systems. Some are described in a recent American report on vegetable farming in China, recounting observations made by a group of visiting American agricultural specialists in 1977. Natural systems of pest control are used which reduce to the minimum the use of chemicals. Vegetables, arranged by rows, are crowded together in plots to mature at different times, and give shade or allow sun at the right moment in the growth cycle. Photographs in the report support the testimony of the observers that 'all crops are carefully hand-tended for maximum yield'.[32] It is an extremely labour-intensive business, but entirely appropriate in China's present economic and social circumstances. In Britain we now face the serious problem of finding enough satisfying work for all. And at the same time we know we have to use our land more economically. The productivity of land per acre under vegetables is very high. Our circumstances are changing in a way that presents the Chinese experience in a new light. For nearly two hundred years, since about 1750, our agricultural landscape has been manipulated in order to economize in the use of labour rather than land. Our priorities may have to be reversed, to use land more economically and labour more generously. If so, more changes in our agricultural landscape undoubtedly lie ahead.

6

Climate and landscape in the British Isles

HUBERT H. LAMB

Introduction

CLIMATE influences the landscape in a host of ways: most comprehensively and continuously through its control of the natural vegetation with which the countryside is clothed and which also provides the habitats for a characterististic fauna. Climate's control over the vegetation is not altogether direct, though when all aspects are considered it is the main control.

The play of the weather provides a range of climatic conditions within which many species can live, though a few will thrive best and in the end become dominant. Those species which finally dominate the natural scene may not have been the first to establish themselves in the landscape after the ice age. The earlier postglacial climates were not the same as the climate we know today. Indeed, the climate is forever changing in greater or less degree. There has been a succession of climate stages—some a bit warmer, some colder than today—and various more or less rapid transitions between them. Moreover, some plant species produce more pollen, or seed more abundantly, than others. Some are spread more widely by the aid of birds and insects as well as by the winds and flowing water. But once the bigger trees were established, they radically changed the environment for the humbler plants and the fauna which must thenceforward live in their shade.

The soil also plays its part in determining how well different plant species will succeed. It is itself, however, partly a legacy of past climates through the nature of the vegetation and the microfauna, mollusca and bacterial life, which those climates supported.

The assemblage of plant species which finally came to dominate the landscape was achieved only gradually, after a succession of developments and changes, over decades, centuries, or thousands of years, as competition from the best-adapted species enabled them to suppress many of the earlier arrivals.

Man's efforts at gardening and growing exotic species are largely a matter of intervening in that continuing competition. We introduce and support certain species of our choice that are capable of thriving in the given climate, but which need our aid in eliminating those competitors which would be more successful without our intervention. We may also, of course, alter the local field climate by providing additional water, or drainage, and controlling or eliminating pests, and so on.

But before the best-suited vegetation—the climax vegetation—is achieved, the climatic conditions themselves undergo continual fluctuations and change, and the climax vegetation is itself in a state of dynamic equilibrium. So one year favours one particular plant or insect much more than others. So, also, killing frosts, or drought, or other events may eliminate or greatly set back certain species and alter the balance of the scene for many years to follow.

These aspects of the landscape therefore betray a dynamic situation in which continual change, usually slow but occasionally conspicuous, is going on.

The most basic item of the natural landscape is, of course, the topography and the geological structure underlying it.[1] The geology determines the nature of the mineral content of the soils and river and lake deposits. The relief is the result of uplift and erosion through weathering, stream flow, and coastal storms, in some cases over many millions of years. The list of processes which have produced the surface land-forms must also include the movement of surface matter by the glaciers of the ice ages, by frost shattering, and by wind and water, including stormy seas, even in our own times. So, once again, climate is for most of the time the main formative influence, even though the land was shaped by major upheavals of the Earth's crust before the erosion which has continued ever since.

We have not space here to dwell on the evidence in our landscape of such things as hot desert climates in the remote geological past, hundreds of millions of years ago. These are seen in the outcrops of red sandstone rocks all the way from the cliffs near Sidmouth in Devon, on the Bristol Channel coast, and through the Welsh borderland, and again in many parts of Scotland, from the Lowland Valley to the fine cliffs of the east coast near Dunottar Castle in Kincardineshire and the Stacks off Duncansby Head, and on to Orkney and beyond. Palaeomagnetic measurements indicate that in the time when the Old Red Sandstone was formed Britain was in the desert zone of the southern hemisphere, near latitude 20°S; and when the Triassic sandstones were formed the latitude indicated is that of the southern Sahara today, near 20°N. The drifting of the continents over hundreds of millions of years will, however, be assigned to geology and the physics of the Earth's crust, and so be beyond the scope of this lecture, even if the climates that went with our changed position in the world are registered in the soils of Devon, Hereford, and Angus.

Neither have we space to look around the country for the occasional evidence of more than one of the ice ages and interglacial periods of the last million years, as in the buried soils and frost features revealed in the soft cliffs of Norfolk near Cromer and Sheringham. We shall take our own survey no farther back than the last ice age and the ten thousand years or so that have elapsed since its ending in this part of the world.

The climatic record

First, we must look over the perspectives of past temperature levels, as far as they are at present known, to provide the necessary framework for our exploration of landscape developments.

The best indication we have of the course of world temperature, going back over the last two million years, is from oxygen isotope measurements on the material at different depths in a core taken from the bed of the Pacific Ocean near the equator.[2] This shows evidence of recurrent ice ages abstracting water from the oceans to form ice masses on land at approximately 100,000-year intervals over the last one million years or more. Of these ice ages at least the last three seem to have produced ice-sheets and glaciers in Britain and Ireland, while ice spreading from northern Scandinavia advanced across the dried-out bed of the North Sea to intrude upon eastern England. Although we like to think of the climate of these islands as being reliably moderated by the warm waters of Gulf Stream origin brought by the North Atlantic Drift—and the year-to-year variability of temperatures which we have experienced in modern times is indeed more moderate here than on the Continent—there was such a great change of the ocean currents in the ice ages that the cooling here and in Ireland was greater than almost anywhere else in the world. The massive cooling of the North Atlantic in our latitudes seen in Figure 6.1—by 12° to 18°C— should be compared with the overall average global cooling amounting to perhaps only 2.5°C.

Figure 6.2 shows a recently published map of Europe and Asia at the height of the last glaciation fifteen to twenty thousand years ago, with most of the British Isles (in the top left-hand corner of the map) covered by ice, and even a separate centre of glaciation in south-west Ireland. The North Sea was reduced to an ice-dammed fresh-water lake in a broad plain draining to the south-west through a valley roughly where the so-called English Channel is today. Much of Russia and Siberia were submerged beneath shallow inland seas and lakes of huge extent. On another view, even the western part of the English Channel may have been filled with an ice tongue spreading from a dome-shaped ice-massif centred on the continental shelf somewhere in the South-western Approaches.

Thus old moraines (see Figure 6.3) and other ice-formed landscape features may be found anywhere in those parts of the north, west, and east of the British Isles that were at one time ice-covered, and periglacial features such as outwash gravels and relics of former permafrost may occur anywhere at all in these islands.

Figure 6.4 shows the apparent changes in the average level of prevailing temperatures in central England over the last 20,000 years, since the height of the last ice age. Within the last thousand years the variability from one century to another can be indicated by the dots that straddle the curves at the right-hand side of the diagram. One must suppose that a somewhat similar variability occurred at all earlier times, perhaps a little less in the periods of warmer climate and possibly up to two, or even three, times greater in the ice-age regime.

We can get an inkling of what such temperature changes as those seen in Figure 6.4

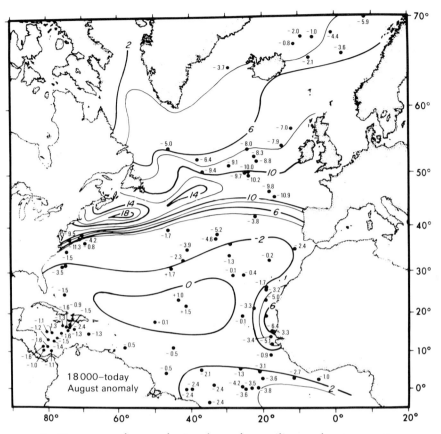

FIG. 6.1 Departures from today's values of prevailing surface temperatures (in °C) in the Atlantic Ocean in the warmest month (August) at the Ice Age climax about 18,000 years ago. (Redrawn from A. McIntyre *et al.*, 'Glacial North Atlantic 18,000 years ago—a CLIMAP reconstruction', in R. M. Cline and J. D. Hays (eds.), *Geological Society of America Memoir 145* (Boulder, Colorado, 1976), pp. 43–76.)

mean for the vegetation cover of the landscape from the changes of height of the upper tree line in central Europe seen in Figure 6.5. Similar histories have been established in other parts of the world, though not yet in Britain. Evidence of such a history is, however, familiar enough in the tree-stumps, dating from about six thousand years ago, on the heights above the present limits of woodland on the Pennines and in Scotland. Of course, when the ice-age glaciers melted there were at first no trees in our landscape, and then for a long time only clumps of birches, and later pines, which gradually spread to form a forest. It took several thousand years for the broad-leafed forest of oak, elm, and lime to arrive from the refuges of these trees beyond the Alps and then to become the dominant feature of our landscape. Later still, the elms and limes declined, rather abruptly (especially in the case of elm) about 3000 BC, and other species such as beech arrived, when the forests were

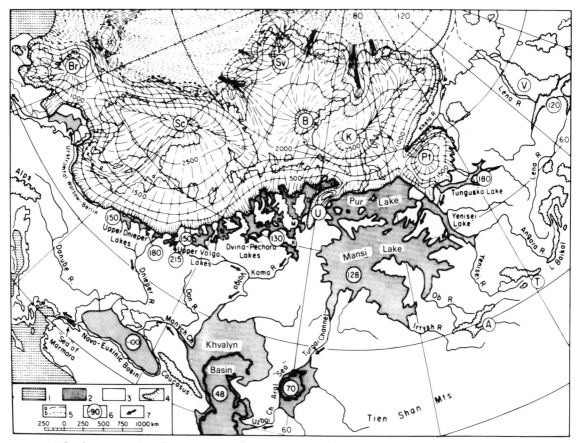

FIG. 6.2 The last great ice-sheet over northern Europe and Asia, and drainage systems. (From M. G. Grosswald, 'Late Weichselian ice sheet of northern Eurasia', in *Quaternary Research*, vol. 13, no. 1 (Academic Press, New York, 1980), pp. 1–32.)

already retreating from the heights and from the western and northern Atlantic coasts. This retreat is thought to register the effects not so much of the cooling as of increasing windiness after the warmest postglacial times and of soil deterioration as the wetness leached soluble nutrients out and peat bogs spread. The process may have been hastened by man-made clearances for crops and pasture and by the grazing of animals.

The temperature history of central England since about AD 800 can be outlined in terms of successive century or half-century averages (Figure 6.6).[3] This recent twelve-hundred-year record reveals an important climatic oscillation, possibly the severest for many thousands of years past, but partly paralleled in each of the last five millennia. There is some ground for believing that the temperatures prevailing in and around the seventeenth century AD were the lowest, and the expansion of the Arctic sea ice and Europe's glaciers the greatest, since the end of the ice age. Indeed, the period from AD 1550 to about 1700 (or, on some criteria, from AD 1300 or 1400 to nearly 1900) is often called the Little Ice Age.

Reconstruction of the prevailing sea surface temperatures at the climax of this period suggests that part of the characteristic switch of ocean currents to an ice-age situation had in fact taken place (see Figure 6.7). Correspondingly, there are indications that the temperatures prevailing in northern Scotland, southern Norway, and Iceland in the late seventeenth century were much more depressed below modern levels than in England—by 2° to 3°C on a thirty-year average as against 1° or 1.1°C depression in central England when the 1670–99 averages are compared with the warmest part of the present century, 1930–59.

The change from the warmest time of similar length in the Middle Ages between about AD 1150 and 1300 to the cold periods around 1560 to 1610 and 1670 to 1700 seems to have meant a fall of the overall average temperatures typical for central England by 1.4° to 1.7°C. The most familiar consequence of this was the onset of the times in which severe winters with frozen rivers were common. Indeed, the great winter of 1564–5, which began the series and which seems to have exceeded the length and severity of any winter in western or central Europe for about 130 years previously, produced such a strong impression on the artists of the time as to set a whole new fashion in landscape painting (which we still like to remember at Christmas-card time). It was followed by about

FIG. 6.3 Old moraine across Glen Strathfarrar, north-west Scotland: view looking down-valley.

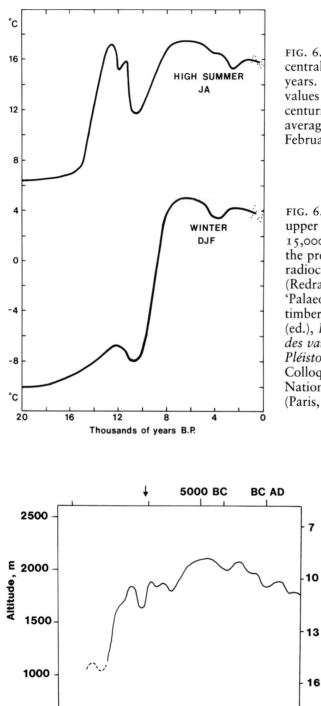

FIG. 6.4 (*left*) Prevailing temperatures in central England over the last 20,000 years. Dots show the summer and winter values derived for the last twelve centuries (JA = July and August average; DJF = December, January and February average.)

FIG. 6.5 (*below*) General height of the upper tree line on the Alps over the last 15,000 years. (Ages BP = years before the present time, actually approximate radiocarbon ages before AD 1950.) (Redrawn from V. Markgraf, 'Palaeoclimatic evidence derived from timberline fluctuations', in J. Labeyrie (ed.), *Les méthodes quantitatives d'étude des variations du climat au cours du Pléistocène*, no. 219 in the series Colloques internationaux du Centre National de la Recherche Scientifique (Paris, 1974), pp. 67–83.)

twenty-five more or less similar winters in the next 280 years. There were other consequences also. For example, the upper limit of cultivation in the hill country of western and northern Britain, which in the thirteenth century had been extended (much higher than in our own day) to about 400 metres above sea level both on Dartmoor and on the Lammermuir Hills in south-east Scotland, descended by 200 metres or so. That this was a change corresponding to the force of natural circumstances is verified by the fact that the upper tree-line on the heights of central Europe, from the Vosges to the Sudeten mountains on the older border of Germany and Czechoslovakia, also fell by about 200 metres between the thirteenth and seventeenth centuries.

These temperature changes certainly brought important changes in the duration of the growing season, which was 10 to 20 days shorter at Oxford even in 1870–95 than between 1930 and 1949. It was probably three to five weeks shorter in most years in the late seventeenth century than in the warmest decades of the present century. The year-to-year variability was also increased.[4] (Since 1960 the growing season in England generally has again been shortened by 9 to 10 days, mostly by later springs.) In the high Middle Ages the growth period may have averaged up to a fortnight longer than in our own century. Similarly, the frequency of frost and snow was increased in the Little Ice Age period of recent centuries. This frequency has varied a good deal in different decades within the present century. The average number of days with snow lying on the low ground of central England between 1670 and 1700 must have been about 20 to 30, as against 5 to 15 in recent decades. In the winter of 1657–8 102 days was the total reported at one place in southern England, compared with 50 to 65 days generally in 1962–3 and 40 days in 1978–9.

There seems to have been a heightened storminess in our latitudes during the late medieval decline. This made itself obvious in the first sharp periods of cooling of the Arctic around 1200–50, 1300–50 and 1400–60. Moreover, the general sea level must have been somewhat raised (by about 50 centimetres?) because of glacier melting in the warmth of several preceding centuries. The incidence of gales, including (it seems) the severest storms known, seems to have been remarkable also in the coldest times around 1560–1610, 1670–1700, and again about 1790–1810, and there were many changes of the coastline by erosion and blown sand.

There is controversy about how close the situation came to the formation of small local glaciers in the seventeenth and eighteenth centuries in a few of the north-east-facing corries in the mountains of Scotland. What is certain is that there were many more persistent snowbeds than now, in shaded corries and clefts in the mountain-sides, that failed to melt in most summers. And there were one or two high-level tarns that bore more or less permanent ice. Many travellers between about 1580 and 1770 referred to permanent snow on the tops of the Cairngorms (1,200 to 1,300 metres above sea level), and in several years between 1805 and 1823 in the English Lake District John Dalton on his yearly climb of Helvellyn (951 metres) in July reported finding a snowdrift remaining 'in the usual place': it is doubtful whether this has ever been present at a similar date in the last fifty to eighty years.[5]

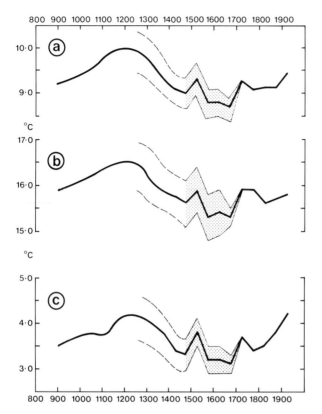

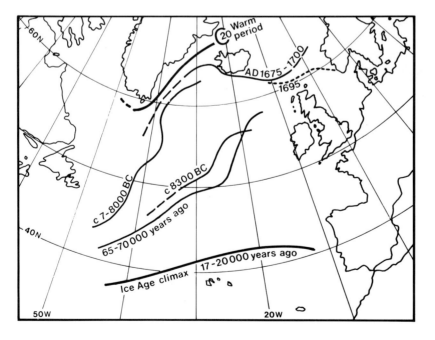

FIG. 6.6 (*left*) Prevailing temperatures in central England since AD 800—probable 50-year averages and margins of uncertainty.

(a) Averages for the whole year
(b) Averages for the high summer—July and August
(c) Averages for the winter—December, January and February.

FIG. 6.7 (*below*) Average positions of the boundary between warm surface water of Gulf Stream origin and the polar water in the North Atlantic at various dates. (From studies by W. F. Ruddiman and H. H. Lamb.)

The average rainfall is also subject to both long- and short-term variations. Thirty to fifty-year averages have been derived for various past epochs, ranging from about 15–20 per cent above the modern figures in the warmest postglacial times to about 10 per cent below today's from around AD 1720 to the 1750s. The effects upon prevailing wetness or dryness of the ground and size of the rivers are, however, complicated by changes in the amount of evaporation, depending on temperature and wind. Variations in these aspects of the landscape certainly have occurred. In this regard studies, aided by radio-carbon dating, of the variations in the rate of peat growth in bogs and the times at which the bogs have dried out are interesting.[6] Most remarkable is the indication of a period of great wetness in the bogs of west Wales between about 800 and 400 BC, when peat growth was at about ten times the long-term average rate; but this period, with presumably very great predominance of westerly winds, may have been relatively dry in the eastern part of the country.

Much greater wetness may have prevailed at times during the melting of the ice-age glaciers. That was the time when, with permafrost still stopping permeability in the chalk of southern England, surface erosion formed the now dry valleys in the Downs (Figure 6.8).

FIG. 6.8 Dry valley, known as the Devil's Kneadingtrough, in the North Downs near Brook in east Kent.

Rainfall variations have to do not only with changes in the amount of water vapour carried by the winds but also with changes in the prevalence of different wind directions and the proximity or otherwise of the storm centres. It seems clear also that, as with temperature, the year-to-year variability of rainfall was enhanced in the colder climatic periods. Despite generally lower total rainfalls, some years and runs of years were very wet and, with reduced evaporation, soils became waterlogged, lakes and rivers overflowed, and landslips and bog-slides were more frequent than at any other time.

Climate and vegetation zones

The variations which we have been discussing mean that in postglacial times moisture has nearly always been sufficient for a complete vegetation cover in these islands, but the changes of prevailing temperature level must have shifted the boundaries of different types of vegetation. There are, in fact, some exceptions even to the sufficiency of moisture. These occur on a local and temporary scale today, when parching easterly or northerly winds blow over open moors at times when frozen soil checks the plants' supply of moisture from the ground, and the surface grasses and heathers and the like are 'burnt' off. Similarly parching conditions sometimes occur on the high ground above 700 to 1,000 metres when very dry air that has subsided from great heights in an anticyclone occasionally reaches the surface there: relative humidities may be as low as 5 to 15 per cent in these conditions. But in the Breckland of west Norfolk and Suffolk over a long period of time, at least from the seventeenth century to the 1920s, the vegetation failed to cover the soil completely (see Figure 6.9): this was evidently due to a combination of the area's very low rainfall (long-term average barely 600 millimetres a year) with the results of past sheep grazing, aggravated sooner or later by rabbits burrowing, and was only cured by the afforestation begun in the 1920s, in the early days of the Forestry Commission. John Evelyn reported in the seventeenth century that the area was liable to frequent storms of blowing sand 'like the sands of Libya', and it is recorded that huge masses of sand were transported up to ten kilometres from about Lakenheath to Santon Downham in one storm in 1668. The situation seems to have been mainly due to a climatic shift, since a quite similar development was affecting inland sandy tracts of the Netherlands over the same period.

The gradations of rainfall from west to east across the country, and of cloudiness and sunshine—and the different liability to occasional extremes of low and high temperature—cause differences in the assemblage of plants in the vegetation cover. An example is the change from west to east in the character of the undergrowth in the remnants of the old Caledonian Forest, the native pinewoods of northern Scotland.

FIG. 6.9 Part of the Breckland in west Norfolk, showing the stony, partly bare ground, photographed about 1920 before afforestation. (Photograph by the late W. G. Clarke, first published in his *In Breckland Wilds*, Robert Scott, London, 1926.)

Amounts of juniper increase in the drier climates towards the east. Similarly, the proportion of ling as against bell heather on the moors, and the quantity of certain berries, increases towards the east.

Average yearly rainfall in the present epoch increases from around 500 mm in the driest districts of East Anglia, and about 650 mm in the driest parts of eastern Scotland, to from 2,000 to locally nearly 5,000 mm in the wettest places in the west, the highest figures being among the mountains in west and north-west Scotland, in Cumberland, and in North Wales. And the average yearly number of 'wet days' with more than one millimetre of rainfall ranges from under 100 in Essex to over 200 in the wetter parts of the western Highlands, the Lake District, and North Wales.

The well-known characteristics of the vegetation in wet localities with abundant surface moisture and restricted evaporation, as in enclosed places beside rivers, swamps and lakes, are the prominence of alder, ferns and mosses, and in the more extreme sites sphagnum bog.

Near most British coasts the sharp increase in windiness results in reduced height, and ultimate disappearance, of trees from the landscape. Surviving trees in the most exposed sites are commonly deformed by the frequency of winds—often strong winds—from the sea. Similar wind-deformation may be seen in the shapes of trees on the heights, but the common characteristic of trees near the natural upper limit of forest is their stunted, slow growth and low stature.

Despite these variations, the vegetation cover of the British Isles today is essentially complete. It is, however, very different in character from what it would be, especially as regards forest cover, had not man's activities largely removed the natural vegetation. The main historical variations since the last ice age have undoubtedly been due to changes in the prevailing temperature level.

The world's climates have long been conveniently classified by Köppen in terms of the distinctive vegetation zones and their temperature requirements.[7] Within the limits of these islands, over the time-span since the climax of the last glaciation, we are concerned with just three of these zones:

1 the *temperate rain-forest climates,* with average temperature of the coldest month not below −3°C: Köppen's type C;

2 the *boreal-forest climates,* with average temperature of the warmest month above +10°C and of the coldest month below −3°C: Köppen's type D; and

3 *cold treeless climates,* with average temperature of the warmest month below 10°C: Köppen's type E.

These can be separated into

(*a*) type ET, the *tundra climates,* with mean temperature of the warmest month above the freezing point and dwarf tree species and mosses present; and

(*b*) type EF, with the average temperature of all months below 0°C, though brief thaws and rain can occur. *Frost climates* of type EF did occur in Britain and Ireland in the Full Glacial period near the ice, that is over most (or all) of the country in the climax phase.

The temperature changes in postglacial times have produced shifts of the CD and DE boundaries. These can be traced as (i) changes in the latitude of the broad-leafed and pine-forest boundary (though for many thousands of years past this has lain somewhere within the northern half of Scotland) and (ii) changes in the height on the mountains of the upper forest limit.

Books illustrating the assemblages characteristic of the natural forest types belonging to zones 1 and 2 in Britain seem to be a rarity, if any exist. Much commoner are illustrations of various mixed agricultural and parkland scenes where the whole landscape registers human control. (There is, however, a good picture of an acid peat bog and pool with sedge border and pine and birch woodland in the background, a typical enough scene for type 1 on p.19 in *Britain's Heritage*, edited by John Julius Norwich, published by Granada, 1983). An interesting indicator of the difference between the open landscapes we are used to and the natural vegetation of most of England may be seen at the agricultural research centre, Rothamsted Experimental Station, Harpenden, Hertfordshire. In the great field known as the Broadbalk, which is divided into a large number of rectangular experimental plots, the half-acre plot number 1 was sown with wheat regularly for thirty-nine years from the beginning in 1843 and then abandoned unharvested from 1882 onwards, to let nature take its course. After 1886 there were no longer any wheat plants to be found. By 1895 the plot had been invaded by oak and ash trees, hazel, rose, and hawthorn. After thirty-six years the trees were dominant, and many brambles, hazels and hawthorns were dying. Other varieties which later established themselves were field maple, holly, sycamore, wild cherry, and blackthorn, with more hawthorns and elderberry at the southern edge. In short, the plot has now become a small sample of mixed oak woodland.

Examples of the natural upper limit of forest are hard to find in the British Isles owing to deforestation and landscape management by man. Figure 6.10 shows the tree-line of natural oak woodland in western North Wales, the wood becoming little more than scrub near its limit at barely 300 metres above sea level, presumably owing to the windiness of the climate (though sheep grazing may also have played a part in determining the limit), and Figure 6.11 shows the pine forest limit in northern central Scotland at about 580 metres on the north side of the Cairngorms.

Let us now consider the chronological sequence of landscape and vegetation development in order to follow the changes of climate that are registered in our landscapes. Within the confines of a lecture samples of only a very limited number of the features and processes registered can be shown.

The former presence of great ice-sheets has left its mark in occasional surfaces of glacier-smoothed rock, often, perhaps usually, with *striae*, or scratches, showing the direction of ice movement through the grinding action of stones that were embedded in the ice. Perched boulders, too, are to be seen today in odd places where the ice-sheets left them when they melted, and others have rolled to where they now lie after being abandoned by the ice or split from rock walls by frost-shattering. There are many in Snowdonia. We have in these islands also the end-moraines, now cloaked in vegetation (as Figure 6.3), of numerous former glaciers. (The late Professor Gordon Manley photographed a whole

FIG. 6.10 Upper forest limit: natural oak woodland in Cwm Nant Col, near Harlech, in western North Wales, here barely 300 metres above sea level.

cluster of moraine remnants, left over from the last phase of the last glaciation, only 10,000 years ago, at the head of Great Langdale.) The corries (great hollows carved in the sides of the mountain and backed by precipices and lesser rock walls) formed by repeated freeze and thaw shattering cracked rock, in places where snow-beds lie long into the summer and ultimately small glaciers form, arc a feature of all our mountain groups, particularly of the north and north-east faces. There are many other relics of the ice-age climate about us, even the marks of old frost cracks, patterning the ground of eastern England as seen from the air and exposed as frost wedges in the cliffs near Sheringham and in the sides of gravel workings. These are cracks that were once filled with ice but are now filled with collapsed or washed-in earth and gravel.[8]

There are also marks to be found of the melting stage towards the end of the glaciation. The gravelly esker in farm and parkland at Hunstanton, Norfolk is an example of a feature attributed to deposition of the debris carried by great outwash streams running on the surface of, and under, the ice. In side-valleys in the central Highlands of Scotland there are the old shore-lines of lakes that existed while the main valleys were still filled with ice deep enough to dam them. The famous 'parallel roads of Glen Roy' are an example. And we have already referred to the dry valleys in the chalk downs of southern England, from

Dunstable to east Kent and Wiltshire, which were formed by water-erosion at a time when the lower layers of the chalk were still impermeable because of permafrost.

Signs of a former climate in mid-postglacial times that was rather warmer than now—though perhaps by only 1° to 2°C—are widespread in the shape of stumps of well-grown trees high on our hills above the present upper tree-line (Figure 6.12) and near the exposed Atlantic coasts of north Scotland. The spread of forest to the very coast is also registered in the exposure of tree-stumps and old forest soils, again of similar age, below the high-tide mark at various places, as at Borth, near Aberystwyth (Figure 6.13). It bears witness also to the somewhat lower sea level that existed at that time when the rebound of the land from the former ice-load was less complete than it now is. Another apparent indication of the warm, and presumably less windy, climate of those same times is found in the size of the biggest oaks whose trunks have been discovered lying in the peat of the Cambridgeshire fenland. Sir Harry Godwin has reported a case where the trunk reached a height of 27.5 metres (90 feet) before the first branch.[9]

FIG. 6.11 Upper forest limit: pines increasingly stunted towards their limit at about 580 metres above sea level on the inhospitable north slope of Creag Mhigeachaidh (Inshriach Forest, Speyside) on the north side of the Cairngorms.

FIG. 6.12 Stumps of full-grown pine trees at about 650 metres above sea level on the northern slope of Cairngorm, only a few kilometres from the present natural limit of stunted pines at 580 metres seen in Figure 6.11. Such tree-stumps in this immediate area, in some cases up to 700 to 800 metres above sea level, have yielded radiocarbon ages generally of 4,000 to well over 6,000 years,* indicating a high-standing cover of pinewoods at these heights between about 5500 and 2000 BC (corrected calendar dates).

*N. V. Pears in *Research papers in forest meteorology* (edited by J. A. Taylor), Aberystwyth symposium, 1972.

The evidence of later climatic changes to be seen in our landscape is very often related to changes in man's ability to exploit the landscape in various ways. The relative warmth of a run of several centuries in the High Middle Ages, between about AD 900 and 1300, is for instance registered in the ridge-and-furrow, bearing witness to former cultivation, up to heights of 300 to 400 metres above sea level in places ranging from Dartmoor to the Lammermuir Hills near Edinburgh. This was also the time when vineyards flourished in many places in England and Wales: some of them were no one man's personal hobby but were kept going for 200 years or more. And some were in exposed sites in the eastern fenland and in valley bottoms elsewhere that would have to be dismissed as frost hollows today.

Many signs are there to be discovered in the landscape of the deterioration of climate from AD 1200–1300 onwards, which led ultimately to the era of frequent great frosts that froze our rivers (though these very rarely occurred more than three to four times in a decade). The great storms which changed the coastline in various places were already prominent in the thirteenth century, and with a probably slightly higher sea level flooding was severe. This was when the Zuider Zee in Holland, and perhaps also the Jadebusen bay in north-west Germany and the Broads in Norfolk, were formed. In the following two or three centuries these embayments of the continental coast were enlarged in further storm floods. Tremendous tracts of land were lost from the west coast of Denmark and Schleswig (then a Danish province). And, step by step, inroads of the sea on England's east coast took the great ports of Dunwich and Ravenspur (or Ravensburgh). Elsewhere former ports were closed, and coastal roads and farmland buried permanently, by blown sand. This deterioration of the climate was the cause of the abandonment of the earlier medieval vineyards, of much tillage of earlier times not only on the heights but apparently also in the Norfolk Breckland, and of the desertion of numerous hamlets and small villages

FIG. 6.13 Forest remains on the west coast of Wales, dating from 5000 to 4000 BC, and traces of the forest floor soil, now submerged and exposed only at low tide, seen on the beach at Borth, near Aberystwyth.

other than those that were wiped out by the Black Death in 1349–50 and subsequent outbreaks of the plague. Desertions occurred also during the later runs of 'failed' summers in the period between 1420 and 1470 and notably in the 1690s.

It seems to be not widely known how much distress prevailed, and how run-down the landscape was, with the frequent harvest failures and famines in the colder climate of the Little Ice Age period. Antonia Fraser has written, of the condition of Scotland from the sixteenth to the nineteenth centuries, that the lowlands were 'dissected . . . by immense watery tracts in the shape of countless lochs and lochans'.[10] In Fifeshire alone there were twenty lochs as big as Loch Leven is now. There is even an anonymous Scots poem, known to have been written around 1300, which seems to record the beginning of the decline, telling how the golden age of King Alexander, with its abundance of ale and bread, and 'of gaming and glee', seemed to have died with him in 1286, and 'the frute failyeit on everilk tree'.[11] Of the situation when the colder climate had reached, and just passed, its climax around 1700, W. M. Thackeray wrote: 'As one views Europe, through contemporary books of travel, in the early part of the last century [that is around 1700 to 1730], the landscape is awful—wretched wastes, beggarly and plundered; half-burned cottages and trembling peasants gathering piteous harvests . . . By these passes my Lord's gilt carriage floundering through the ruts as he swears at the postillions and toils on to the Residenz. Hard by, but away from the noise of citizens . . . is Wilhelmslust . . . or Versailles—it scarcely matters which—near to the city, shut out by woods from the beggared country . . .'[12] (At such a time many of the great parks of the palaces and squires' halls of Europe, that broad sections of the public enjoy today, were planned and laid out.) How similar this description is to the Discourse given by Andrew Fletcher of Saltoun in Midlothian in 1698 to the old Scots parliament, criticizing the well-to-do of the more comfortable cornland counties like his own in the eastern lowlands for their unconcern over the starving population of the upland parishes all over Scotland, after six successive years of harvest failure, with a third of the population dead or dying.

Climate and Landscape Management

Many factors undoubtedly played a part in the recovery of Europe after 1700, the increasing freedom from famines, and the explosive growth of population which has continued to our own day. The planting of hedges and greater shelter-belts of trees, started in Norfolk by the first Thomas Coke of Holkham in the first half of the eighteenth century, and the agricultural improvements—fertilizers, drainage, pesticides, and improved strains of the various crops—were certainly very important. Others have stressed the shift away from rye, which, despite its virtues of productivity in poor soils and in surviving severe winters, is liable to the ergot fungus which was formerly the cause of widespread debilitating diseases and deaths. It is not so widely known that the results of the improved agriculture owed a good deal to the better, warmer summers in much of the eighteenth century. Nowadays the diseases of rye, as of other crops, are under better control and there are many who are gaining a taste for rye bread. But the value of hedges and shelter-belts seems to have been forgotten by all too many modern mass-production farmers with their giant equipment.

The ever-shifting sands that had overwhelmed the rich farms of the Culbin estates near the southern shore of the Moray Firth, reputedly in 1694, and the sand-blows and inadequate vegetation of the East Anglian Breckland, were only halted in the 1920s and after by carefully worked out plans of afforestation. The success of this parallels the successes of modern engineering in draining the Zuider Zee in Holland as well as many marshy and formerly waterlogged valley areas in the British Isles. The same may be said of the coastal sea defences which have lessened the hazards of storm floods, particularly around the North Sea, where repeated incidents in the Middle Ages brought disasters as great as the Bangladesh cyclone of 1970. Reported death tolls were counted in hundreds of thousands. The Thames Barrier is the latest development in this story, and it is hoped that it will protect London against the flood threat posed by the rising sea level in the southern North Sea and apparently increasing storminess.[13]

In other ways, however, the works of man have increased the risks—and the frequency—of flooding in valleys and in urban areas. Through improvements in field and urban drainage and the asphalted and paved surfaces of towns the speed of run-off has been increased. Hence, individual heavy or prolonged rains and thawing of snow are the more liable to produce sudden flooding of the lower-lying areas. We have also increased our vulnerability to climate's fluctuations and changes by our supposed rationalization of agriculture, concentrating once more on almost one-crop cultivation in huge areas where that crop usually grows best.

Many studies of local climate in towns and cities have indicated the importance of the 'urban heat island', attributable partly to artificial heat generated in the buildings and partly to the responses of the paved surfaces to weather. Perhaps the most general conclusion is the virtue of avenues of trees and open spaces in cities in moderating these effects.

Other points too numerous to go into here, and requiring more detailed study, are concerned with man's pollution of the atmosphere and the possibility that our technology and energy-production is reaching such a scale that the whole Earth's climate may soon be affected, supposedly in the direction of a rapidly increasing warming due to the radiation properties of the increasing carbon dioxide in the atmosphere. As we have seen, nature too is continually producing changes of climate, and the present natural trend seems to be in the direction of cooling.[14] Whichever way the climate develops over the coming decades, the changes will offer opportunities to be exploited as well as threats to existing ways. The greater warmth of the present century, as compared with at least the last five centuries, has encouraged the opening of many vineyards in England and the cultivation of peaches and apricots, though these seem to have done less well in the rather cooler years since 1950. Exploitation of conditions to the limit of what the climate for the time being allows— whether, for instance, for exotic crops or flat-roofed, and even glass-roofed, triumphs of architectural engineering—is always vulnerable to climatic change.

We must be both alert and cautious, imbued too with a good understanding of what we attempt to conserve, because conservation is often not nature's way. Most of all, I believe we must not squander limited resources of either energy or land in trying to create and maintain too artificial an environment in our overheated buildings and treeless townscapes with their excessive paving.

7

Towns, industry, and the Victorian landscape

F. M. L. THOMPSON

THERE was little doubt in William Cowper's mind when he pronounced that 'God made the country, and man made the town' that the former had made a pretty good job of it, and the latter a pretty frightful mess.[1] Some eighteenth-century opinion, to be sure, was scared or bored by the country in its more desolate or dull-witted aspects, and warmed to the town as the cradle and nursery of culture and pleasure. Dr Johnson, it is well known, thought that 'when a man is tired of London he is tired of life', and the urbane Pope bid an emotional farewell to the 'dear, damn'd, distracting town' when leaving London.[2] But, while acknowledging that, as regrettable necessities, different towns had their points— 'Oxford for learning, London for wit, Hull for women, and York for a tit' as the proverb ran—the main stream of literary opinion, swollen by romanticism, flowed strongly through the next two centuries in favour of the virtues of the natural, as expressed in the countryside, and in condemnation of the havoc and degradation wrought by men as they created monster towns and monstrous industrial landscapes in the cause of greater production and larger profits. D. H. Lawrence, writing in 1929 that 'the real tragedy of England, as I see it, is the tragedy of ugliness. The country is so lovely: the man-made England is so vile', was plumb in the middle of the Cowper tradition as sharpened by Thomas Carlyle, Ruskin, William Morris, and a host of Victorian critics of the handiwork of industrial man.[3] It was, no doubt, less demanding for poets and writers to wax lyrical about the countryside than to make the effort needed to conceptualize and then verbalize the perplexing complexities of urban life; simpler to commune with nature and versify daffodils or cooling streams than to worry over a new phraseology capable of capturing the inner meaning of blast furnaces or bottle ovens; more comforting to accept ancestral and religious traditions which equated nature with innocence and beauty than to struggle to express the allure of industrial and urban landscapes which manifestly contained many appalling affronts to human dignity and the human eye. Nevertheless, the increasingly dominant cult of the country was not just the mentally lazy way of summarizing aesthetic and social criticism of industrialization: it also expressed many hard, grim, truths about the effects of men and society on the landscape; but it happened to be wrong-headed.

In their descent from prosperity and world mastery the English have become a nation of preservationists, and chief among the objects to be preserved is the landscape. It is to be preserved from thoughtless or wanton desecration or destruction by late twentieth-century vandals who mainly bear the guise of property developers, planners, bureaucrats, or giant corporations, nationalized or not, but who are in essence no more than the most visible and identifiable manifestations of the general menace to whatever happens to exist at any given moment in the physical landscape, which is posed by changing, expanding, or new technologies or material needs. There is, however, considerable confusion over what it is that is to be preserved. Is it landscape untouched by human hands? In which case preservationists might as well pack up shop in Britain and go off to the Amazon or Tasmania to fight for the few remaining regions of natural wilderness. Is it countryside not much altered in its appearance by human activity since some point in the past? In which case is the approved cut-off date, after which change is impermissible, 54 BC, AD 1066, 1600, 1800, 1914, or 1983? Is the landscape to be protected a purely rural category, a stretch of country which is not completely uninhabited, to be sure, but is inhabited by not too many people tastefully disposed in a few isolated houses of distinction or in small clusters of lesser dwellings of pleasingly picturesque quality? Or does the concept of the landscape which is worth preserving embrace those parts of the man-made built environment, in towns, in houses and buildings, and in industrial operations, which the beholder—architect, industrial archaeologist, Georgian or Victorian Society enthusiast—chances to find pleasing and interesting? Beneath such questions lie deeper confusions and ambiguities in attitudes towards the processes which have created the landscapes that it is now sought to conserve, and a reluctance to sort out the implications of admiring the relics and remains of past changes and obsolete and dead technologies, while striving to hide or chase away the visible effects of current developments and technologies.

It may well be that in a hundred years derelict nuclear power stations will have merged into the landscape and have acquired admirers and defenders of their irreplaceable contribution as relict features. Certainly one does not have to look far today to find admirers of railway lines which were once denounced as raw scars on the scenery, reservoirs which were bitterly condemned as drowners of old villages, or mill chimneys which were the very fount of atmospheric pollution; many of these, fallen silent or by nature silent, have become accepted as familiar and hence in some sense natural parts of the landscape. The distance of time and memory lends charm and fascination to many strange objects, as well as unlikely events, and maybe the general law of landscape appreciation amounts to little more than the proposition that yesterday's blot on the landscape is today's beauty spot. Nostalgia is an essential clue to landscape sentiment and landscape definition. It does not in itself explain why certain scenes, settings, and structures touch nostalgic chords at certain times, and are found to be evocative and admirable, while others remain below the dignity of landscape status, or if considered at all excite ridicule or disgust. An explanation of these moods and attitudes lies in the realms of the sociology of culture and the aesthetics of taste. Today's nostalgia, however, is a reminder to the historian of the landscape that anything done to the land, or erected upon it, necessarily produced a visible, physical, effect on the scene, and may have survived long enough to trigger the subsequent emotional and artistic responses needed to make it part of the scenery. It is also a hint that not everything the Victorians did with, to, and on the land was frightful, ugly, and regrettable.

For the most part, of course, Victorians got on with whatever business was in hand, and any effect on the appearance of the landscape of what they did was unintended and incidental to the object of growing food, producing coal or cotton, providing transport, housing workers, or whatever. There were exceptions, and, particularly in the housing of the better-off, the appearance not only of individual houses but of whole streets and districts was a prime concern, because prices and profits were strongly influenced by overall impressions of status and attraction. Streetscapes and urban landscapes were not, therefore, entirely a chance by-product of the building industry, but in certain locations were the deliberate, calculated, product of commercial enterprise: there was an economics of urban landscapes, and the total effect of a development scheme could be the subject of

FIG. 7.1 The country landscape left by the Victorians. James McIntosh Patrick, 'Autumn, Kinnordy' (1936). (Courtesy Dundee Art Gallery and Museum, and the artist.)

market forces. More rarely a Titus Salt appeared, conceiving a large mill and attendant workers' housing as an entity, and perceiving that it could and should be designed both as an agreeable industrial feature and as a development to harmonize with the existing landscape. 'I looked around for a site suitable for a large manufacturing establishment,' he recorded on the opening of Saltaire in 1853, 'and I fixed upon this as offering every capability for a first rate manufacturing and commercial establishment. It is also, from the beauty of its situation, and the salubrity of the air, a most desirable place for the erection of dwellings. Far be it from me to do anything to pollute the air or the water of the district . . . I hope to draw around me a population that will enjoy the beauties of this neighbour-hood—a population of well-paid, contented, happy operatives.'[4] This passage suggests the commercial motive for such industrial paternalism: landscape design was expected to pay, by assuring a more productive workforce living in it. The example, engulfed in modern Bradford, may not impress, since it cannot now be viewed against its country background. It was in any case not widely followed. The late twentieth differs from the mid-nineteenth century in that the Salt approach, though not the Salt solution, to considering the impact of large development schemes on the environment has become the general rule. The consideration is given by architects, civil servants, and officials, under town and country planning rules, rather than by millowners under the influence of profit and philanthropy: the general public is unconvinced that the results are any better, although they undoubt-edly look different.

The deliberately conceived urban and industrial landscape did, then, have its place in the Victorian outlook on building and construction, and it would find its place in a more complete treatment of the subject of this essay. But the actual language of 'urban landscape' and 'industrial landscape' is a modern usage, developed by planners in the 1920s and given wider currency by urban historians and historical geogaphers within the last twenty years.[5] To the Victorians themselves the concept of landscape had essentially, perhaps exclusively, rural and country connotations: it was what landscape artists painted or what landscape gardeners created. It was also what towns and industry gobbled up, obliterated, ravaged, polluted, and destroyed. Temple Thurston, writing at the end of a century of industrial growth, summed up the prevailing sentiments:

You have only to go into the Black Country [he wrote in *The Flower of Gloucester*] to know what can be done with a wonderful world when God delivers it into the hand of man. I know very well that there is the pulse of England's greatness, that out of Bradford, Halifax, Huddersfield, Rochdale, and Burnley, the stream of molten metal flows through the veins and arteries of a great nation . . . But what a price to pay and what a coinage to pay it in . . . those belching furnaces and that poisoned land must make you marvel as you pass it by. The black sweeping hills with scrubby bushes, leafless and dead; the men and women, white-faced and dirty with the everlasting falling of the sooty air; the thousand factories and the countless furnaces; the utter lifelessness in all this seething mass of life.[6]

In a more personalized vein H. G. Wells said the same thing when he mourned the vanished fields and lanes and paddling brook of his Bromley youth, crushed under the heel of the speculative builder.[7]

FIG. 7.2 'Train Landscape' by Eric Ravilious (1939). (Courtesy Aberdeen Art Gallery and Museum.)

Accepting for the moment that loss of attractive country and pleasant farmland was the price paid in landscape terms for the growth of population and industry, it is important to try and put two central matters into perspective: the size of the price, and the quality of the relationship between what was lost and what was retained. All building, all commercial activity, all industrial operations, require some land; the Victorian descriptive evidence gives the impression that the new forms of machine industry and large cities were more greedy in their appetites for land than older forms had been, and consumed gargantuan quantities. It is, of course, perfectly obvious that in absolute terms towns, factories, and the whole complex of non-agricultural activities occupied far more land in 1900 than they had done in 1800, if only because population had increased fourfold and industrial output well over tenfold. It is by no means so obvious that post-Industrial Revolution non-farming activities were relatively more land-hungry than pre-industrial ones had been. On the one hand, housing clearly came to occupy more land per dwelling. There was an increase in room sizes and in the overall size of houses, slight maybe in houses for the masses but far from imperceptible, noticeable in its effects when aggregated over hundreds of thousands of houses, and becoming more marked from the 1850s onwards. Some of this increase went upwards, into more storeys, and had no effect on the size of building plots; but part went sideways and expressed itself in using more land per dwelling, for the building itself, for backyards, even for gardens.[8] Of greater importance for land usage was the tendency towards lower densities per acre in housing layouts, for status, fashion, and health reasons. Low densities of 6 to 12 houses to the acre, in contrast to classically urban eighteenth-century densities of perhaps 40 or 50 to the acre, were already in vogue for high-class suburban developments in the 1830s and 1840s. The downward trend, although not the exact densities, spread to middle- and lower-middle-class districts at least by the 1860s, and was affecting purpose-built working-class developments by the 1890s. England—although not Scotland, with its attachment to tall tenements—had moved from being a country of tight-packed towns in 1800 to being by 1900 the most profligate country in the industrialized world in its use of land for housing.[9] The overall impact should not be exaggerated, and average housing densities per acre were to fall more dramatically in the inter-war years, which was the time when the true urban or suburban sprawl in all its Betjeman glory was created: before 1914 Metroland was only a dream in the mind of an ambitious Metropolitan Railway director, and until the 1920s there were no sepia views of leafy lanes in Pinner, morning villas at Neasden, or bank clerks kept warm inside by the thought of Ruislip, while before the 1930s it would have been pointless in more ways than one to long for friendly bombs to fall on Slough.[10] By the standards of the 1930s or the 1980s, the Victorians were frugal in their use of land for housing; by those of the early 1800s, or by comparison with their European contemporaries, they were extravagant.

On the other hand, the general tendency of industrial, commercial, and mining operations was to become more rather than less land-intensive. In terms of demand for space, at least for surface area, that after all was the object of the exercise in mechanization, factory organization, and growth in the size of individual firms and units of production. An increase in the productivity of land employed for non-agricultural purposes may well have been an incidental and unintended by-product of innovations and investments designed to increase the productivity of labour or capital, but nevertheless it did occur. A mildly lunatic calculation from the heart of the Industrial Revolution, the cotton industry, may illustrate the point. With traditional single-spindle spinning wheels, one to a cottage and 50 cottages to the acre, one acre was required for 50 spindles. The earliest spinning jenny, with 16 spindles, raised the capacity of an acre to 800 spindles; the most highly developed jenny, still hand-operated and cottage-housed, increased this still further by the 1780s to around 4,000 spindles. By contrast, cotton mills of modest size, of which four could be comfortably fitted on one acre and use less than one-third of that area for actual buildings, were by the early 1830s using early versions of the self-actor mule, at 500 spindles per mule, 5,000 spindles per mill, and 20,000 spindles per acre.[11] In other words, one acre of space devoted to cotton mills accommodated as much crude productive capacity as would have covered 400 acres of spinning wheels or 25 acres under spinning jennies. While powered machinery was more compact, in relation to output, than the traditional methods it replaced, the buildings which housed it frequently themselves economized on land by going upwards; mills were often of five or six storeys, where hand spinners and weavers had worked in single- or two-storey cottages. In mining, the move towards deeper levels, with a single pit working more extensive areas underground, meant declining demand for surface area for the pithead gear in relation to tonnage output; the reversion to large-scale opencast mining since 1945 is a reminder of the enormous appetite for land which can be stimulated by techniques for ripping coal from shallow depths. In commerce and trade, never large consumers of land under any system of organization, the trend towards larger individual concerns in banking, in insurance, or in merchant houses, probably produced some decline in demand for land; while the department stores of the late nineteenth century did something like ten to twenty times as much trade on their sites as could have been done by small shopkeepers with small shops on an equivalent area.

No precise measure can be given for the land-economizing effects of Victorian industrial and commercial development. Over the period the composition of industrial output and personal consumption changed so much, so many totally new commodities

FIG. 7.3 Victorian townscape: Saltaire, Bradford. Modern aerial photograph. (Courtesy City of Bradford Metropolitan Council.)

appeared or entered into general use, and so many familiar articles, like fabrics, clothes, or furniture, changed in type and quality, that comparisons of land requirements related to volumes or values of output can be no more than highly impressionistic. It is, nevertheless, salutary to remember that if one imagines a weird counterfactual world in 1901 in which the actual 1901 levels of output and consumption were achieved, but by the employment of exclusively pre-Victorian or pre-industrial techniques and methods, then in such a Britain manufacturing and extractive industry, commerce, trade, and business would have occupied anything from ten to fifty times as much land as they did in fact occupy in the real world. If landscape is a matter of country prospects and agricultural land, then the amount which survived would have been much shrunken; this is some indication of the sheer scale of landscape loss from which Britain was rescued by Victorian industrialization and urbanization.

Just how much land was turned into urban and industrial landscape during the nineteenth century, or to put it the other way round, was lost to agriculture, is another question, to which available studies and statistics provide surprisingly inadequate answers.[12] The problem can be tackled in descending order of certainty by looking at those activities which have come under the notice of the State. Those industries and utilities which have been nationalized since 1945 have generated figures of their landholdings, and although these relate to the 1970s they can be projected backwards to the end of the nineteenth century, with varying degrees of confidence.[13] The oldest State-owned enterprise, the Post Office, admitted to owning nothing but farmland, 5,500 acres (2,226 hectares) of it in Britain, and although there could be a worthy study of the postal landscape and the different layers of telegraph poles pinned into the landscape, it can easily be ignored in a general survey. Even the pleasing thought that its twentieth-century possessions represent a relict feature left over from the days when the Post Office might have kept paddocks for the horses which drew its mail coaches should be dismissed as a figment of imaginary bureaucratic sloth. Pride of place, unsurprisingly, is taken by British Rail, which in 1971 had about 220,000 acres (89,032 hectares) of land. By then Beeching had begun to bite and there had been some branch-line closures, incidentally introducing new landscape features and novel opportunities for observing the process of reversion to climax vegetation, which is more scruffy than exciting. All-time maximum railway route mileage came earlier, and although it had not quite been attained by 1901 it is a safe guess that the railways of Britain had by then control of about 240,000 acres (97,122 hectares). Some of this railway land was buried in towns, some of which in turn had been created by the railways, but most of it was out in the country, widely scattered since by the early twentieth century there was scarcely a spot in England—Scotland was rather different, given its Highland mass—more than five miles from a railway. This railway intrusion into the landscape was almost entirely a Victorian event, though the initial spurt had of course begun a few years before the Queen's accession, and it took place on a scale, in relation to total land area, unequalled in any other country in the world except Belgium. This newcomer might be regarded as the mechanized successor of canals as a segregated form of transport using a specialized track, and in the terms of the land budgeting discussed earlier it made more extensive demands on space, using land at 11 to 12 acres per mile or between two and three times the canal rate. Its total consumption of land, equivalent to about half the surface of Oxfordshire, was indeed very considerable, and although there was no particular railway concentration, outside the railway towns like Crewe, Swindon, Eastleigh, or Wolverton, or the vast complexes of junctions, sidings, and marshalling yards like the Battersea Tangle, Stratford, or Cricklewood, of which one could say that a true railway landscape had been fashioned, its very ubiquity made the railway a part of almost every landscape in England except for the highest mountains and most inaccessible uplands.

Wordsworth, it is well known, thought that the railway threatened to approach the high mountains altogether too close for comfort. 'Is then no nook of English ground secure from rash assault?' ran his sonnet on the Projected Kendal and Windermere Railway in 1844, in words echoed down the years by countless people who see their familiar peace menaced by the construction gangs of progress. A second anti-railway poem, 'Proud were ye, Mountains', failed to do the trick but dignified Worsworth's élitism with the righteousness of an unselfish defender of nature:

> Now, for your shame, a Power, the Thirst of Gold,
> That rules o'er Britain like a baneful star,
> Wills that your peace, your beauty, shall be sold,
> And clear way made for her triumphal car
> Through the beloved retreats your arms enfold!
> Heard ye that Whistle? As her long-linked Train
> Swept onwards, did the vision cross your view?
> Yes, ye were startled; and, in balance true,
> Weighing the mischief with the promised gain,
> Mountains, and Vales, and Floods, I call on you
> To share the passion of a just disdain.

The nub of his argument, set out in his letters to the press, was that the beauty of the Lakes was essentially and permanently a minority taste which could only be experienced by a special kind of cultivated, educated, and leisured person, who by definition must be sufficiently persistent to be capable of contriving to reach the scenery without railway assistance. In his eagerness to explain and justify this point of view, however, he fell into grave logical confusions. On the one hand he argued that multitudes of day trippers would trample down and destroy the very attractions they came to see: what would become of the little town of Bowness, he asked, in 'the Advance of the Ten Thousand? Leeds, I am told, has sent as many at once to Scarborough. We should have the whole of Lancashire, and no small part of Yorkshire, pouring in upon us to meet the men of Durham, and the borderers from Cumberland and Northumberland.' They would create, or have created for them, 'for the profit of the shareholders and that of the lower class of inn-keepers . . . wrestling matches, horse and boat races without number, and pot-houses and beer-shops would keep pace with these excitements and recreations, most of which might too easily be had elsewhere'. On the other hand he argued that 'the imperfectly educated classes are not likely to draw much good from rare visits to the lakes' since in their eyes 'a rich meadow, with fat cattle grazing upon it, or the sight of what they would call a heavy crop of corn, is worth all that the Alps and Pyrenees in their utmost grandeur and beauty could show to them', while the capacity to appreciate the picturesque and romantic scenery could be acquired 'only by a slow and gradual process of culture' not available to the masses. From this the conclusion ought to be have followed that the masses would not in fact come to a place they were incapable of appreciating and hence did not want to visit. In other words, the railway was not worth opposing because it could never be popular or profitable. Artisans and labourers, and the humbler classes of shopkeepers, instead of rambling in the Lakes, would do better to 'make little excursions with their wives and children among neighbouring fields, whither the whole of each family might stroll' close to their homes.[14]

The clergyman who visited Wordsworth at Rydal and enquired whether by any chance he had written anything else besides the *Guide to the Lakes,* was perhaps more than an ignorant buffoon: a poet may be well advised to stick to poetry. In the long run Wordsworth was correct. The problem of how to preserve the characteristics which make a landscape beautiful and wonderful beyond description from being altered and obliterated by the means of access and accommodation designed to make them available to the masses, is insoluble. The preservationist who is a purist must inexorably make five-star landscapes into class landscapes kept for the few by ensuring that access is too expensive and difficult for the many. In the particular case he was wrong. The railway stopped short of Bowness and the lakeside, frustrated by the resistance of highly local property interests. Instead, around its greenfield terminus at Windermere, it generated a little new town, all stone and slate of a retiring middle- and upper-middle-class decorum and opulence. The railway did bring excursion trains, but little sign of vulgarity and spoliation—unless the lake paddle steamers, a rather charming element in the mobile landscape to mid-twentieth-century nostalgic vision, appeared as the symbol of snorting philistinism to the nineteenth-century aesthete. The millowners of Yorkshire and Lancashire did indeed launch their masses by the trainload, but the trains headed for Blackpool or Scarborough; by the 1890s Bass, the Burton brewers, were sending twelve special trains, marshalled with military precision, on the annual works' outing, but the destination was Skegness[15] Railways, in fact, protected the Lakes by funnelling the masses to the seaside, which from his argument about working-class tastes and preferences is what Wordsworth should have expected. He was, perhaps, premature by a century in his forebodings, shooting at a target he could not have foreseen. If improved communications are responsible for bringing in the hordes, it is the motorway which has opened up the Lakes, not least to the minor hordes from a conveniently sited new university which epitomizes the partial spread of culture to wider social levels which Wordsworth felt to be a prerequisite of landscape appreciation.

Motorways lead back to the main theme as well as to the Lakes. They consume about 25 acres to the mile (6.2 hectares per kilometre) and are at least twice as land-hungry as railways. In proportion to length the impact of surface transport doubles or trebles with each major innovation, while in proportion to output the impact of industry declines, as the microchip will no doubt presently confirm. That will be testable in the future. At present, the historian can be confident that the electrically powered industry of the twentieth century is cleaner than the coal-fired, steam-driven industry of the Victorians, but less certain that there was much difference between their respective demands for standing room. The implications of this can be examined presently, but first something must be said about the energy landscape which underpinned Victorian industry.

By the end of the reign energy meant coal: surviving users of power from water, wind, or horse were, outside agriculture, more curiosities than serious parts of the industrial structure, although manual power, turning such things as sewing machines, remained important in workshop and home industries. The transition to this state of affairs was a Victorian phenomenon, for in 1837 even in the cotton industry, the technological leader, water provided nearly a quarter of total power needs; figures for power used in industry at large are not available for this date, but it seems likely that in 1850 water-power still accounted for at least one-third of all industrial power used, and in 1870, after another twenty years of rapid extension of steam-power outside its initial narrow front in textiles, iron smelting, and coal mining itself, into the broad fields of general manufacturing, between 10 and 12 per cent of total power was still generated by waterwheels.[16] In absolute terms the industrial use of steam-power moved from about 300,000 h.p. in 1850, to about 1.7 million h.p. in 1870, and nearly 10 million h.p. by 1907: in very crude terms the landscape had to find room for a multiplication of coal-fired factories and works by 30 or 40 times in the Victorian period, or an increase in all forms of works of about 20 times.

A watery industrial landscape is a very different thing from a steamed industrial landscape; and the provision of the energy itself has very different effects. Harnessing water for power requires some construction work, but Victorian diggings of watercourses and mill-races and building of weirs, dams, and reservoirs, were of pygmy proportions in comparison to modern hydroelectric works; such Victorian workings have in any case merged into the scenery and, hallowed by the patina of age, disuse, and neglect, are generally accepted without reflection as part of the natural landscape. It was otherwise with the getting of coal. Awesome, grimy and distinctive colliery landscapes of pithead gear, coal heaps, slag heaps, and a maze of tramroads and colliery railways, usually accompanied by colliery villages and always by a thick layering of the surrounding country with coal dust, proliferated as the output of coal climbed from 27 to 230 million tons a year. The character of these micro-landscapes altered and became more locally dominant during the century, as winding gear, ventilation equipment, or pithead transport became more elaborate and more prominent, and as individual collieries became large-scale concerns. The geographical impact of these landscapes also spread and shifted over the century, as activity expanded on the coalfields which were already old-established by the 1830s, such as the North-East, West Cumberland, or Lancashire; as coalfields which were virtually newcomers to national importance, such as South Wales or South Yorkshire, were colonized; and as some older fields, such as those of the ten-yard seam in Staffordshire, became worked out. Before Victoria was dead Kent was being introduced to the experience of the colliery landscape. Within any particular mining locality, however, growth in the size of the individual enterprise and deeper working meant that the physical presence on the surface became more concentrated and probably less space-consuming than had been the case with pre-Victorian petty landsale collieries (which catered purely for the local market) and their surface scratchings. Unless the official history commissioned by the National Coal Board is about to inform us, however, we do not and cannot know what the aggregate impact of coal mining was in terms of surface area occupied. The National Coal Board does appear as a considerable landowner in the 1970s, owning 255,000 acres (103,561 hectares) in Britain, and a further 32,000 acres (13,194 hectares) as leasehold; 138,000 acres (55,989 hectares) of this is, however, farmland let to tenant farmers—a relic, maybe, of the time when collieries needed hay farms to supply their pit ponies, as well as a by-product of the land needs of opencast mining. Something under 150,000 acres (60,701 hectares) may, therefore, represent the area used for strictly colliery purposes in the 1970s. Without knowing something about the effectiveness of land-disposal operations by collieries since the beginning of the century, or about their land acquisitions for new sinkings, it is impossible to say how much land had been taken for colliery use during the nineteenth century, but 150,000 acres (60,701 hectares), or about one-third of the county of Oxfordshire, may suggest the order of magnitude reasonably well.

Similarly, the 59,000 acres (23,958 hectares) owned and 15,000 acres (5,989 hectares) leased by British Steel in the 1970s gives only the roughest of indications of the land which may have been taken by the iron and steel industry in the nineteenth century; likewise the 6,000 or so acres (2,343 hectares) occupied by British Gas may or may not understate the global impact of Victorian gasworks and gasometers. At this point the nationalized industries cease to assist the Victorian historian, since the holdings of the Electricity Board were overwhelmingly, and those of the Civil Aviation Authority exclusively, acquired after 1901. Those which do help—railways, coal, steel, and gas—suggest that something like 455,000 acres (184,128 hectares) may have gone their way during the Victorian period: that is, less than 1 per cent of the total land area of Britain, which may not sound very much, or an area the size of Oxfordshire, which does.

Beyond this, all is conjecture and surmise. There are no national statistics for the areas taken by the non-ferrous metal industries, the stone and slate quarries, the gravel pits and cement works, or the brick-fields, all of which made dents and marks on landscapes outside the urban setting. Manufacturing industry, which over the course of the period became almost entirely concentrated in towns, is unrecorded except in the diffuse, but in principle highly informative, Ordnance Survey maps, which, however, remain unstudied for this purpose. Even the towns themselves, containing the industrial and commercial as well as residential areas, generated no statistics of this kind, and local case studies are not yet sufficiently numerous or sufficiently area-conscious to make generalizations possible. Figures for administrative areas are, of course, quite simple to come by, but of more than doubtful value when the object is to find the size of built-up areas at different dates. Generally speaking, the areas of what look from their names to be town authorities are likely to be smaller than the actual built-up areas at the beginning of the period, because local government institutions and boundaries lagged well behind reality; while by the end of the period the administrative areas are likely to be far larger than the actual built-up areas, because local imperialism and aggrandizement, coupled with administrative convenience, had led boroughs to inflate their boundaries to embrace as much surrounding open country as they could plausibly collar. There were exceptions, the most obvious being that the 74,816 acres (30,276 hectares) of the County of London was a great deal smaller than the continuous built-up areas of Greater London in 1901, perhaps little more than one-half of the size.[17] The census authorities did not catch up with this anomaly until 1951, when they recognized that 'for some time it has been felt that the customary analysis of the population by types of Administrative Area may not give an accurate picture of urban development. Areas administered by Borough or Urban District Councils may contain tracts of land that cannot fairly be called urban in character; areas administered by Rural District Councils may contain some land that should be called urban in

FIG. 7.4 Towns invading the country: 'London Going Out of Town', by George Cruikshank (1829). (Courtesy the London Borough of Camden.)

character.' The solution was to classify every ward or parish as either 'built-up' or 'non-urbanized', on the basis of the Ministry of Housing's population density map; the exercise showed that the Urban Administrative Authorities of England and Wales had, in 1951, a truly urbanized population of 30.9 million, while their total population was 35.3 million, and that Rural Authorities had an urbanized population of 0.5 million and a total population of 8.4 million. This implied that the previous conventional measure of urban population, relying on administrative units, overstated the true position by about 11 per cent. Whether this demographic correction factor could be translated into an urban space correction factor is extremely doubtful; it is even more doubtful if either could be adapted for retrospective application to 1901, let alone to early Victorian censuses. It is, however, a useful reminder that urban populations consumed comparatively little space to see that, in 1951, the six large English conurbations contained 54 per cent of the total urban population but occupied only 25 per cent of the land area administered by all urban authorities. Clearly some towns were then, and were at earlier dates, more closely packed and densely built than others; but it is at least plausible to suggest that the figures for urban administrative areas overstated the actual physical extent of built-up landscapes by a factor of two or more.[18]

Thus armed, we can proceed to make some guesses at the scale of the urban impact on the landscape in 1901. The upper limit is set by taking the raw figure of 25 million, which is an overstatement, for the total urban population, and assuming that the quarter of this which lived in Greater London occupied also a quarter of the urbanized area, another overstatement since the area ascribed to Greater London was computed in 1951 after fifty further years of massive encroachment on the countryside, and in 1901 a great deal of it was still farmland. This procedure suggests a total urban presence for England and Wales in 1901 of 1.8 million acres (728,000 hectares). A middle estimate is provided by taking the recorded area of the twenty-two largest county boroughs in 1901, which was 294,000 acres (118,975 hectares); these twenty-two towns had half the English urban population, so that 600,000 acres (242,806 hectares) might account for the entire urban surface. A lower limit is set by taking the 'true' urban population of 1901 as 22 million; the population of the LCC area was one-fifth of this, and since the LCC people managed to make do on 74,816 acres (30,276 hectares), all the towns of England and Wales ought to have been able to stand on 375,000 acres (151,754 hectares).

It is impossible to be sure whereabouts reality lay between these estimates, but probably it was to be found towards the lowest. Housing densities, after all, were thought to be rather low and spacious at 30 to the acre in the late Victorian period, fit for highly respectable lower-middle-class occupation, and 41 houses to the acre could easily be achieved under enlightened municipal by-law rules in the early twentieth century.[19] The housing stock of 1901 included a large proportion, perhaps a third or more, which had been built to considerably higher densities before by-laws began to bite in the 1850s and 1860s, and to assume an overall average density in 1901 of 40 houses to the acre is not unreasonable. In which case, the 4.6 million houses recorded in the Urban Districts would not have required more than 115,888 acres (46,897 hectares) to stand on, complete with their streets.[20] Residential housing, of course, only forms part of any town area; but if double that area, another 230,000 acres (93,075 hectares), is set aside for business and commercial quarters, shopping streets and main thoroughfares, and industrial zones, with a bit over for open spaces, it would seem to be a generous allowance. That would leave the total urban surface of 1901 at less than 350,000 acres (141,637 hectares).

It is, no doubt, more fun to generate such statistics than to try to evaluate them; but steering a course between guesses produces 400,000 acres (161,871 hectares) as a plausible, round figure for the aggregate size of late Victorian towns. From what base did they start in the 1830s? The twenty-two largest boroughs, whose populations trebled between 1841 and 1901, did no more than double their recorded administrative areas, and that would imply that at the beginning of the period towns were already occupying as much as 200,000 acres (80,935 hectares).[21] But to allow for the greatest conceivable impact of Victorian building on the countryside a rather smaller starting point might be thought more suitable; to accommodate such feelings one might hazard that since town populations grew by rather under four times during Victoria's reign, perhaps town areas grew by exactly four times, implying a base in the 1830s of around 100,000 acres (40,467 hectares). Hence something of the order of 300,000 acres (121,403 hectares) was the size of the Victorian urban bite into the countryside. The twentieth-century bite, by contrast, has quite likely already exceeded 1 million acres (404,678 hectares).

That, to be sure, was quite a lot of space to turn over from farmland to bricks and mortar, an area as large as Bedfordshire laid down to houses and factories. But, at under 1 per cent of the total land surface of England (Scotland and Wales have to be left out of account in these urban calculations, because their urban acreages were not recorded in the census), hardly enough to justify the frequently hysterical outbursts of contemporaries at the remorseless onward march of the army of builders into the country. Those outbursts, such as Cobbett's fear at the start of the period that the Great Wen would shortly stretch in solid unbroken ugliness from the Thames to Brighton's beaches, or the eugenicists' gloomy prophecies at the end of it that continued unbridled urban expansion would shortly generate a nation of malformed half-wits, are more indicative of contemporary alarms about the dangers to society from excessive wealth or excessive poverty than they are rational responses to the facts of urban growth. They are also expressions of a fear and loathing of really large towns as somehow alien, unprecedented—except for London, and, as an overblown monster, that had been dreaded and denounced at least from the mid-sixteenth century—and apparently launched on an uncontrollable, self-perpetuating, headlong advance which looked as if it would go on for ever, quite literally under its own steam. From the point of view of the articulate classes, the opinion-formers, the 1 per cent of the surface which was changing into townscape was a critical fraction, since it was the one on which most of them lived and which supplied the everyday prospect from their windows. Not only did they live where the action was, even if it was taking place on a relatively minute stage, but the other 1 per cent of the surface which was changing from country into non-country was quite largely taken up by the railways on which they rode from city to city; it formed the narrow corridors from which they viewed the landscape,

FIG. 7.5 The industrialist in the countryside: Wyfold Court, Oxfordshire, 1872–6. Built for Edward Hermon, partner in Horrocks, Miller & Co. Preston, cotton manufacturers; architect, G. Somers Clarke. (Courtesy The National Monuments Record.)

and since railways naturally attracted industries to their sides the view tended to contain a lot of visible evidence of the dismemberment and disfigurement of rural scenes.

Such horror sentiments are thus entirely understandable as indicators of the perceptions of one party in the perpetual division in English opinion and literature over what attitudes to strike towards the town/country dichotomy. These feelings and perceptions cannot be dismissed or refuted by an appeal to the overall facts of the matter, since they were rooted in prejudices or value-systems whose validity was not open to empirical verification of that sort, and they were held by people with passionate loyalties to highly specific and particular little places, which might indeed have changed from summer hayfield, redolent with romantic memories of half-perceived youthful love, to rows of pitifully pretentious semi-detacheds, with harsh reminders of petty Pooterdom, in much less than half a lifetime. If someone wished to grieve over the vanished green hills of Penge, sunk beneath the weight of terraces filled with clerks, no one could deny that they had indeed disappeared. The historian, however, is not for that reason obliged to jump from the particular to the general, and to accept the same blinkered vision that led some observers to imagine that the urban flood was actually one of colossal proportions.

In any case—and here at last I can turn from considering the size of the loss of country or farmland landscape to towns and industry, to the second issue, of the quality of the relationship between what was lost and what was retained—there was a town/country symbiosis which was far more important in the real world of economic and social living than any town/country dichotomy in the world of the emotions. At a relatively trivial level, if industry went to the towns, industrialists planted themselves in the countryside, and many country landscapes of today are given point and interest by the country houses of Victorian manufacturers and city men. There are the large and famous, like Cragside in Northumberland, built for the greatest armaments manufacturer of his day, Sir William Armstrong; and the lesser but notable, like the half-timbered revivalist Wightwick Manor in Staffordshire, built for the varnish and paint manufacturer, Theodore Mander. If one looks at the Victorian country houses in Oxfordshire which Mark Girouard finds worthy of notice, all five were contributed by manufacturers or businessmen: Eynsham Hall was built for the Mason family who ran copper mines in Portugal; Heythrop Hall for Albert Brassey, son of the greatest Victorian railway contractor; Kiddington Hall for the banker, Mortimer Ricardo; Shiplake Court for a London stockbroker, R. H. Harrison; and Wyfold Court for Edward Herman, partner in Horrocks of Preston, probably the largest cotton manufacturers of their time.[22] To these could be added Flint House for a wholesale grocer, F. N. Garrard; Friar Park for Sir Frank Crisp, London solicitor; Huntercombe Place for W. B. Close, London engineering consultant; and Ewelme Down for Frank Lawson, London financier. The only new country house in Oxfordshire of the nineteenth or twentieth centuries built for the traditional landed aristocracy was Middleton Park; that was built in 1938, for the seventh Earl of Jersey, one of the last great country houses to be built in Britain, and the only one which Lutyens designed for a member of the established aristocracy.[23] All of these were carefully contrived additions to the country scene, urban businessmen's personal contributions to the rural landscape.

Of much greater general consequence was the flip side of the process of industry going to the towns. The characteristic locational process of the steam age was, of course, the concentration of manufacturing industry on the coalfields; but even outside the coalfields industry was tending, by the second half of the nineteenth century, to concentrate in the middle-sized towns. A brief trawl of the big manufacturers of agricultural implements in the 1880s and 1890s, who were not in coalfield sites, yields Aveling and Porter in Rochester, Barford and Perkins in Peterborough, Clayton and Shuttleworth in Lincoln, Hornsby in Grantham, Howard in Bedford, Ladd in London, Marshall in Gainsborough, Ransomes in Ipswich, Ruston in Lincoln, and Samuelson in Banbury. London manufactured many things, and was far and away the largest industrial town in Britain; but all the others were in decidedly urban settings, county towns and important market towns close to some of their customers, but far away from the coal which supported some of their competitors like Bradbury of Manchester or Fowler of Leeds. If industry went to the towns, then industry left the country. More to the point, new industries, new firms, and new businesses chose urban, not rural, locations. The whole thrust of Victorian industrialization meant that isolated rural sites and small village locations were completely out of court for factory building, and it was therefore the great force which spared the countryside from any indiscriminate scattering of industrial developments, the force which quite simply created the country landscape and denuded it of many of the industrial features which had previously adorned, or disfigured, the prospect. Here and there remains of earlier, rural, phases of industry survive: early cotton mills beside their streams, water-wheels and mills once geared to all sorts of industrial processes, cottages of domestic outworkers in cloth, lace, or straw hats, village sites where once pins, nails, horseshoes, or wheels were made. Yesterday's industry, dead industry, makes today's landscape. It is technological and locational obsolescence which has given a picturesque quality to these relics, and that obsolescence stemmed directly from the economics of Victorian industry and its urban imperative. Motor transport and electrification, the

FIG. 7.6 Industry in the Victorian town: Preston, the source of Wyfold Court. Aerial view of Preston. (Courtesy Aerofilms Ltd.)

twentieth-century locational liberators, have opened up the countryside for industrial penetration and created the possibility of landscapes peppered with the unpicturesque.

The countryside became, then, by the late Victorian period, a place where farming, hunting, and shooting were carried on, and little else save, maybe, a spot of fishing. The Victorians, inadvertently no doubt, created more sharply segregated landscapes—country, urban, industrial—than had ever existed before or since. In creating them, the Victorians also created the basic image, and the essential structure, of the rural landscape which late-twentieth-century enthusiasts struggle to preserve in the mistaken belief that they are defending ancient traditions from modern vandals. The farming landscape itself probably enjoyed an unaccustomed general stability in the Victorian years, sandwiched as it was between the earlier phase of parliamentary enclosure, which radically changed the physical appearance of Midland England in particular, and the later and still continuing phase of heavily subsidized agribusiness, which is radically changing the appearance of most of arable England. The countryman of the 1830s, revisiting Britain in 1901, would have noticed small changes in the farming landscapes almost everywhere, but no large widespread unfamiliar features. What he would have found most striking is what may be called the landscape of agricultural depression, which differed visually in superficial ways from the landscape of prosperity in such things as the balance between grass and crops and the scruffiness of the hedges, and which had little room for signs of bustling activity and enterprise in the countryside. The impression that the farming landscape is timeless and unchanging is, indeed, almost entirely the result of a long period, from 1880 to 1940, during which farming, while not exactly undergoing prolonged and unrelieved depression, was never in a sufficiently profitable condition to sustain developments leaving great physical imprints on landscape features.

That interlude was an unusual state of affairs, caused in large measure by the growth and successes of Victorian industry which made it possible and sensible for Britain to import a rapidly growing proportion of its food supply, and to make relatively smaller, and changing, demands on its own agriculture. Nevertheless, the farming landscape remained man-made, and man-maintained or neglected. If one may hark back to William Cowper or D. H. Lawrence, God or nature only supplied the bare canvas: farmers and landlords actually painted the landscape. Until the 1880s at least they were busily altering the details of the picture, not with the bold strokes of the straight roads and rectangular fields of new enclosures, maybe, but with the more selective touches of new farm buildings and the more subtle hues of field drainage which changed the colour as well as the texture of the land. Here and there, of course, a local landscape could be totally transformed, as when a large part of Wychwood Forest was grubbed up in the 1860s by the Crown Estate and turned into somewhat unprofitable farmland at the cost of disrupting the local deer- and girl-chasing Whitsun ceremonies.[24] The reverse process, the afforestation of vast stretches of poor-quality upland rough grazing and waste land, has been an entirely twentieth-century development, and the appearance of over $2\frac{1}{4}$ million acres (915,018 hectares) of Forestry Commission landscape on the scene is emphatically post-Victorian: frequently criticized for spoiling the views, this has been quantitatively the largest single landscape change since enclosures dwindled away after 1815, and dwarfs any spatial impact of Victorian towns and industry.[25]

Today the country landscape is becoming a place in which a car can be parked while its occupants read the Sunday newspapers; a place maintained in good order at the taxpayers' expense by farmers and landlords who screen their private opulence behind a public façade of impoverished hill sheep farmers and anxiety-ridden battery hen keepers. For the Victorians the country landscape was something from which a living had to be earned by farming operations which paid for themselves on the open market (at least after 1846). The market was provided by towns and industry, and their growth was the condition of survival for the rural landscape, not something which farmers and landlords resented. To be sure, particular farmers on the urban fringes were harassed by urban multitudes trampling down the country they came to enjoy, and particular landlords on the urban fringes rejoiced at the chance to grow houses instead of crops. In general, however, the encroachment of towns and industry was seen by the agricultural community as an opportunity, not as a loss. It was an opportunity which led farmers, to all appearances, to extend the margins of cultivation more rapidly than any shrinkage of farmland through the advance of the urban frontiers. The total cultivated area, under crops and grass, was expanding until the close of the Victorian area: between 1866 and 1906 3 million acres (1.2 million hectares) were added to the officially recorded cultivated acreage of England and Wales, and 700,000 acres (283,274 hectares) to that of Scotland; the all-time historical peak in intensity of cultivation was reached at this time, with 75 per cent of the total land area of England and Wales being used as agricultural land, and 25 per cent of the area of Scotland (the proportions subsequently declined, by 1966, to 65 and 22 per cent respectively).[26] Much of this registered expansion was purely a statistical illusion, caused by changes in the classification of lands at the margin between 'permanent grass' and 'rough grazing', and by changes in the threshold size of holdings which were included in the Agricultural Returns. But much of it, also, was real expansion, a continued colonization of moorland and heath into the sheep-grazed section of the farming landscape, so that one may guess that for every acre which was shifted from farm landscape to urban landscape, at least two more were added to the cultivated landscape from the reserves of the truly natural landscape. The ultimate natural landscape, left as God made it, was of course the bare rock of the mountain tops, incapable of being grazed by anybody. For between those tops and the barely cultivated land lay the grouse landscapes and the deer-stalking landscapes, prominent in parts of Yorkshire and the north-east, dominant in the Highlands, and scarcely untrodden by man even if not much touched by his hands.

The object of asking for friendly bombs to fall on Slough, you will recall, was 'To get it ready for the plough'.[27] Whatever may have been necessary in the 1930s, such ruthlessness was not required in the more civilized years of Queen Victoria, when the country landscape grew, changed, and flourished precisely because the towns were cramped, crowded, and in many respects extremely ugly: 'beauty must suffer', as the 1930s would have said.

8

Agriculture, forestry and the future landscape

M. E. D. POORE

I FEEL a great responsibility in having undertaken to deliver the last of this series of Wolfson lectures—to leave the final taste in the mouth at the end of such a noble feast. It makes me feel very humble, and more than a little apprehensive.

The trouble is that much has taken place in the time since I accepted the invitation. Then the Wildlife and Countryside Bill was in its infancy; Marion Shoard's *Theft of the Countryside* had only recently appeared; and I had no suspicion that I was to become a member of the Nature Conservancy Council. What a chance this offered to be provocative, even irresponsibly provocative!

But since then there has been a flood of literature and a deluge of conferences—on aspects of the British response to the World Conservation Strategy, on forestry and conservation, on broad-leaved woodlands, on a new policy for the uplands, and on the triumph and shame of agriculture. These have carried both debate and action several steps forward and have set up some valuable pointers for the future. Above all looms the ponderous mass of the Wildlife and Countryside Act which became law in 1982. The Act, along with the debate that preceded it and the events that have followed it, have all demonstrated that the future of the countryside has become a political issue of great public concern. Nothing will ever be quite the same again.

The earlier lectures have shown vividly how the landscape has been constantly changing. Within the physical constraints of land-form and fluctuating climate, it has evolved in response to economic influences and social preferences. It is my task to try and project this into the future, to use an appreciation of history to speculate—guess, if you like—about what *may* happen. This is all I can do. Any attempt at scientific prediction would be absurd. The uncertainties are too great.

To quote Professor Claude Henry of Paris: 'In the seventeenth century Colbert, Minister to Louis XIV, felled the most beautiful oaks in the king's forest to build warships to fight the British fleet. At the same time, he decided to have the oaks replanted, because he said that two hundred years later the king would need full-grown oaks to build warships to fight the British fleet. Was Colbert stupid? Ships are no longer made of oak and, since Trafalgar, France is not very keen on trying to fight the British fleet. Nevertheless, we are very happy to have the oaks; their wood fetches a high price and they have re-seeded, so we can enjoy the environmental values of the forests they constitute.'

The rural landscape has not been shaped only by agriculture and forestry: industry and transport have done much to open up, transform, and finally restrict the countryside. Although I shall be concentrating on farming and forestry, it is as well not to forget that growing population and thrusting technology—both largely urban-based—provide much of the driving force behind rural land use, in the technical advances they pioneer and in their demand for produce.

We are now, more tightly than ever before, economically tied to other parts of the world. The provisions of the Treaty of Rome affect every one of us; even the Outer Hebrides are the subject of an Integrated Development Programme of the European Economic Community. Our news bulletins are full of reports of unfair competition from abroad and protectionism, trade wars, sale of American grain to the USSR, and so on; our new landscapes are mountains, rivers, and lakes of solid or liquid commodities. The supply and price of energy dominates all. A far cry, you may say, from the character of the British landscape; yet factors such as these, and the technology that drives them, are one of the main determinants of the kind of landscape that we will have in the future. The other will be the kind of landscape we wish to have.

Now, to the main subject. When launching a rocket into the unknown it is as well to know where one is and which way the thing is pointing. So I should like to begin by considering the development, during the last few decades, of policies and practice in agriculture, forestry, and some of the other activities that impinge on the landscape. This will necessarily be in bare outline, designed to bring out the broad trends that seem important in understanding the ways we may go.

To take agriculture first. A great impetus was given to farming during the war years in an effort to reduce as far as possible the dependence on imported foods which tied up shipping badly needed for other purposes. At this time was born the vision of moving towards self-sufficiency in temperate foodstuffs and reducing the import bill for food. Ever since, this has been the mainspring of government policy in making every effort to increase food production. The policy has been conspicuously successful. Enormous technical strides have been made by British agriculture. Yields per acre have vastly increased owing to improved practices based on research: better varieties, better understanding of soil properties and drainage, improved techniques of tillage, fertilizers, pesticides, animal nutrition and health. The list is impressive and so is the achievement. Between the late 1940s and late 1970s average yields of wheat, barley, potatoes, and milk have doubled, or nearly so. An average hen produces 240 eggs a year; thirty years ago she achieved a mere 114.

This has been accompanied by a surge of mechanization. New machines allow tasks to be carried out more effectively; a combine harvester will allow much better advantage to be taken of brief spells of good weather and will pick up lodged grain that defeated the old-fashioned binder. Making silage, too, is not so weather-dependent as hay making. But they also lead to the shedding of labour. Only 2.7 per cent of the working population was engaged in agriculture in 1971 compared to 5.6 per cent in 1950 (in Western Europe it averaged 30 per cent). Very rarely today does one see the spectacle of communal labour— hop pickers, stookers, hay makers, potato lifters—that was still a feature of the landscape even in my boyhood, and in which I helped. The average cereal field now only contains a working man on about 12 days of the year.

Machines and techniques, driven by strong commercial pressure, determine the jobs to be done and the way that they are done. The shape of hedges, the way rough grass is cut, the nature of ditches, the size of fields, are dominated by machines designed to do the various jobs in the most cost-effective manner—and this usually means with the least labour. Technology has become the master rather than the servant of human purpose.

This has led to the effects on landscape that are now notorious and have been well documented for England and Wales in the Countryside Commission's New Agricultural Landscapes—larger fields, fewer hedges, disappearance of trees and ponds, ploughing of grassland and moorland, drainage, greater uniformity of crops, stubble burning, absence of people, increase in mechanical noise, closer penning of animals, no winter stubbles— countless changes, some ubiquitous, others confined to certain parts of the country.

In overgrazed and eroding parts of the world, one frequently recommends increasing the productivity of the more fertile soils in order to release pressure from the less good and allow them to recover. So one might naïvely have supposed that the enormous increases in productivity brought about by our new agricultural revolution would have allowed other less-favoured soils to be used for different purposes. But no: the opposite has been the case. Every new technique and machine has made possible fresh inroads into the dwindling stocks of uncultivated land. In the interests of greater agricultural production, if something is possible it should be done, provided of course that it is economic. And the price-support systems tend constantly to push back the frontiers of the economic just as the machines do of the technically practicable.

So agriculture is seen from within as a magnificent technical achievement, an industry which has accomplished higher gains in productivity than any other. It puts the land, too, to highly productive use, contributes to domestic self-sufficiency in food and to the feeding of a hungry world. Farmers are proud of their achievements and of their success in contributing towards national objectives. There are anxieties also, it must be admitted. In a sense they are caught in a technology trap—advance or go under. There is therefore a high degree of indebtedness. Land values and the amount of capital required are so high that there is little opportunity for the young to enter farming except by inheritance. There are fewer tenanted farms.

Perhaps their greatest anxiety, though, is to find that the world outside does not view them as they view themselves. They feel that this is unjust: many care for conservation and have done much to accommodate it on their farms. In spite of this, the agricultural industry—and I make the distinction deliberately—is looked upon by many as a jug- gernaut that is driving small farmers out of business, depopulating the countryside, making great inroads into uncultivated lands—the heaths, marshes, grasslands that used to be a feature of most landscapes—and generally treating the countryside as one would treat the factory floor; and doing this at great expense to the taxpayer.

In the late 1940s agriculture was viewed as the guardian and custodian of the countryside; hence the fact that it was exempted from planning control. Now it is viewed as the main threat. Two things have contributed to this reversal of attitude: agricultural policy and a very much greater interest and awareness by the general public. My guess is that this awareness and its political power will continue to grow: the changes in the last few years have been startling; against this background, present agricultural policy may prove to be the farmers' worst enemy. It has already been the end of many a small farmer. One must ask whether the time has not come to change its direction.

The position of forestry is in a number of important ways different. To begin with, forests occupy a much smaller proportion of the land surface—only 8 per cent in 1978 compared with about 78 per cent in agricultural use (of which 30 per cent is in arable and 48 per cent is grassland). This is the lowest proportion in Europe except for Eire (the average for the European Community countries is 21 per cent); even if planting took place at the highest practicable rate proposed by the Centre for Agricultural Strategy, it would only reach 15 per cent by 2030. Britain has a high annual bill for timber imports (about £3,000 million in recent years) and is only about 8 per cent self-sufficient in wood and wood products. The doubling of forest area proposed by CAS would lead to an ultimate self-sufficiency of only about 25 per cent. There has never been any suggestion that Britain should become totally self-supporting.

In land-use terms forestry has always taken second place to agriculture; it receives only a fraction of the financial support that goes to farming, and there is no common forestry policy in the EEC. Moreover, a large proportion (45 per cent) of the area under forest is owned and managed by the equivalent of a nationalized industry, the Forestry Commission, whose policies also have a considerable influence on the forests in private ownership. Forestry is undoubtedly the poor relation; but, in compensation, it can and could respond more flexibly to changes in government policy and public priorities.

To simplify greatly, we have to consider two completely different kinds of forest: on the one hand are those which have continuity with the original forest of Britain—of oak, ash, beech, lime and elm, and of pine and birch—which are rich in indigenous plants and animals and are a valued part of the landscape (see Oliver Rackham's account of these in Chapter 3); on the other are the new plantations, often resented as an intrusion, displacing wild communities to which we have become accustomed. The potential of these lies in the future when, with good design and management, they can become rich in wildlife and an accepted part of the scenery.

The forest is quite a different kind of cropping system from the farm. A well-established and mature forest is a stock of capital on the land which, if well invested—in the case of forest, managed—will appreciate in value and can yield an income represented by the annual increment of the growing stock. This wealth can be tapped when there is a good market or when the owner wishes for some ready cash. There is not the compulsion for constant management that is imposed by the annual cycle of farming operations. Trees do not lamb, or suffer from swine fever, or have to be harvested between two summer thunderstorms. Most operations, even thinning, can be treated in a more relaxed way.

Much of British forest is, of course, not yet in this stable state in which the crop has balanced proportions of different ages, and the area planted each year approximately equals the area felled. Because of the high rate of new planting in the last thirty-five years there is still a preponderance of young plantations, especially in the uplands, where the bulk of this planting has taken place (70 per cent of British conifer crops have been established since 1950). Only some of the older forests, such as the Forestry Commission Drummond Hill or the Atholl estates in Perthshire, have reached a condition of maturity and balance. The phase of reforestation through which we have been passing should be looked upon as one of rebuilding the capital of standing timber (and, incidentally, of forest soils) that had been dissipated by the reckless and prodigal deforestation over the centuries, aggravated by two world wars. This idea of capital was implicit in the early policies of the Forestry Commission (1917 and 1943) in which a principal objective was to build up a strategic reserve of home-grown timber sufficient to secure supply in case of a future war lasting from three to five years and to provide for about one-third self-sufficiency. Since 1958 the notion of a strategic reserve has been largely abandoned. As a consequence, a narrow accountant's view tends often to be taken of the financing of forestry which neglects its role in accumulating a national capital asset. Such a policy brings the same kind of pressure for intensification that has led agriculture to have such an adverse effect on the landscape.

Another fundamental difference between forestry and farming is the relative permanence of forestry. A crop of trees, once planted, seems there for keeps. Corn may change to oilseed rape or a field full of sheep but sitka spruce, once there, stays. This has a strong influence on people's perception of afforestation and greatly influences the effect it has on landscape, nature conservation, and access. Upland afforestation has probably brought about the most sweeping change in rural land use since the enclosures.

Even more significant is the need to make a virtue of uncertainty. The time at which a forestry operation is carried out, planting, thinning, underplanting, is often widely separated from the time at which the final crop is harvested (30 or 40 years in a fast-growing crop and 200 in oak). There is therefore a great likelihood that market conditions will be totally different at the time of harvesting and that the original assumptions may prove to have been baseless. The recent collapse of the pulp mill at Fort William has created serious problems for the forests in west and north Scotland where this mill was an integral part of the planning of forestry development of the region in the 1950s.

An excellent example of this uncertainty was found by Dr Dawkins in Uganda and I quote it now with his kind permission. In the 1920s *Eucalyptus saligna* was widely planted to provide fuel for the railways, but in the late twenties the railways took to oil and coal. By this time it was found that eucalyptus plantations were effective in drying out malarial swamps, and more were planted in the 1930s to do just this. By the end of the thirties, however, it was found better to control the mosquitoes by spraying with creosote and later with DDT. In the early 1940s a new value was found for eucalyptus wood as fuel for the growing city populations, but this was soon replaced by the more convenient paraffin and electricity. The eucalyptus was in great demand in the 1950s for power transmission lines until it was found that cement and steel were more durable and termite-resistant. A new use was then found for the wood as charcoal for the cement and steel industries. All these uses had their origin in technological advances and in rising standards of living and of organization. Now, sadly, one of the main uses is once again as firewood. The lesson is that wood is always useful, but it is difficult, if not impossible, to predict for what.

Although British forestry may not perhaps be subject to these extreme vagaries, the long time-scale can and does produce problems. There are coming to be two divergent ways of looking at forestry: the tree-farming view in which a crop is grown as efficiently and rapidly as possible for a defined market, and the view of the forest as a standing asset. Much of importance to the landscape depends upon this distinction. The former is akin to equating trees to an agricultural crop with most of the accompanying problems of intensification (heavy use of machines, pesticides, fertilizers and the rest); though, even so, because of the longer life of the crop, much more of the natural can and does insert itself. The latter view–forest as a standing asset—permits a much more flexible approach.

It is for these various reasons, I assume, that the Government has for many years taken a wider view of forest policy. Although the objective of timber supply has retained pride of place, the social and environmental benefits to be derived from forestry have not been neglected, and the present policies for the Forestry Commission embrace considerations of rural employment, landscaping, access, and nature conservation. As a result forestry has managed to avoid the excesses attributed to agriculture. It has generally responded to reasonable criticism, sometimes slowly and reluctantly, but eventually with some conviction. But the tree-farming attitude has bitten much more deeply into our forestry philosophy and practice than it has in continental Europe. This is perhaps understandable in Britain, with the urgent need to reforest, Treasury pressure, and conspicuous success in increasing yields. Nevertheless, the dedication to production has not been wholesale; policies for the New Forest have been imaginative; criticism of forest design led rapidly to the landscaping by Sylvia Crowe and her successors; and there has been a liberal policy for access and recreation.

The very hard-nosed attitude to nature conservation of the 1950s, which would not recognize that a site suitable for forestry should under any circumstances be reserved for nature conservation, soon became modified. The practice of converting oakwoods to conifers by spraying with herbicides from the air was abruptly abandoned. The main issues of debate now are about details rather than concepts: how large an area in the uplands should be left unplanted in the interests of nature conservation and where; how far should the most efficient silviculture make concessions to wildlife; how many lowland broad-leaved woods should be managed primarily for nature conservation. The recent strong initiatives about broad-leaved woods are designed to find ways of reconciling wood production with retaining other values—of landscape, history, and wildlife.

In spite of the rigorous constraints imposed by their financing, both the Forestry Commission and private forestry have largely avoided the clash with public opinion that is developing in the case of agriculture. Some issues remain—notably afforestation in National Parks—but conditions are favourable for resolving them. What has not emerged, however, is any clear policy about the relative weight that the Forestry Commission should give to the various elements in its terms of reference; nor is there any real move to integrate agriculture and forestry in a wider land-use policy in the use of land, fiscal incentives, education, and advice to landowners. Except in large private estates, the two pursue their independent ways.

The growth of official concern for scenic beauty, recreation, access to the countryside, and nature conservation, led to the establishment of organizations interested in the quality and enjoyment of the landscape which were quite separate from those responsible for its productive use. It is very odd that there has never been an authority with responsibility for the survival and vigour of rural communities. The Highlands and Islands Development Board is interested, in its region; the Rural Development Boards might have been, had they survived. The Development Commission has done as much as many. But a great part of the running has been made by voluntary organizations, the Councils for the Preservation of Rural England, and Wales (CPRE and CPRW), the Rural Community Councils, the Council for Small Industries in Rural Areas (COSIRA), and now Rural Voice. Why? It seems that, unlike communities of animals and plants, villages and hamlets must be left to economic forces—consolidation of farms, depopulation, decay of bus services, the closing of village schools. This is somehow acceptable. To reverse it deliberately is stigmatized as social engineering. It can be done for the lady's slipper orchid or avocet (though agricultural scientists have been known to sneer and call it gardening) but not for Lesser Mouldering-in-the-Marsh. Again why? If the focus of countryside policies had not been on the frills but on the solid framework of landscape conservation—vigorous communities of people living, working, and caring for the landscape around them—we might not be in the pickle we are in now.

The late 1940s saw the birth of the authorities that have now become the Nature Conservancy Council (NCC) and the Countryside Commissions (CCs). With the possible exception of the Countryside Commission for Scotland, their history has generally been one of battling against the big battalions, with budgets that were derisory in comparison with those backing the 'productive' uses of the land. In its early days under the Privy Council the Nature Conservancy interested itself in broader problems of rural land use. The Committee for Agricultural Research and Nature Conservation, set up in 1949 under the chairmanship of the Lord President of the Council, had as members all the land-use Ministers. It could have fulfilled this wider function but, as far as I can gather, it never met and the Nature Conservancy's original interests have progressively narrowed to a concentration on wildlife conservation. There was lost an opportunity which has never been taken since. Much of the effort of the NCC and CCs has gone into defending areas against development in the sense of the 1947 Town and Country Planning Act—by National Parks, Areas of Outstanding Natural Beauty (AONB), and Sites of Special

Scientific Interest (SSSI)—and in managing for nature conservation in the National Nature Reserves. There have also been many positive steps, the encouragement of voluntary bodies in conservation (the figure of three million is quoted as their combined membership), setting up Country Parks, tree planting, the setting up of the Farming and Wildlife Advisory Groups (FWAGs), and the promotion of continuous discussion and exchange of views. Much, however, was essentially defensive.

In 1949, as I have mentioned, it had been assumed that agriculture and forestry would be the best guardians of the countryside, but already in the 1950s it was clear that this was not necessarily so. Gradually it became apparent that the direction of modern farming was a much greater threat, to nature conservation especially, than developments under planning control. The hazard of pesticides was detected in time, their worst effects were avoided and they were brought under control, but the rare plants of arable land have gone. The debate continued on shrinking ground through the Countryside in 1970 Conferences and with the publication of Norman Moore's *Nature Conservation and Agriculture* in 1977, but nothing effectively stemmed the tide in agriculture, though it did to some extent in forestry. Many small measures were taken, planting field corners with trees, digging ponds and so on—all admirable, but no substitute for keeping grasslands, wetlands, and heaths under unintensive, non-destructive use. In the last two years the extent of the damage to SSSIs and the loss of species has become better documented and more widely known. It was in this hotbed of conflicting interests and public anxiety that the egg of the Wildlife and Countryside Act was laid, incubated, and hatched.

The pattern has now been set by this Act, whether we like it or not. It has been described as the most advanced wildlife legislation in the world, and in other ways that are far less polite. In a sense both are right. It is, however, now the framework within which we must work in the next few years and every effort must be made to make it succeed or know the reason why. There are certainly several good points: the Act is expected to work through discussion, persuasion, and compromise rather than compulsion; it should give an opportunity to explain to farmers and foresters the natural-history interest of their land and how they can manage it to maintain this—in the end it should lead to much greater understanding of the aims of nature conservation; it is based on the principle that no one who manages in the interest of nature conservation should be financially disadvantaged by so doing. Against this one must set a number of weaknesses: the most serious is that the operation of the Act will lie within the financial environment of present-day farming in which both the differences in profitability between the intensive and unintensive and the differences in capital value between these two states are greatly exaggerated; the financial burden of providing inflated compensatory payments will lie with the conservation organizations whose resources are minuscule in comparison with those at the services of agricultural production—it seems unlikely that Government will increase them to match their new obligations if there should be a run on the bank, though this will only be known when tested. The existing polarization between the two interests will be increased unless the agriculture departments act vigorously in withholding grants on conservation grounds; the Act will lead to a great increase in bureaucracy in notification, consultation, placing SSSIs on the land register, calculating financial compensation and so on; apart from the SSSIs and areas in National Parks, there will be no protection whatever for uncultivated land which is not of 'special scientific interest', yet there is plenty of such land which has got some natural-history interest and is most valuable for informal access and recreation—SSSI status has almost by accident become the last defence of uncultivated land.

The future, therefore, is very uncertain. The effectiveness of the Act will depend on a real spirit of compromise. This means that there should be very few unnecessary or irresponsible applications for 'improvement' on the part of the land-owners and occupiers, and no unreasonable rigidity from the NCC in laying down specifications for management agreements. It depends also on a willingness of the agriculture departments to withhold grants on conservation grounds. Yet so much has already been lost in present-day Britain that the starting point of any compromise is very strongly on the side of agriculture. You will know well of the protest that the area of 2,500 acres of West Sedgemoor notified as an SSSI is much too large. But this 2,500 is only a fraction of the 169,000 acres in the neighbourhood which was once of high wildlife quality or even of what remained forty or fifty years ago; and a very small part indeed of the wetlands in the flood-plains of English lowland rivers that remained at the beginning of the nineteenth-century. Read, for example, of the richness of Whittlesea Mere near Peterborough, drained in the middle of the last century. In lowland Britain very little is left of a former abundance.

The other great uncertainty is the will on the part of Government to provide the funds that are needed to make the Act work: to increase the capacity of the NCC to cope with the greatly enhanced responsibilities and to provide the compensatory payments required by the Act.

The Act is framed in such a way that very careful detailed discussions will be necessary with farmers to explain what they should or should not do to maintain the features of interest and value on their land. Often the restraints will be very slight—refraining from using fertilizer here, or leaving a patch undrained there—but they have to be carefully explained to reassure farmers who have become understandably worried at the way the ponderous machinery of the law has intruded on the use of their land. So the NCC must give generously of the time of knowledgeable, patient, and sensitive field staff—if it is given the resources to do so.

An even greater amount of uncertainty hangs over the willingness of Government to pay, through the NCC and the Countryside Commission, the compensatory payments that may be required. The annual amounts could be enormous in terms of the budgets of the two organizations; though not, in contrast, in relation to the money flowing into agriculture through the agriculture ministries, the European Community, and by tax and rate concessions. There is the looking-glass situation of large amounts of taxpayers' money being used to promote activities that the law requires to be countered using more of the taxpayers' money. Surely an infallible recipe for expensive Government.

Another great uncertainty hangs over those parts of the countryside that lie outside specially scheduled sites. By implication they have been left without any protection at all. Is it reasonable that only sites which are of proven *scientific* interest should have safeguards against change?

So the outlook is far from sure? Looked at in the long run one must hope that the Wildlife and Countryside Act is replaced by measures of a different kind. It has a number of serious philosophical faults. It develops a polarization between the interests of conservation and agriculture; aid for farming comes from one source, for conservation from another. It singles out scientific interest (outside the National Parks) and makes it into the last bastion of uncultivated land against the plough or the conifer. It is essentially defensive in posture. But perhaps the most serious of all is that it addresses symptoms rather than causes, because it is set in the context of massive financial support for the increase of agricultural productivity rather than support of the rural economy as a whole.

What then of the more distant future, when the Wildlife and Countryside Act has run itself in or worked itself out? Is there any possibility of radical change? Are we to hope for changes through new technology or by an altogether new approach? Going back to Colbert, will it be metal ships or the dawning of a new love for the French?

Let us look at technology first and see what we may expect. I suspect not too much that will revolutionize the landscape. We have already gone a long way along the path of mechanization and increased yield based on good scientific research, and we clearly can go some way further. Genetic engineering would perhaps push us far and fast, so could revolutionary discoveries in the efficiency of photosynthesis, but these would not, I suspect, change our direction. The industrial production of edible (and palatable) plant protein could perhaps influence us, but I guess that we are too conservative in our eating habits to be shifted much except in emergencies: good as reserve rations or for mountain camping, but no substitute for grilled sole or a good slice of roast beef.

What else might happen?—changes in communication and control systems, much-improved weather forecasting, and perhaps limited climatic control. All these could lead to greater efficiency, higher predictability, and ever-increased productivity. They could all be directed to using less land for the same amount of production; but, on past showing, they will not. So we come back to economics and attitudes.

Looking back, one can see that the present crisis of confidence has been caused by following isolated sectoral interests—a policy for farming, a policy for forestry, for nature conservation, for amenity, for access, tourism and so forth. I think that there is a stage when this separation and identification of interests is essential in order to sort out their similarities and differences, but also to ensure that the weaker interests are not lost sight of. If nature conservation had been bulked with forestry or with natural resources, it could too easily have been swamped by the other more dominant or immediate interests. But if these sectoral approaches are not blended eventually into a coherent national approach to the use of the countryside, they can lead to unnecessary polarization of attitudes, waste of resources, proliferation of bureaucracy and, worst of all, serious damage to the resource which all are, in one way or another, dedicated to looking after—the landscape of Britain.

This is exactly where we find ourselves now. Reaction against it could be extreme—to the extent of planning control or even nationalization of the land.

In spite of many recent calls for a national land-use policy, there is remarkably little government interest. It is easier to allow things to sort themselves out through the balance of forces between government agencies and interest groups. But this is essentially an example of the hidden exercise of power. The ultimate sanction of money is at the disposal of Government and the balance of interest will eventually be determined by the way the domestic purse-strings are controlled. Imagine how dramatic could be the effect on landscape if the funds available to the NCC and CCs were increased tenfold and those for agricultural support quartered.

What then is the alternative? Here we really start guessing. For the sake of argument let us remove the most devastating futures: let us assume that there will not be another world war or nuclear holocaust. This still leaves plenty of choice: on the domestic scene, a complete change of policy in relation to agricultural support; in relation to Europe, the breakdown and recasting of the Common Agricultural Policy or a breakaway Britain; in relation to the world at large, the abandonment of trade protectionism and adoption of a policy that is more in the long-term interests of the developing world. There are plenty of possible futures.

Would it not be possible to turn the problem inside out, to look at objectives first and then the means to attain them? In this we should be thoroughly modern and advanced, and follow the prescriptions of the best schools of management. Why do we not do so? Why does the Government not promote a national debate on a national rural land-use policy? I suspect that it may be because we are scared of the answers we may get—like the reluctance to consult the doctor of one who suspects he has an incurable disease.

The question we need to ask ourselves is: what kind of a countryside do we want? Then we can go on to consider whether it is attainable and, if so, how? First, and perhaps most important, one would like to see thriving, prosperous, vigorous communities—villages, hamlets, farmsteads—in which a proportion of the inhabitants at least was occupied gainfully in the management and care of the countryside. This means a reasonable population engaged in agriculture, forestry, and other aspects of rural land management. It also means sufficient services—housing, transport, schools, doctors, shops, church, and so forth—to make these attractive places to live in for those with reasonable present-day expectations.

Secondly, one would like to see everywhere a reasonable balance between the intensively cultivated and thus inaccessible land and the uncultivated and accessible. This balance would of course vary greatly between one part of the country and another. In some upland areas it would be entirely appropriate to bring some more areas into more intensive use; but in highly cultivated parts of the lowlands there would be great social and ecological benefit in relaxing pressure slightly. If 1 per cent of arable land in the most intensively farmed parts of England were to be removed from arable and devoted to less intensive management it would fulfil almost all needs for additional wildlife habitat, and informal recreation. This is nothing in comparison with the increase of production on these same acres during the last twenty years. Moreover, the land need not revert to totally unproductive use; it could be readily used for grazing or for hay, for example. What one is asking is that the owner should be satisfied with the products of a less exacting kind of agriculture.

As an example I should like to talk about my own village. This is not atypical, I think, with its mixture of established families and incomers; some work in and around the village and there is one small but flourishing local industry; most work in nearby towns. There is a network of paths, some statutory, others not, which are well and fully used. We could do with more. We are blessed with a common (natural grassland and river bank) which is greatly frequented by young and old alike (including many from further afield), a dry valley of unimproved grassland full of cowslips, and a much loved piece of woodland which foresters would describe as neglected and unproductive—as indeed in a sense it is. This is walked through, used by children for 'cowboys and indians', is a source of firewood, full of birds and flowers, and no doubt a source of other delights. We are very lucky, by accident of topography and history (the common and tips of mine waste) and because those who own or occupy the land have not been interested in pushing its use to the limits of efficiency. Many villages are not so fortunate. One must remember that the country lanes which were a pleasure to walk when I was young are now metalled roads and are neither pleasant nor safe. By contrast I remember spending a long time in a car in the East Anglian peat fens looking for somewhere to have a picnic and having to settle for the bank of a sterile ditch cheek by jowl with a patch of nettles. Much of the lowland countryside requires more, much more, space for informal access. We have much to learn from our neighbours in continental Europe.

If an initiative such as this—relaxing the intensive farming on a minute fraction of the agricultural area—were to be taken widely by the farming community, they would have the conservationists eating out of their hands; it would be appreciated that this was real, not merely cosmetic as much (sometimes wrongly) is suspected to be today. The foresters have already taken this kind of initiative, for example in their strong drive to develop a policy for broad-leaved woodlands which would demonstrate that they can become profitable while maintaining or even increasing their interest for wildlife and their value as an amenity. An alternative worth trying would be for such areas to be owned or leased by the community itself and managed for conservation, informal access, and limited production of firewood or hay, for example. What I am proposing are commons with a modern face. The third element would be in the maintenance and management of features of importance for landscape and nature conservation—hedges, walls, ditches, ponds, trees, roadside verges, and so forth.

These three would provide a framework for the future of the whole rural landscape—for its productive use, settlement, employment, services, scenery, nature conservation, and informal access. Over this would be superimposed the special heritage sites such as National Parks, AONBs, SSSIs, ancient monuments and the like; although, as the basic structure became stronger, some of the special categories might become unnecessary.

The aim would be to direct the enormous amounts of money which now go solely to support increases in agricultural productivity into support for integrated rural policies of this kind, including, of course, productive agriculture. This is by no means a new proposal. To some extent it has been applied by the Development Boards; and detailed proposals which would begin to lead in this direction appear in three new discussion documents: *What Future for the Uplands?* by the Countryside Commission for England and Wales; *Putting Trust in the Countryside*, which is part of the UK response to the World Conservation Strategy; a *New Life for the Hills* from the Council for National Parks. There has even been a tentative and experimental scheme funded by the European Community in the Peak Park. So the conditions would be created in which those who own and manage the land would be able to look after all aspects of it; to replace the single-minded pursuit of production by the idea of trusteeship or stewardship—for all aspects of the landscape. Would a change in the financial framework be enough? What about attitudes?

The Ministry of Agriculture seems to have done a pretty thorough job in converting the modern farmer to production at any price. But I am not sure that appearances do not mislead. A carrot has been used that would win the first prize at any horticultural show; but I suspect that many farmers and most foresters are reluctant vandals. A change in the emphasis of education and advice, together with the work of the Farming and Wildlife Advisory Groups *and* a new financial framework, would bring a total change in a decade. In the perspective of history the present fetish could prove only a seven-day wonder.

A digression on forestry, which I have rather neglected. I see a fair increase in the area of upland forest and in the degree of self-sufficiency in timber. For the balance I tend to think we will support and encourage production in the tropics, import, or substitute. Because of the long-term nature of the crop the contribution to landscape is largely set; but there could be a number of changes. An integrated policy would mean more trees on the farm; energy plantations for fuelwood will appear; and there will be an increase of purely local markets once again, perhaps even village forests.

In general I see a growing divergence between tree farming and extensive forestry: the former very capital-intensive, efficient, adapted to a precise market; the latter, extensive, opportunistic. Much upland forestry may fall in this category as it enters its second or third generations. There will be design for landscape and wildlife, more diversity in structure, age, and composition; and on this will be imposed natural irregularity caused by windblow, frost, deer, invasion by birch, rowan, willow, and natural regeneration of spruce, fir, larch, and pine. The plantations of today will become the forests of the future.

I can imagine some of you asking whether a move towards the less intensive use of the land is in harmony with the spirit of the age. This is a matter of opinion, but I think that perhaps it is, whether you look at it in the context of Britain, Europe, or the world. I say this because I am convinced that we shall have to move during the next few decades towards what Lester Brown has called a sustainable society and towards a much greater sensitivity to the problems of the poorer nations.

To take the British scene first. The moves I have suggested would centre round reversing the drift to the cities by creating jobs in the country: making small farms viable, increasing the labour force on larger farms, encouraging combinations of agricultural and forestry work, building up the conservation work force, and setting up small industries. The services would follow. As it seems that the revolution of the silicon chip is unlikely to create jobs in industry as did the first industrial revolution, it would seem no bad thing to boost rural employment instead. In a world in which oil will (in spite of temporary gluts) become inexorably scarcer and more expensive, dispersal of the work-force may also seem more prudent and attractive, to make use of more dispersed sources of energy and economize in its use. In this we could take a leaf out of the Chinese book.

Exactly the same conditions apply to Europe. Some of the Alpine countries have already adopted policies of this kind in relation to their mountain valleys, with results that we flock to see. Intensified cultivation will lead to depopulation and the decay of rural life in all the more marginal areas. This was the trend that the Less Favoured Areas Directive of the EEC was designed to stem, but the Directive is being used in ways that have exactly the opposite effect. It is an astonishing misnomer that the EEC's *Integrated* Development Programme for the Western Isles should concentrate solely on agricultural improvement.

There is no contradiction either at the world scale. The Food and Agriculture Organization of the United Nations (FAO) has made a detailed study of the needs of agriculture into the next century. The conclusion is perhaps surprising—that the only way of meeting the needs of the hungry and undernourished in the developing countries is to increase production in these countries themselves, where there are still areas to be opened up for agriculture and yields are low and can be greatly raised. These increases, the Report argues, will be quite impossible unless the developed countries provide encouragement by liberalizing their trade and importing from the developing countries. A grain store for famine relief is certainly needed, but, apart from that, what will be required from the developed nations will be aid, trade, and the ability to respond flexibly in their production to the needs of the poorer nations. The conclusions are clear: less protectionism (by Britain and Europe); use grass rather than grain to feed livestock; and there is no need to bring every inch into cultivation to feed the starving millions.

So it seems that in the long run what is good for our landscape is also what will fit in best with the needs of both Europe and the developing world. It is bizarre that we are pursuing our present agricultural intensification so ruthlessly at a time when *rural community development* is the centrepiece of present policies for helping the rest of the world, and the blind pursuit of productivity is being blamed for many of the failures of development in recent decades. Is it possible that the recipe that we recommend for the underdeveloped could also be good medicine for us?

What then are our hopes for the future landscape? First, that we should deliberately build up a living, lively, and varied rural economy; and, secondly, that we should create the conditions in which those who live and work on the land become its trustees: conditions in which they are enabled to make a proper livelihood managing it for all the purposes that society values, and in which they wish and are proud to do so. In this way we shall develop a genuine land husbandry and show that we are truly civilized. With restraint there is room for all. Or am I too optimistic?

Epilogue

S. R. J. WOODELL

IT is the editor's good fortune to be in the position to have the last word. Being in this privileged position I feel that I should express my own concern, a concern that I know is felt by many others, about some aspects of the future of our landscape. In doing so I may be accused of partiality towards one small part of the landscape mosaic. That is fair enough, but we are all partial, and in my view what is happening to this small facet of the landscape is symptomatic of what is taking place in general. Therefore I make no apology for bringing this volume to a close on a gloomy note.

The term 'naturalist' may be defined in various ways. It can include amateurs who take an active interest in observing plants and animals in the wild, and professional scientists who study the workings of natural ecosystems, who are going well beyond mere observation. Naturalists have been scorned in the past, especially the recent past, but only by those who do not understand that good natural history is true science, and that great biological scientists of the past, such as Darwin, Huxley, Linnaeus, Cuvier, and many others were basically naturalists.

Many naturalists have become conservationists. Darwin spoke out more than once in defence of areas of great natural-history value that he thought might be threatened. The concern of naturalists with conservation is more general today than at any time in the past, because they see natural environments all over the world under their greatest threat ever. Both naturalists and conservationists are deeply interested in landscape; perhaps more often with its intimate detail than its broad sweep. They see wildlife under threat and they try in a variety of ways to do something to save it. One of the most effective ways is to publicize the threats. What naturalists are trying to save is as important a part of our landscape as are many of the other parts discussed in this book. Some of the destruction is the result of ignorance or carelessness, some the consequence of extraction of maximum profit from the land. I make no apology for pointing out what is happening in Britain, nor for suggesting that much more needs to be done to prevent it.

In this book, changes have been discussed which have taken place over millions (Jones, Lamb), thousands (Cunliffe, Rackham) or hundreds of years (Thirsk, Beresford). Professor Thompson described change taking place over a few decades. Those which Professor Poore refers to have taken only thirty years and are still going on. It may seem superfluous to say more about what is happening to the countryside now, since we are bombarded from so many quarters with so much rhetoric. Yet despite the amount that has been and is being said I am constantly dismayed not only by the indifference that many people display, but also by how unaware so many of our fellow citizens are about what is happening. Why is this?

We are mainly city dwellers. Most of us pass through the countryside infrequently, though millions of commuters see parts of it every working day. How many of them, as they pass through it, actually *see* it and observe it closely enough to notice change? Even country dwellers often allow change to go unremarked. If, on one's daily journey or trip to an annual holiday destination, a hedge disappears here, an old meadow is ploughed up there, part of an ancient woodland elsewhere is felled, how many of us take more than casual note? Of those who do, how many do no more than say to themselves that it is a pity but there is nothing they can do about it?

This is understandable. Observation requires effort; action demands more effort. Most of us are too busy even to sit down and write a letter to somebody who might be able to take action. So changes are allowed to continue. Individually they are small, cumulatively they have a tremendous impact on our environment. Even those who are professionally concerned may find it difficult to grasp the scale of the changes. Of course it differs in various parts of England. East Anglians are familiar now with prairie-like landscapes resulting from post-war hedge clearance, while those living in the counties bordering Wales have so far seen little of this kind of change. Travelling from one end of the country to the other, the magnitude of habitat destruction becomes more and more apparent to the discerning observer.

Professor Poore has documented the effects that membership of the European Economic Community are having on agricultural practice in Britain. These come on the heels of an already more efficient agriculture than existed before the war. We now grow far more cereal, and some other crops, than we require, or indeed than our European partners need. He has dealt with some of the political implications of this and I do not propose to pursue them further. What must concern us here are the environmental effects. Apart from Professor Poore, one other contributor to this volume, Oliver Rackham, has expressed some of this concern.

At this juncture the reader may think that I am straying from the theme of the lecture series, and that even if my worries about present-day change are justified, surely this whole volume is a document of change. Our speakers have demonstrated that our present landscape in all its complexity is itself a record of the changes we have imposed upon it for millennia. Further (one might argue), at some time in the future the late twentieth century will be regarded as just one more period of change which, in the context of the overall history of the landscape, will have added merely one more facet to the many-splendoured kaleidoscope that is our present landscape. Support for this view can be found in Professor Thompson's lecture. He has shown in a masterly manner that a period of our history that has been regarded as highly destructive of our landscape had in fact less impact than is generally believed. (Though the less immediately obvious effects of redistribution of population from country to town had both visual and social effects far beyond the direct impact of the Industrial Revolution that he was discussing.)

Other speakers surprised many of us with their accounts of large-scale change in the past. Dr Rackham's evidence that the 'wildwood' had been so extensively cleared by Norman times was no doubt new to many. Dr Thirsk clearly demonstrated how transient agricultural fashions have been; no doubt they will be just as volatile in the future. Does it really matter, then, that the domination of our agricultural policy by the EEC, with its concomitant intensification of the destruction of semi-natural vegetation, is bringing about rapid effects on our wildlife now?

Following that line of argument, it can be suggested that future changes in agricultural policy may release land from cultivation and allow it to 'revert' to a semi-natural state. It has happened before, most recently in the pre-war priod. In the present state of world food supplies it seems unlikely, but this is a notoriously difficult area in which to make predictions. If land was allowed to fall out of cultivation, would our landscape not once more take on a more attractive appearance? Indeed it would, but there are considerations other than visual ones involved, and my contention is that, although visually attractive, it would be a biologically impoverished landscape; impoverished, that is, unless we can arrest the present rate of loss of wildlife habitat.

A sceptical reader may agree that loss of wildlife and biological impoverishment are happening, and are undesirable, but what have they to do with *landscape?* I would answer by pointing out that for very many people, not just naturalists, what little remains of our semi-natural vegetation, with its array of animals and plants, is the part of the landscape that attracts their attention and interest; that gives it variety, both biological and visual. The hundreds of thousands of people who are members of County Naturalists Trusts, the Royal Society for the Protection of Birds, the Woodland Trust, and other organizations which are devoted to saving this part of the landscape, are witness to that fact. Without its remaining wildlife the landscape would still retain many of the elements which make it beautiful, but it would have lost some of its most attractive features. Wildlife suffers now the most severe pressures it has ever had to withstand, and it is less well equipped to withstand them than it has ever been since human beings returned to Britain after the last glaciation.

Why is this so? Because now only a very small percentage of the surface area of England is still occupied by semi-natural vegetation: a much smaller amount than existed during earlier periods of rapid change. This small percentage is steadily being eroded. Recent studies have shown that Sites of Special Scientific Interest, which are intended to represent and conserve the 'best' examples of various habitats, have been lost at the rate of 4 per cent per year. It is difficult to know whether the less well protected sites are disappearing more rapidly. The pressures on habitats are both more intense than and different in degree from those of the past. As the area of semi-natural habitat decreases, so the chance of species extinctions grows greater. Plants and animals which were common only a few decades ago are now scarce. Examples of this rapid decline are the common frog and all newts.

The loss of a few plant and animal species may be unfortunate, but are we not again getting away from our theme, the landscape? Indeed not: these losses are signposts to much more fundamental changes. For instance, frogs and newts are dependent on open water for breeding. Much of their decline has resulted from drainage, the filling in of ponds, and pollution of some of the waters that remain. Water adds variety to any landscape. Crowds of people flock to areas of water in our countryside. They are evidence that water is much appreciated as a landscape feature. If the loss of amphibians is an indicator of loss of open water, then one of the most attractive features of the landscape is being eroded.

Most readers will be able to think of other examples which show similar trends. The loss of any animal or plant is an indication that some part of the natural environment has gone or has been changed fundamentally. Some of the most sensitive indicators of change are among the least conspicuous—mosses and lichens, for example. The actual loss of individual species is itself unfortunate to say the least. What the loss indicates is very important indeed. Even if the present trends are reversed, some elements of our landscape will be lost for ever, or at least may take hundreds or thousands of years to re-create. There are schemes afoot to re-create 'instant' ancient grassland. They may work, after a fashion, but though the grassland created may be attractive it will take much longer to stabilize than to create, and its potential animal inhabitants will take even longer to recolonize it, if indeed they ever do.

What I have attempted in this epilogue is to point out the relative scales of change, and the relative time periods during which the changes documented in this book have taken place. Both the scale and the time have accelerated alarmingly.

I am writing this in a very different landscape, one in which European man has had major, sometimes disastrous, impacts. Partly this is the result of attempts to introduce European agricultural and pastoral methods to a very arid climate. Other areas of the world have suffered similarly at our hands. We seem to find it hard to learn from our mistakes; even after they have been pointed out, we go on making them. We in Britain and north-west Europe are lucky to have a benign climate. Our landscape has considerable resilience, and the capacity to absorb change. It also has the capacity to regenerate after it is damaged. As I said in the Introduction, people have been exerting their influences on it for millennia. In the main these influences have been gradual and gentle.

The fortuitous combination of a benign climate and relatively slow change has served us well. But can the landscape survive rapid change? Much depends on agricultural policies during the next few decades, and these in turn depend on forces beyond our immediate control. Those who actually own the land and work on it have a great responsibility.

To use an analogy from my own experience: I am one of the many people who collect old books. It can be said that I am the owner of the books in my collection. I do not see it quite like that and I know that many other collectors feel the same way. We see ourselves more as the custodians of these books, looking after them, and of course enjoying them, during our period of possession. We are also ensuring that they survive for future generations of booklovers to enjoy. We take steps to conserve them and repair them if they are damaged.

The analogy can be extended to works of art, furniture, and, perhaps more appositely, to buildings. The owners of buildings scheduled as worthy of conservation have imposed upon them considerable restrictions on what can be done in the way of alterations. The legislation is not completely effective, but it helps. Why should land not be submitted to similar constraints? Why should landowners not be required to hand on their land, having used it for their own purposes, in a condition that reflects good management? You may regard this as an unreasonable restriction of freedom, but the land, and the landscape, belongs to us all, and all those who make use of it should be responsible. This includes not only the owners and those who grow food upon it, but everyone who uses it for recreation.

We are all custodians of our landscape. Will our descendants, in a few hundred years or less, praise us for the care which we gave to our landscape, or condemn us for the damage we did to it? It is up to all of us to ensure that it is praise, rather than condemnation, that we receive.

Notes and references

Notes to Chapter 1 (pp. 1–47)

1. The attributes of rocks that influence topographic development are generally outlined in Sparks 1971.
2. There are many published subdivisions of England into relief regions. That used in this chapter is adapted from Warwick 1964.
3. There is an enormous range of literature on the relationships of geology and topography. The most readable general account is Trueman 1971. Regional accounts are contained in the eleven volumes of British Regional Geology published by HMSO (for example, Gallois 1965) and volumes in the 'Geology Explained' series published by David and Charles (such as Dreghorn 1967). More localized descriptions can be found in the New Series Sheet Memoirs published by HMSO, the Geological Association Field Guides, and in the 'Landscapes Through Maps' series published by the Geographical Association.
4. The nature and operation of geomorphological processes are discussed in Rice 1977, Derbyshire *et al.* 1979, and Embleton and Thornes 1979. The influence of man on environmental systems and thereby on the operation of geomorphological processes is examined in Goudie 1981, and in the two anthologies Hollis 1979, and Gregory and Walling 1980.
5. There remains considerable speculation about the duration of the Pleistocene, owing to disagreements about where to place the basal boundary, problems of correlation, and difficulties with absolute dating. For a discussion see Bowen 1978. Most writers have supported one of two distinct schools of thought, favouring either a 'short' Pleistocene, beginning about 1.6–1.75 Ma, or a 'long' Pleistocene extending back to 2.4–2.5 Ma. Although a 'long' Pleistocene has been adopted in this chapter, support has strengthened recently for the 'short' interpretation, despite the fact that there is clear evidence for significant climatic deterioration about 2.4 Ma, including a continental-scale glaciation of the Northern Atlantic region at 2.37 Ma (Shackleton *et al.* 1984).
6. For general discussions of Pleistocene environmental change see Bowen 1978 and Goudie 1983.
7. Detrital evidence in nearby strata indicates that the Dartmoor granite was exposed in the Permo-Triassic (Laming 1982) and Lower Cretaceous (Groves 1931), submerged and buried during the early Upper Cretaceous (Cenomanian = Lower Chalk) (Smith 1961), and then re-exposed by the early Eocene (Hamblin 1973).
8. Jones 1980a.
9. Jones 1980a.
10. For a review see Young 1974.
11. Dangerfield and Hawkes 1969; Isaac 1981.
12. Jones 1980a.

13. There is a vast recent literature on global tectonics. Useful introductory reviews include Wilson 1972, Hallam 1973, Tarling and Tarling 1974, and Oxburgh 1974. For a more advanced review with specific reference to Britain see Dewey 1982. The rifting and opening of the northern North Atlantic Basin is discussed in Hallam 1971, Laughton 1972, Phillips and Forsyth 1972, and Roberts 1974.

14. There is no one book that adequately deals with the geomorphological evolution of England. The best discussions are to be found in the Methuen series on 'The Geomorphology of the British Isles': King 1976, Straw and Clayton 1979, and Jones 1981. For a description of the role of human activity in landform creation see Brown 1970.

15. For a review of the geological evolution of the British Isles see Anderton *et al.* 1979.

16. Sparks 1971.

17. Anderson and Owen 1982; Anderton *et al.* 1979.

18. The five granite masses of Devon and Cornwall are known to be bosses of a major granite pluton (batholith) dated at 280 ± 10 Ma and intruded at depth into the sedimentary pile. For details see Brammall and Harwood 1932, and Anderson and Owen 1982. For details of the exposure of the Dartmoor granite see note 7 and Dangerfield and Hawkes 1969.

19. Wooldridge and Linton 1955.

20. Lake 1975; Jones 1980a; Stoneley 1982.

21. See Kent 1949, Naylor and Mountenay 1975, and the 1:1,584,000 scale *Tectonic Map of Great Britain and Northern Ireland* (1966), Institute of Geological Sciences.

22. Brown 1960.

23. The word isostasy describes the way in which the relatively light rocks which form the outermost rigid shell of the Earth (Crust and Upper Mantle = Lithosphere) float on a zone in the Mantle, known as the Asthenosphere, where the denser rocks are near their pressure-melting point. It is this weak zone, extending usually from 50 km to 250 km depth, which facilitates the horizontal motion of plate tectonics as well as relatively rapid vertical movements when the balance is disturbed. The best-known of these vertical, or isostatic, movements is glacio-isostasy which is concerned with both the subsidence of areas when loaded with large volumes of glacial ice and their subsequent uplift, or rebound, on deglaciation, the latter at rates of 5,000 to 16,000 B. Isostatic movements can also result from sedimentary loading—the North Sea Basin subsidence—and erosional unloading or denudation, when the removal of strata over areas greater in size than the Weald can eventually result in imbalance and uplift. Such movements are both pulsed and damped. Nevertheless, it is considered likely that to achieve an overall lowering of 300 metres over an extensive area involves the denudational removal of 1,500 metres of strata, due to repeated isostatic uplift.

24. Roberts 1974.

25. Read and Watson 1975.

26. George 1974.

27. Hancock 1975.

28. See Hancock 1975; Hay and Pitman 1973; Vail *et al.* 1977; Vail, Mitchum and Thompson 1977.

29. Terris and Bullerwell 1965.

30. Linton 1951a; Linton 1951b.

31. Edwards 1976.

32. Richey 1961; Curry *et al.* 1978.

33. Sissons 1967; Sissons 1976; Herries Davies and Stephens 1978.
34. Herries Davies and Stephens 1978.
35. George 1966.
36. Hamblin 1973; Edwards 1976.
37. Early supporters of the Chalk Cover hypothesis tended to reconstruct the base of the Chalk so that it lay just above the highest elements in the present topographic landscape of Dartmoor, the Pennines and Wales, e.g. Linton 1951a, Linton 1956a, Brown 1961, and Orme 1964. While there is remaining uncertainty as to the extent to which the Chalk Sea submerged Highland Britain—e.g. George 1966 and Sissons 1967—there is growing support for the view that the late Cretaceous surface lay well above the present upland summits—e.g. George 1974.
38. See Curry *et al.* 1978, and Jones 1981.
39. Jones 1981, pp. 70–6.
40. Catt and Hodgson 1976; Jones 1981.
41. Wooldridge and Linton 1955.
42. Wooldridge and Linton 1955; Linton 1956c.
43. Jones 1974.
44. Jones 1981.
45. Jones 1974.
46. Montford 1970; Curry *et al.* 1978.
47. Summerfield and Goudie 1980; Isaac 1981, 1983.
48. Several different phases of sarsen formation have been postulated, all of them in the Palaeogene; for a review see Summerfield and Goudie 1980. An Oligocene age was favoured in Clark *et al.* 1967 and subsequently received much support. More recent research has suggested earlier formation: three phases of formation during the Eocene have recently been favoured in Small 1980, while an early Palaeocene age has been postulated for Devon sarsens in Isaac 1983. The proposed age of sarsen formation is of considerable significance for the reconstruction of geomorphological evolution: the older the sarsens, the less the potency that can be ascribed to subsequent denudation. The interpretation employed here is for several formative phases with the bulk of sarsens on the higher chalklands dating from the late Palaeogene.
49. Bristow 1968; Edwards 1976. A third basin has recently been identified at Dutson, Cornwall: see Freshney *et al.* 1982.
50. Hamblin 1973; Isaac 1981, 1983.
51. Linton 1955.
52. Palmer and Radley 1961; Palmer and Neilson 1962; Gerrard 1974.
53. Vail *et al.* 1977.
54. Walsh *et al.* 1972.
55. Worssam 1963; Curry *et al.* 1978.
56. Jones 1980a; Small 1980.
57. Topley 1875; Davis 1895; Wooldridge and Linton 1955.
58. For a review see Linton 1964.
59. For a review see Goudie 1983. In this context it is important to note the work of Shakleton *et al.* 1984 which suggests that the first continental-scale glaciation occurred at 2.37 Ma.
60. For a review see Bowen 1978.
61. Catt 1981.

62. Gray and Lowe 1977; Sissons 1979.
63. Straw and Clayton 1979.
64. Bowen 1981.
65. Sissons 1976; Gray and Lowe 1977.
66. Straw and Clayton 1979; Straw 1979.
67.   Bristow and Cox 1973.
68. Cox 1981.
69. Stephens 1970.
70. The southward displacement of the ice limit so as to butt against the Thanet Dome and penetrate into the Straits of Dover, as shown in Figure 1.18, is based on D'Olier 1975 and Destombes *et al.* 1975.
71. Kellaway *et al.* 1975. For a rejection of these suggestions see Jones 1981, pp. 191–6.
72. Boulton *et al.* 1977.
73. Linton 1957.
74. Boulton *et al.* 1977.
75. For a general review of ideas concerning the evolution of the Lower Thames see Baker and Jones 1980.
76. Shotton 1953.
77. The extent and significance of pro-glacial Lake Lapworth is a matter of controversy. Poole and Whiteman 1961 concluded that a very extensive lake was created. Others appear unconvinced; see Worsley 1975. It is now concluded that the Ironbridge Gorge may have been initiated by ice-marginal or subglacial flows although it was probably subsequently enlarged by overflow; see Straw and Clayton 1979, pp. 217–21.
78. See Straw and Clayton 1979.
79. See Bowen 1973. For reviews of models of Quaternary sea-level change see Bowen 1978 and Goudie 1983.
80. The best presently available general review is Mitchell 1977.
81. Stephens and Synge 1966; Stephens 1970; Bowen 1973.
82. For a general discussion of periglacial processes see Washburn 1973. For a review of the significance of periglacial activity in Britain see Worsley 1977 and Waters 1978.
83. See Briggs and Gilbertson 1980.
84. See Green and McGregor 1980.
85. There are numerous papers with published sections through periglacial deposits; see, for example, Kerney 1965.
86. Palmer and Radley 1961; Palmer and Neilson 1962.
87. See Jones 1981, pp. 240–4.
88. Catt 1977; Catt 1979.
89. The significance of periglacial fashioning was first highlighted, and extra-glacial southern England described as a 'typical periglacial landscape', in Te Punga 1957.
90. The fullest synthesis of recent sea-level change is contained in the theme issue of *Proceedings of the Geologists' Association* entitled 'I.G.C.P. Project 61: Sea-level movements during the last deglacial hemicycle (about 15,000 years)', Vol. 93, 1 (1982), pp. 1–125.
91. D'Olier 1972; Jones 1981, pp. 263–70.
92. The best review of coastal features remains Steers 1964. For other discussions see Steers 1962 and Steers 1966.

93. Valentin 1971.
94. Everard 1954.
95. Prince 1964; Lambert *et al.* 1970.
96. See Jones 1982.
97. Although archaeologists have long used human artifacts for stratigraphic purposes, the first use of more recent 'rubbish' is contained in Hunt 1959.
98. Goudie 1981.
99. There is an enormous literature on underfit streams: see, for example, Dury 1954; Dury 1958; Dury 1964; Dury 1970; Dury 1977.
100. Straw and Clayton 1979, pp. 116–24; Jones 1981, pp. 284–94; Burrin and Scaife 1984.
101. Burrin 1981.
102. Burrin and Scaife 1984.

References to Chapter 1 (pp. 1–47)

Anderson, J. G. C., and Owen, T. R. 1982, *The Structure of the British Isles* (Pergamon Press, Oxford).

Anderton, R., Bridges, P. W., Leeder, M. R., and Sellwood, B. W. 1979, *A Dynamic Stratigraphy of the British Isles* (Allen and Unwin, London).

Baker, C. A., and Jones, D. K. C. 1980, 'Glaciation of the London Basin and its influence on the drainage pattern: a review and appraisal', in Jones 1980b, 131–75.

Boulton, G. S., Jones, A. S., Clayton, K. M., and Kenning, M. J. 1977, 'A British ice sheet model and patterns of glacial erosion and deposition in Britain', in Shotton 1977, 231–46.

Bowen, D. Q. 1973, 'Time and place on the British coast', *Geography,* **58,** 207–16.

—— 1978, *Quaternary Geology* (Pergamon Press, Oxford).

—— 1981, 'The "South Wales End-Moraine": Fifty years after', in Neale and Flenley 1981, 60–7.

Brammall, A., and Harwood, H. F. 1932, 'The Dartmoor Granites', *Proceedings of the Geologists' Association,* **88,** 171–237

Briggs, D. J., and Gilbertson, D. D. 1980, 'Quaternary processes and environments in the upper Thames valley', *Transactions of the Institute of British Geographers,* NS **5,** 53–65.

Bristow, C. M. 1968, 'The derivation of the Tertiary sediments in the Petrockstow Basin, North Devon', *Proceedings of the Ussher Society,* **2,** 29–35.

Bristow, C. R., and Cox, F. C. 1973, 'The Gipping Till: a reappraisal of East Anglian glacial stratigraphy', *Journal of the Geological Society,* **129,** 1–37.

Brown, E. H. 1960, 'The building of southern Britain', *Zeitschrift für Geomorphologie,* NS **4,** 264–74.

—— 1961, 'Britain and Appalachia', *Transactions of the Institute of British Geographers,* **29,** 91–100.

—— 1970, 'Man shapes the earth', *Geographical Journal,* **136,** 74–85.

—— and Waters, R. S. (eds.) 1974, *Progress in Geomorphology,* Institute of British Geographers Special Publication 7.

Büdel, J. 1982, *Climatic Geomorphology* (Princeton University Press, Princeton).

Burk, C. A., and Drake, C. L. (eds.) 1974, *The Geology of the Continental Margins* (Springer-Verlag, Berlin).

Burrin, P. J. 1981, 'Loess in the Weald', *Proceedings of the Geologists' Association*, 92, 87–92.

—— and Scaife, R. G. 1984, 'Aspects of Holocene valley sedimentation and floodplain development in southern England', *Proceedings of the Geologists' Association*, 95, 81–96.

Catt, J. A. 1977, 'Loess and coversands', in Shotton 1977, 222–9.

—— 1979, 'Distribution of loess in Britain', *Proceedings of the Geologists' Association*, 90, 93–5.

—— 1981, 'British pre-Devensian glaciations', in Neale and Flenley 1981, 9–19.

—— and Hodgson, J. M. 1976, 'Soils and geomorphology of the Chalk in south-east England', *Earth Surface Processes*, 1, 181–93.

Clark, M. J., Lewin, J., and Small, R. J. 1967, 'The sarsen stones of the Marlborough Downs and their geomorphological implications', *Southampton Research Series in Geography*, 4, 3–40.

Clayton, K. M. 1974, 'Zones of glacial erosion', in Brown and Waters 1974, 163–76.

Cox, F. C. 1981, 'The "Gipping Till" revisited', in Neale and Flenley 1981, 32–42.

Curry, D., *et al.* 1978, *A Correlation of Tertiary Rocks in the British Isles*, Geological Society Special Report No. 12, 30–7.

Dangerfield, J., and Hawkes, J. R. 1969, 'Unroofing of the Dartmoor granite and possible consequences with regard to mineralization', *Proceedings of the Ussher Society*, 2, 122–31.

Davis, W. M. 1895, 'On the origin of certain English rivers', *Geographical Journal*, 5, 128–46.

Derbyshire, E., Gregory, K. J., and Hails, J. R. 1979, *Geomorphological Processes* (Dawson, London).

Destombes, J.-P., Shephard-Thorn, E. R., and Reddings, J. H. 1975, 'A buried valley system in the Straits of Dover', *Philosophical Transactions of the Royal Society of London*, A279, 243–56.

Dewey, J. F. 1982, 'Plate tectonics and the evolution of the British Isles', *Journal of the Geological Society of London*, 139, 371–412.

D'Olier, B. 1972, 'Subsidence and sea-level rise in the Thames Estuary', *Philosophical Transactions of the Royal Society of London*, A272, 121–30.

—— 1975, 'Some aspects of the Late Pleistocene–Holocene drainage of the River Thames in the eastern part of the London Basin', *Philosophical Transactions of the Royal Society of London*, A279, 269–77.

Dreghorn, W. 1967, *Geology Explained in the Severn Vale and Cotswolds* (David and Charles, Newton Abbot).

Durrance, E M., and Laming, D. J. C. (eds.) 1982, *The Geology of Devon* (University of Exeter, Exeter).

Dury, G. H. 1954, 'Contributions to a general theory of meandering valleys', *American Journal of Science*, 252, 193–224.

—— 1958, 'Tests on a general theory of misfit streams', *Transactions of the Institute of British Geographers*, 25, 105–18.

—— 1964, 'Principles of underfit streams', *US Geological Survey Professional Paper*, 452–A.

—— (ed.) 1966, *Essays in Geomorphology* (Heinemann, London).

—— 1970a, 'General theory of meandering valleys and underfit streams', in Dury 1970b, 264–77.

—— (ed.) 1970b, *Rivers and River Terraces* (Macmillan, London).

—— 1977, 'Peak flows, low flows and aspects of geomorphic dominance', in Gregory 1977, 61–74.

Edwards, R. A. 1976, 'Tertiary sediments and structure of the Bovey Basin, south Devon', *Proceedings of the Geologists' Association*, 87, 1–26.

Embleton, C., Brunsden, D., and Jones, D. K. C. (eds.) 1978, *Geomorphology: Present Problems and Future Prospects* (Oxford University Press, Oxford).

—— and Thornes, J. B. (eds.) 1979, *Process in Geomorphology* (Edward Arnold, London).

Everard, C. E. 1954, 'The Solent River: a geomorphological study', *Transactions of the Institute of British Geographers*, 20, 41–58.

Freshney, E. C. *et al.* 1982, 'A Tertiary basin at Dutson, near Launceston, Cornwall, England', *Proceedings of the Geologists' Association*, 93, 395–402.

Gallois, R. W. 1965, *The Wealden District* (HMSO, London).

Geologists' Association 1982, 'I. G. C. P. Project 61: Sea-level movements during the last deglacial hemicycle (about 15,000 years)', *Proceedings of the Geologists' Association*, 93, 1, 1–125.

George, T. N. 1966, 'Geomorphic evolution in Hebridean Scotland', *Scottish Journal of Geology*, 2, 1–34.

—— 1974 'Prologue to the geomorphology of Britain', in Brown and Waters 1974, 113–25.

Gerasimov, I. B. 1969, 'Degradation of the last European ice sheet', in Wright 1969, 72–8.

Gerrard, A. J. W. 1974, 'The geomorphological importance of jointing in the Dartmoor granite', in Brown and Waters 1974, 39–51.

Goudie, A. S. 1981, *The Human Impact* (Blackwell, Oxford).

—— 1983, *Environmental Change,* 2nd edn. (Oxford University Press, Oxford).

Gray, J. M., and Lowe, J. J. 1977a, 'The Scottish Lateglacial environment: A synthesis', in Gray and Lowe 1977b, 163–81.

——, —— (eds.) 1977b, *Studies in the Scottish Late Glacial Environment* (Pergamon Press, Oxford).

Green, C. P., and McGregor, D. F. M. 1980, 'Quaternary evolution of the River Thames', in Jones 1980b, 172–202.

Gregory, K. J. (ed.) 1977, *River Channel Changes* (Wiley, Chichester).

—— and Walling, D. E. (eds.) 1980, *Man and Environmental Processes* (Butterworth, London).

Groves, A. W. 1931, 'The unroofing of the Dartmoor granite and the distribution of its detritus in the sediments of southern England', *Quarterly Journal of the Geological Society of London*, 87, 62–96.

Hallam, A. 1971, 'Mesozoic geology and the opening of the North Atlantic', *Journal of Geology*, 79, 129–57.

—— 1973, *A Revolution in the Earth Sciences* (Oxford University Press, Oxford).

Hamblin, R. J. O. 1973, 'The Haldon gravels of south Devon', *Proceedings of the Geologists' Association*, 84, 459–76.

Hancock, J. M. 1975, 'The petrology of the Chalk', *Proceedings of the Geologists' Association*, 86, 499–535.

Hay, J. D., and Pitman, W. C. 1973, 'Lithospheric plate motion, sea-level changes, and climatic and ecological consequences', *Nature*, **246**, 18–22.

Herries Davies, G. L., and Stephens, N. 1978, *The Geomorphology of the British Isles: Ireland* (Methuen, London).

Hollis, G. E. (ed.) 1979, *Man's Impact on the Hydrological Cycle in the United Kingdom* (Geobooks, Norwich).

Hoskins, W. G. 1955/1970, *The Making of the English Landscape* (Hodder and Stoughton/ Penguin, London).

Hunt, C. B. 1959, 'Dating of mining camps with tin cans and bottles', *Geotimes*, 8–10 and 34.

Institute of Geological Sciences 1966, *Tectonic Map of Great Britain and Northern Ireland*, 1:1,584,000 scale.

Isaac, K. P. 1981, 'Tertiary weathering profiles in the plateau deposits of east Devon', *Proceedings of the Geologists' Association*, **92**, 152–68.

—— 1983, 'Tertiary lateritic weathering in Devon, England, and the Palaeogene continental environment of South-west England', *Proceedings of the Geologists' Association*, **94**, 105–14.

Johnston, R. J., and Doornkamp, J. C. (eds.) 1982, *The Changing Geography of the United Kingdom* (Methuen, London).

Jones, D. K. C. 1974, 'The influence of the Calabrian transgression on the drainage evolution of south-east England', in Brown and Waters 1974, 139–58.

—— 1980a, 'The Tertiary evolution of south-east England with special reference to the Weald', in Jones 1980b, 12–47.

—— (ed.) 1980b, *The Shaping of Southern England* (Academic Press, London).

—— 1981, *The Geomorphology of the British Isles: South-east and Southern England* (Methuen, London).

—— 1982, 'Human occupance and the physical environment', in Johnston and Doornkamp 1982, 327–61.

Kellaway, G. A., Redding, J. H., Shepard-Thorn, E. R., and Destombes, J.-P. 1975, 'The Quaternary history of the English Channel', *Philosophical Transactions of the Royal Society of London*, **A279**, 189–218.

Kent, P. E. 1949, 'A structure contour map of the surface of the buried pre-Permian rocks of England and Wales', *Proceedings of the Geologists' Association*, **60**, 87–104.

Kerney, M. P. 1965, 'Weichselian deposits in the Isle of Thanet, East Kent', *Proceedings of the Geologists' Association*, **76**, 269–74.

King, C. A. M. 1976, *The Geomorphology of the British Isles: Northern England* (Methuen, London).

Lake, R. D. 1975, 'The structure of the Weald—a review', *Proceedings of the Geologists' Association*, **86**, 549–57.

Lambert, J. H., Jennings, J. N., Smith, C. T., Green, C., and Hutchinson, J. N. 1970, *The Making of the Broads: A reconsideration of their origin in the light of new evidence*, Royal Geographical Society Research Series, No. 3.

Laming, D. J. C. 1982, in Durrance and Laming 1982, 148–78.

Laughton, A. S. 1972, 'The Southern Labrador Sea—a key to the Mesozoic and early Tertiary evolution of the North Atlantic', in National Science Foundation 1972.

Lewis, C. A. (ed.) 1970, *The Glaciation of Wales and Adjoining Regions* (Longman, London).

Linton, D. L. 1951a, 'Problems of Scottish scenery', *Scottish Geographical Magazine*, **67**, 65–85.

—— 1951b, 'Midland drainage: some considerations bearing on its origin', *Advancement of Science, London*, **7**, 449–56.

—— 1955, 'The problem of tors', *Geographical Journal*, **121**, 470–87.

—— 1956a, 'Geomorphology', in Linton 1956b, 24–43.

—— 1956b, *Sheffield and its Region* (British Association, Sheffield).

—— 1956c, 'The Sussex Rivers', *Geography*, **41**, 233–47.

—— 1957, 'Radiating valleys in glaciated lands', *Tijdschrift van het Koninklijke Nederland, Aardrijkskundig Genootschap*, **74**, 297–312.

—— 1964, 'Tertiary landscape evolution', in Watson and Sissons 1964.

Mackinder, H. J. 1902, *Britain and the British Seas* (Heinemann, London).

Montford, H. M. 1970, 'The terrestrial environment during Upper Cretaceous and Tertiary times', *Proceedings of the Geologists' Association*, **81**, 181–204.

Mitchell, G. F. 1977, 'Raised beaches and sea-levels', in Shotton 1977, 169–86.

National Science Foundation 1972, *Initial Reports of the Deep Sea Drilling Project*, Vol. 12 (National Science Foundation, Washington).

Naylor, D., and Mountenay, S. N. 1975, *Geology of the North-West European Continental Shelf*, Vol. 1 (Graham and Trotman, London).

Neale, J., and Flenley, J. (eds.) 1981, *The Quaternary in Britain* (Pergamon Press, Oxford).

Orme, A. R. 1964, 'The Geomorphology of southern Dartmoor', in Simmons 1964.

Oxburgh, E. R. 1974, 'The plain man's guide to plate tectonics', *Proceedings of the Geologists' Association*, **85**, 299–357.

Palmer, J., and Neilson, R. A. 1962, 'The origin of granite tors on Dartmoor, Devonshire', *Proceedings of the Yorkshire Geological Society*, **33**, 315–40.

—— and Radley, J, 1961, 'Gritstone tors of the English Pennines', *Zeitschrift für Geomorphologie*, **5**, 37–52.

Payton, C. E. (ed.) 1977, *Seismic Stratigraphy* (American Association of Petrological Geology).

Phillips, A. D. M., and Turton, B. J. (eds.) 1975, *Environment, Man and Economic Change*, (Longman, London).

Phillips, J. D., and Forsyth, D. 1972, 'Plate tectonics, palaeomagnetism and the opening of the Atlantic', *Bulletin of the Geological Society of America*, **83**, 1579–600.

Poole, E. G., and Whiteman, A. J. 1961, 'The glacial drifts of the southern part of the Shropshire–Cheshire basin', *Quarterly Journal of the Geological Society*, **117**, 91–130.

Prince, H. C. 1964, 'The origin of pits and depressions in Norfolk', *Geography*, **49**, 15–32.

Read, H. H., and Watson, J. 1975, *Introduction to Geology: Vol. 2, Earth History, Part II—Later Stages* (Macmillan, London).

Rice, R. J. 1977, *Fundamentals of Geomorphology* (Longman, London).

Richey, J. E. 1961, *Scotland: The Tertiary Volcanic Districts* (HMSO, London).

Roberts, D. G. 1974, 'Structural development of the British Isles: the continental margin, and the Rockall Plateau', in Burke and Drake 1974, 343–60.

Shakleton, N. J. *et al.* 1984, 'Oxygen isotope calibration of the onset of ice-rafting and history of glaciation in the North Atlantic region', *Nature*, 307, 620–3.

Shotton, F. W. 1953, 'The Pleistocene deposits of the area between Coventry, Rugby and Leamington and their bearing on the topographic development of the Midlands', *Philosophical Transactions of the Royal Society of London*, B237, 209–60.

—— (ed.) 1977, *British Quaternary Studies* (Oxford University Press, Oxford).

Simmons, I. G. (ed.) 1964, *Dartmoor Essays* (The Devonshire Association, Exeter).

Sissons, J. B. 1967, *The Evolution of Scotland's Scenery* (Oliver and Boyd, Edinburgh).

—— 1976, *The Geomorphology of the British Isles: Scotland* (Methuen, London).

—— 1979, 'The Loch Lomond Stadial in the British Isles', *Nature*, 280, 199–203.

Small, R. J. 1980, 'The Tertiary geomorphological evolution of south-east England: an alternative explanation', in Jones 1980b, 49–70.

Smith, W. E. 1961, 'The detrital mineralogy of the Cretaceous rocks of south-east Devon with particular reference to the Cenomanian', *Proceedings of the Geologists' Association*, 72, 303–32.

Sparks, B. W. 1971, *Rocks and Relief* (Longman, London).

Steers, J. A., 1962, *The Sea Coast* (Collins, London).

—— 1964, *The Coastline of England and Wales* (Cambridge University Press, Cambridge).

—— 1966, *The English Coast* (Fontana, London).

—— (ed.) 1971, *Applied Coastal Geomorphology* (Macmillan, London).

Stephens, N. 1970, 'The West Country and Southern Ireland', in Lewis 1970, 267–314.

—— and Synge, F. M. 1966, 'Pleistocene shorelines', in Dury 1966, 1–51.

Stoneley, R. 1982, 'The structural development of the Wessex Basin', *Journal of the Geological Society*, 139, 543–54.

Straw, A. 1979, 'The geomorphological significance of the Wolstonian glaciation of eastern England', *Transactions of the Institute of British Geographers*, NS 4, 540–9.

—— and Clayton, K. M. 1979, *The Geomorphology of the British Isles: Eastern and Central England* (Methuen, London).

Summerfield, M. A., and Goudie, A. S. 1980, 'The sarsens of southern England: their palaeoenvironmental interpretation with reference to other silcretes', in Jones 1980b, 71–100.

Tarling, D. H., and Tarling, H. P. 1971/1974, *Continental Drift* (Bell/Penguin, London).

Te Punga, M. T. 1957, 'Periglaciation in southern England', *Tijkschrift van bet Koninklijke Nederland. Aardrijkskundig Genootschap*, 64, 401–12.

Terris, A. P., and Bullerwell, W. 1965, 'Investigations into the underground structure of southern England', *Advancement of Science, London*, 22, 232–52.

Topley, W. 1875, *The Geology of the Weald,* Memoir of the Geological Survey UK.

Trueman, A. E. 1971, *Geology and Scenery in England and Wales* (Penguin, London).

Vail, P. R., *et al.* 1977, 'Seismic stratigraphy and global changes in sea level', in Payton 1977, 49–212.

——, Mitchum, R. M., and Thompson, S. 1977, 'Global cycles of relative changes of sea level', in Payton 1977, 83–97.

Valentin, H. 1971, 'Land loss at Holderness', in Steers 1971, 116–37.

Walsh, P. T., Boulter, M. C., Ijtaba, M., and Urbani, D. M. 1972, 'The preservation of the Neogene Brassington Formation of the southern Pennines and its bearing on the evolution of upland Britain', *Journal of Geological Science,* **128,** 519–59.

Warwick, G. T. 1964, 'Relief and structure', in Watson and Sissons 1964, 91–109.

Washburn, A. L. 1973, *Periglacial Processes and Environments* (Edward Arnold, London).

Waters, R. S. 1978, 'Periglacial geomorphology in Britain', in Embleton *et al.* 1978, 154–61.

Watson, J. W., and Sissons, J. B. 1964, *The British Isles* (Nelson, London).

Wilson, J. T. (ed.) 1972, *Continents Adrift* (Freeman, Oxford).

Wooldridge, S. W., and Linton, D. L. 1955, *Structure, Surface and Drainage in South-east England* (George Philip, London).

Worsley, P. 1975, 'An appraisal of the glacial Lake Lapworth concept', in Phillips and Turton 1975, 98–118.

—— 1977, 'Periglaciation', in Shotton 1977, 205–19.

Worssam, B. C. 1963, *The Geology of the Country around Maidstone,* Memoir of the Geological Survey UK.

Wright, A. E., and Moseley, F. (eds.) 1975, *Ice Ages: Ancient and Modern* (Seel House, Liverpool).

Wright, H. E. (ed.) 1969, *Quaternary Geology and Climate* (National Academy of Sciences, Washington).

Young, A. 1974, 'The rate of slope retreat', in Brown and Waters 1974, 65–78.

Zagwijn, W. H. 1975, 'Variations in climate as shown by pollen-analysis especially in the Lower Pleistocene of Europe', in Wright and Moseley 1975, 137–52.

Notes to Chapter 2 (pp. 48–67)

1. The literature is extensive, but for general works using the results of pollen analysis see Godwin 1956 and Pennington 1974, both with extensive bibliographies. An up-to-date account demonstrating the intimate relationship between pollen studies and archaeology is given by Simmons and Tooley 1981.
2. Evans 1972.
3. For example, Robinson 1981; Osborne 1982.
4. Bell 1982; Keeley 1982.
5. Fowler 1978, pp. 5–6; Cunliffe 1978.
6. Godwin 1956.
7. Godwin 1960.
8. Hibbert *et al.* 1971.
9. Godwin 1940.
10. The most important recent works on this theme include Jacobi *et al.* 1976; Simmons 1979; Simmons and Dimbleby 1974; Smith 1970; Jacobi 1978; all with full bibliographies.
11. Jacobi *et al.* 1976.

12. Simmons 1979.
13. Jacobi 1978.
14. Simmons and Dimbleby 1974.
15. Case 1976; Whittle 1978.
16. Evans 1972, pp. 242–79.
17. Waton 1982.
18. Pennington 1975.
19. The most up-to-date summary of the problem will be found in Simmons and Tooley 1981, Chapter 4. Detailed references are given there in full.
20. Dimbleby 1962.
21. Fox 1954; 1964.
22. Simmons 1969.
23. Clayden and Manley 1964.
24. Flemming 1978.
25. Wainwright *et al.* 1979, 1980; Smith *et al.* 1981.
26. Lamb 1982, p. 55.
27. Fox 1953.
28. Cunliffe 1978b, pp. 197–200.
29. Cunliffe 1976, pp. 135–45; 1978b.
30. Bell 1981.
31. Shotton 1978.
32. For example, Wainwright 1979; Davies 1981; Monk and Fasham 1980.
33. The excavations of the hill-fort of Danebury, directed by the writer, are shortly to be published (Cunliffe 1984). The analysis of the animal remains was undertaken by Annie Grant. The plant remains were studied by Martin Jones. Their full reports will be in Vol. II of the excavation report.
34. Cunliffe 1973.
35. The literature relevant to farming is very considerable. Applebaum 1972 gives a personal overview while White 1970 provides a general empire-wide survey of farming practices.
36. Riley 1980.
37. Wilson 1981.
38. Cunliffe 1963b.
39. Simmons 1979.
40. Simmons 1980.
41. Cleere 1976.
42. Cleere 1976.

References to Chapter 2 (pp. 48–67)

Applebaum, S. 1972, 'Roman Britain', in Finberg, H. P. R. (ed.), *The Agrarian History of England and Wales* (Cambridge University Press, Cambridge).

Bell, M. 1981, 'Valley sediments and environmental change', in Jones, M., and Dimbleby, G. (eds.) 1981, 75–91.

—— 1982, 'The effects of land-use and climate on valley sedimentation', in Harding, A. (ed.) 1982, 127–42.

——, and Limbrey, S. (eds.) 1982, *Archaeological Aspects of Woodland Ecology* (British Archaeological Reports, International Series 146, Oxford).

Case, H. J. 1976, 'Neolithic explanations', *Antiquity*, **43**, 176–86.

Clayden, B., and Manley, D. J. R. 1964, 'The soils of the Dartmoor granite', in Simmons, I. (ed.) 1964, 117–40.

Cleere, H. 1976, 'Some operating parameters for Roman ironworks', *Institute of Archaeology Bulletin*, **13**, 233–46.

Cunliffe, B. 1973a, 'Chalton, Hants: The evolution of a landscape', *Antiquaries Journal*, **53**, 173–90.

—— 1973b, chapters in Pugh, R. B. (ed.), *The Victoria History of Wiltshire* (Institute of Historical Research, University of London) 1:2, 439–67.

—— 1976, 'The origins of urbanisation in Britain', in Cunliffe, B., and Rowley, T. (eds.) 1976) 1976, 135–61.

—— 1978a, 'Settlement and population in the British Iron Age: some facts, figures and fantasies', in Cunliffe, B., and Rowley, T. (eds.) 1978, 3–24.

—— 1978b, *Iron Age Communities in Britain*, 2nd edn. (Routledge and Kegan Paul, London).

—— 1984, *Danebury: An Iron Age Hillfort in Hampshire. The excavations of 1969–78*, Vols. I and II (Council for British Archaeology Research Reports, 52, London).

——, and Rowley, T. (eds) 1976, *Oppida: The Beginnings of Urbanization in Barbarian Europe* (British Archaeological Reports Supplementary Series II, Oxford).

——, and Rowley, R. T. (eds.) 1978, *Lowland Iron Age Communities in Europe* (British Archaeological Reports International Series 48, Oxford).

Davies, S. M. 1981, 'Excavations at Old Down Farm, Andover. Part II: Prehistoric and Roman', *Proceedings of the Hampshire Field Club and Archaeological Society*, **37**, 81–163.

Dimbleby, G. W. 1962, *The Development of British Heathlands and their Soils* (Oxford Forestry Memorandum 23, Oxford).

Evans, J. G. 1972, *Land Snails in Archaeology* (Seminar Press, London).

——, Limbrey, S., and Cleere, H. (eds.) 1975, *The Effects of Man on the Landscape: The Highland Zone* (Council for British Archaeology Research Report II, London).

Flemming, A. 1978, 'The prehistoric landscape of Dartmoor Part I: South Dartmoor', *Proceedings of the Prehistoric Society*, **44**, 97–123.

Fowler, P. J. 1978, 'Lowland landscapes: culture, time and personality', in Limbrey, S., and Evans, J. G. (eds.) 1978, 1–12.

Fox, A. 1953, 'Hill-slope forts and related earthworks in South-West England and South Wales', *Archaeological Journal*, **109**, 1–22.

—— 1954, 'Celtic fields and farms on Dartmoor', *Proceedings of the Prehistoric Society*, **20**, 87–102.

—— 1964, South West England (Thames and Hudson, London).

Godwin, H. 1940, 'Studies in the post-glacial history of British vegetation. III. Fenland pollen diagrams. IV. Post-glacial changes of relative land- and sea-levels in the English Fenland', *Philosophical Transactions of the Royal Society of London* (B), **230**, 239–303.

—— 1956 (Second Edition 1975), *The History of the British Flora* (Cambridge University Press, Cambridge).

—— 1960, The Croonian Lecture, 'Radiocarbon dating and Quaternary history in Britain', *Proceedings of the Royal Society of London* (B), **153**, 287–320.

Harding, A. (ed.) 1982, *Climatic Change in Later Prehistory* (Edinburgh University Press).

Hibbert, A. *et al.* 1971, 'Radiocarbon dating of Flandrian pollen zones at Red Moss, Lancs', *Proceedings of the Royal Society of London* (B), **177**, 161–76.

Jacobi, R. M. 1978, 'Population and landscape in Mesolithic lowland Britain', in Limbrey, S., and Evans, J. G. (eds.) 1978, 75–85.

Jacobi, R., Tallis, J. H., and Mellars, P. 1976, 'The southern Pennine Mesolithic and the archaeological record', *Journal of Archaeological Science*, **3**, 307–20.

Jones, M., and Dimbleby, G. (eds.) 1981, *The Environment of Man in the Iron Age to the Anglo-Saxon Period* (British Archaeological Reports International Series 87, Oxford).

Keeley, H. 1982, 'Pedogenesis during the later prehistoric period in Britain', in Harding, A. (ed.) 1982, 114–26.

Lamb, H. H. 1982, 'Climate from 1000 BC to 1000 AD', in Jones, M., and Dimbleby, G. (eds.) 1981, 53–65.

Limbrey, S., and Evans, J. G. 1978, *The Effect of Man on the Landscape: The Lowland Zone* (Council for British Archaeology Research Report 21, London).

Monk, M. A., and Fasham, P. J. 1980, 'Carbonized plant remains from two Iron Age sites in central Hampshire', *Proceedings of the Prehistoric Society*, **46**, 321–44.

Osborne, P. J. 1982, 'Some British later prehistoric insect faunas and their climatic implications', in Harding, A. (ed.) 1982, 68–74.

Pennington, W. 1974, *The History of British Vegetation*, 2nd edn. (English Universities Press, London).

—— 1975, 'The effect of Neolithic man on the environment in north-west England: the use of absolute pollen diagrams', in Evans, J. G., Limbrey, S., and Cleere, H. (eds.) 1975, 74–86.

Riley, D. N. 1980, *Early Landscapes from the Air* (University of Sheffield).

Robinson, M. 1981, 'The Iron Age to Early Saxon environment of the Upper Thames Terraces', in Jones, M., and Dimbleby, G. (eds.) 1981, 251–86.

Shotton, F. W. 1978, 'Archaeological inferences from the study of alluvium in the lower Severn–Avon valleys', in Limbrey, S., and Evans, J. G. (eds.) 1978, 27–32.

Simmons, B. 1979, 'The Lincolnshire Car Dyke', *Britannia*, **10**, 183–96.

—— 1980, 'Iron Age and Roman coasts around the Wash', in Thompson, F. H. (ed.) 1980, 56–73.

Simmons, I. (ed.) 1964, *Dartmoor Essays* (Devonshire Association, Exeter).

—— 1969, 'Environment and Early Man on Dartmoor, Devon, England', *Proceedings of the Prehistoric Society*, **35**, 203–19.

—— 1979, 'Late Mesolithic societies and the environment of the uplands of England and Wales', *Institute of Archaeology Bulletin*, **16**, 111–29.

—— and Dimbleby, G. W. 1974, 'The possible role of ivy (*Hedera helix* L.) in the Mesolithic economy of Europe', *Journal of Archaeological Science*, **1**, 291–6.

—— and Tooley, M. (eds.) 1981, *The Environment in British Prehistory* (Duckworth, London).

Smith, A. G. 1970, 'The influence of Mesolithic and Neolithic man on British vegetation: a review', in Walker, D., and West, R. G. (eds.) 1970, 81–96.

Smith, K., Coppen, J., Wainwright, G. J., and Beckell, S. 1981, 'The Shaugh Moor Project: Third Report—settlement and environmental investigations', *Proceedings of the Prehistoric Society*, **47**, 205–73.

Thompson, F. H. 1980, *Archaeology and Coastal Change* (Society of Antiquaries Occasional Paper (NS) 1, London).

Wainwright, G. J. 1979, *Gussage All Saints: An Iron Age Settlement in Dorset* (HMSO, London).

——, Flemming, A., and Smith, K. 1979, 'The Shaugh Moor Project: First Report', *Proceedings of the Prehistoric Society*, **45**, 1–33.

—— and Smith, K. 1980, 'The Shaugh Moor Project: Second Report—the enclosure', *Proceedings of the Prehistoric Society*, **46**, 65–122.

Walker, D., and West., R. G. (eds.) 1970, *Studies in the Vegetational History of the British Isles* (Cambridge University Press, Cambridge).

Waton, P. V. 1982, 'Man's impact on the chalklands: some new pollen evidence', in Bell, M., and Limbrey, S. (eds.) 1982, 75–91.

White, K. D. 1970, *Roman Farming* (Thames and Hudson, London).

Whittle, A. W. R. 1978, 'Resources and population in the British Neolithic', *Antiquity*, **52**, 34–42.

Wilson, D. H. 1981, *Pollen analysis and settlement archaeology of the first millennium BC from North-East England* (M.Phil. dissertation, University of Oxford).

Notes to Chapter 3 (pp. 68–105)

1. Mellanby 1982.
2. Ministry of Agriculture, Fisheries, and Food, press notice, 19 May 1982.
3. Rackham 1976, p. 17.
4. Turner and Hodgson 1979; Rackham 1980, Ch. 8.
5. Rackham 1980, Ch. 9.
6. Rackham 1980, p. 7.
7. Rackham 1980, pp. 106–7.
8. Rackham 1980, p. 130.
9. British Library: Cott. Claud. C.xi, f.149. Gonville and Caius College, Cambridge: MS 485–9, f.149. Ely Diocesan Registry (in Cambridge University Library): G/3/27. My translation.
10. Rackham 1975, Ch. II.
11. Rackham 1967.
12. Rackham 1976, pp. 66–8.
13. Rackham 1976, pp. 80–3.
14. Rackham 1980, p. 141.
15. Rackham 1975, pp. 28–31.
16. Rackham 1972; Rackham 1980, pp. 145–9.
17. Rackham 1982a.
18. Rackham 1980, pp. 165–8.
19. Rackham 1980, p. 9; Rackham 1976, p. 174.

20. Rackham 1976, pp. 70–1, 115–17; Rackham 1980, p. 130.

21. Rackham 1976, pp. 118–19.

22. Rackham 1980, Chs. 13–24; Peterken 1981, Pt. 2.

23. Rackham 1980, pp. 239–41.

24. Rackham 1976, p. 29; Rackham 1975, pp. 90–2.

25. Peterken 1982, pp. 52–4.

26. Rackham 1980, Ch. 12.

27. Rackham 1976, pp. 115–16.

28. Rackham 1978.

29. Rackham 1976, pp. 162–4.

30. Peterken 1969; Rackham 1980, pp. 263–4.

31. Rackham 1980, pp. 241, 293; Rackham 1982b.

32. Rackham 1976, pp. 149, 172.

33. Rose and James 1974; Rackham 1980, pp. 199–200.

34. Rackham 1983.

35. Suffolk Record Office, Ipswich; HD/323/1.

36. Gonner 1911.

37. Tusser 1984, p. 139.

38. Brandon 1974.

39. Merton College (Oxford) Record 6/17.

40. Public Record Office: E134/1649 Easter/1.

41. Cambridge Record Office: 152/P11.

42. Moore 1897.

43. Ault 1972.

44. Merton College (Oxford) Record 5382.

45. Essex Record Office: D/DK M1.

46. Eland 1949, p. 51.

47. Turner, W. 1548, *The names of herbes*.

48. Emmison 1976.

49. Suffolk Record Office, Ipswich: T1/1/16.

50. Pollard, Hooper, and Moore 1974.

51. Willmot 1980.

52. Addington 1982.

53. Thorold Rogers 1866, Vol. 2, p. 594.

54. Davenport 1967.

55. Rackham 1976, pp. 130–2.

56. Rackham 1980, Ch. 9.

57. Birch 1885–93, No. 207.

58. Birch 1885–93, No. 816.

59. Birch 1885–93, No. 751.

60. Birch 1885–93, No. 1139.

61. Birch 1885–93, No. 594.

62. Drury and Rodwell 1980.

63. Columella, *De re rustica*, XI. iii. 3–5 (1st century BC); Palladius Rutilius, *Opus agriculturae*, I. 34 (4th century AD).

64. Siculus Flaccus, *De condicionibus agrorum* (1st century AD).
65. Julius Caesar, *De Bello Gallico*, II. xvii (51 BC).
66. Robinson 1978.
67. Powell 1963.
68. Royal Commission on Historical Monuments 1968, p. 203.
69. Rowley 1978.

References to Chapter 3 (pp. 68–105)

Addington, S. 1982, 'Landscape and settlements in South Norfolk', *Norfolk Archaeology*, **38**, 97–139.

Ault, W. O. 1972, *Open-field Farming in Medieval England* (Allen and Unwin, London).

Bell, M., and Limbrey, S. (eds.) 1982, *Archaeological Aspects of Woodland Ecology*, British Archaeological Reports International Series 146.

Birch, W. de G. 1885–93, *Cartularium Saxonicum*.

Bowen, M. C., and Fowler, P. J. (eds.) 1978, *Early Land Allotment* (Council for British Archaeology Research Report 48, London).

Brandon, P. 1974, *The Sussex Landscape* (Hodder and Stoughton, London).

Buckley, D. G. (ed.) 1980, *Archaeology in Essex to AD 1500* (Council for British Archaeology Research Report 34, London).

Corke, D. (ed.) 1978, 'Epping Forest—the natural aspect?' *Essex Naturalist*, NS 2.

Davenport, F. G. 1967, *The Economic Development of a Norfolk Manor 1086–1565* (Cass, London).

Drury, P. J., and Rodwell, W. 1980, 'Settlement in the later Iron Age and Roman periods', in Buckley 1980, 59–75.

Duffey, E. (ed.) 1967, *The Biotic Effects of Public Pressures on the Environment* (Natural Environment Research Council).

Eland, G. 1949, *At the Courts of Great Canfield, Essex* (Oxford University Press, Oxford).

Emmison, F. G. 1976, *Elizabethan Life: Home, work and land* (Essex Record Office, Chelmsford).

Gonner, E. C. K. 1911, *Common Land and Enclosure* (Macmillan, London).

McGrail, S. (ed.) 1982, *Woodworking Techniques before AD 1500*, British Archaeological Reports International Series 129.

Mellanby, K. 1982, 'Hedges—habitat or history', *Natural World*, **5**, 27–9.

Moore, S. A. 1897, *Cartularium monasterii Sancti Johannis Baptiste de Colecestria* (Chiswick, London).

Peterken, G. F. 1969, 'Development of vegetation in Staverton Park, Suffolk', *Field Studies*, **3**, 1–39.

—— 1982, *Woodland Conservation and Management* (Chapman and Hall, London).

Pollard, E., Hooper, M. D., and Moore, N. W. 1974, *Hedges* (Collins, London).

Powell, S. C. 1963, *Puritan Village: The formation of a New England town* (Middleton, Connecticut).

Rackham, O. 1967, 'The history and effects of coppicing as a woodland practice', in Duffey 1967, 82–92.

—— 1972, 'Grundle House: on the quantities of timber in certain East Anglian buildings in relation to local supplies', *Vernacular Architecture*, **3**, 3–8.

—— 1975, *Hayley Wood: Its history and ecology* (Cambridgeshire and Isle of Ely Naturalists' Trust).

—— 1976, *Trees and Woodland in the British Landscape* (Dent, London).

—— 1978, 'Archaeology and land-use history', in Corke 1978, 16–57.

—— 1980, *Ancient Woodland: Its history, vegetation and uses in England* (Edward Arnold, London).

—— 1982a, 'The growing and transport of timber and underwood', in McGrail 1982, 199–218.

—— 1982b, 'The Avon Gorge and Leigh Woods', in Bell and Limbrey 1982, 171–6.

—— 1983, 'Observations on the historical ecology of Boeotia', *Annual of the British School at Athens*, **78**, 291–351.

Robinson, M. 1978, 'The problem of hedges enclosing Roman and earlier fields', in Bowen and Fowler 1978, 155–9.

Thorold Rogers, J. E. 1866, *A History of Agriculture and Prices in England* (Oxford University Press, Oxford).

Rose, F., and James, P. W. 1974, 'The corticolous and lignicolous [lichen] species of the New Forest, Hampshire', *Lichenologist*, **6**, 1–72.

Rowley, T. 1978, *Villages in the Landscape* (Dent, London).

Royal Commission on Historical Monuments 1968, *West Cambridgeshire* (HMSO, London).

Turner, J., and Hodgson, J. 1979, 'Studies in the vegetational history of the northern Pennines', *Journal of Ecology*, **67**, 629–46.

Tusser, T. 1984, *Five Hundred Points of Good Husbandry* (Oxford University Press, Oxford). The first edition was published by R. Tottell in 1573.

Willmot, A. 1980, 'The woody species of hedges with special reference to age in Church Broughton Parish, Derbyshire,' *Journal of Ecology*, **68**, 269–86.

Notes to Chapter 4 (pp. 106–128)

1. For a bibliography see his Festschrift, Chalklin and Havinden 1974, pp. 342–50.
2. Hoskins 1946.
3. Hoskins 1949.
4. Hoskins 1954; Beresford 1943.
5. Published as Hoskins 1945 and Beresford 1946.
6. The surveyor's name was Captain Bayly, RE; for an example of his work see Beresford 1951a, Pl. 2.
7. Crawford 1925.
8. Beresford 1950.
9. But by 1930 he had transferred to the History Faculty to teach ecclesiastical history: personal

communication dated 23 June 1983 from Professor H. C. Darby who attended his classes in 1925.

10. Seebohm 1883, frontispiece.

11. Mowat 1888.

12. Fowler 1936.

13. Tawney 1912, p. 163.

14. Tawney 1912, p. 223; the map was redrawn and simplified with some inaccuracies. For the original see Beresford 1947, 2nd edn. 1971, pl. 9.

15. In a review of Derek Fraser (ed.), 'A History of Modern Leeds', in *Northern History*, 18 (1982), 285.

16. Royal Commission on Historical Monuments 1968, p. 113; for the text of the terrier of 1352 see Beresford 1948, p. 38; Saltmarsh's field excursions are mentioned in his *Times* obituary (27 September 1974).

17. Maps but not field-work were involved in Beresford 1941–2.

18. Giving rise to Beresford 1946a which had neither maps nor illustrations.

19. Orwin and Orwin 1938, endpieces.

20. Orwin and Orwin 1938, p. 11a.

21. As shown in Beresford and St Joseph 1958, 2nd edn. 1979 pp. 40–1.

22. Orwin and Orwin 1938, 3rd edn. 1954, p. 49 and fn.: 'of course it may be, but . . . '. Kerridge 1951 will be found in their updated bibliography but not Beresford.

23. Birmingham Reference Library MS 379051 (1752).

24. Birthplace Library, Stratford-upon-Avon, MSS (1778).

25. Northampton City Library MSS (1766); RCHM 1975, fig. 22.

26. As explored by Clark 1960 and Pocock 1968; for more remarkable speculations see McCloskey 1976.

27. Birthplace Library, Stratford-upon-Avon, Wheler MS 41: 'the first column from the left hand numbereth all the ridges from one side the furlong to the other according as they are used and belong to the several persons'. The 'persons' in the late sixteenth century included Hathaways.

28. Chambers 1930, pp. 141–9.

29. For developments in air photography at that time see Wilson 1982.

30. Beresford 1948.

31. 'I fully expect to be in Leicester on the 25th and have made a note of the date for our discussion of the ridge and furrow theory': Hoskins to Beresford, letter of 4 September 1947.

32. Oxford, All Souls College, Hovenden maps portfolio; another copy in Martin, no. 219, and a third 'formerly in the Bursary'. Beresford 1947, 2nd edn. 1971, Pl. 9 is a reproduction of the whole sheet.

33. Hoskins 1949b, pp. 77–126.

34. British Library MS Harley 6288; part of map reproduced in Beresford 1954a, Fig. iv.

35. For an account of these visits and papers at a seminar read by Hilton, Hoskins, and Beresford, see Steensberg 1982.

36. Clapham 1949, p. 197; modified by his editor at 80, fn.

37. M. W. Thompson in *Medieval Archaeology*, 15 (1971), p. 182 reviewing Beresford and Hurst 1971.

38. The initial stimulus was the writing of *The Lost Villages of England*, commissioned by

Margaret Stewart of the Lutterworth Press after reading my article, 'Tracing lost villages' in *Country Life,* 15 October 1948.

39. Beresford and Hurst 1971, pp. 34–40.
40. Beresford 1954b, Ch. 6.
41. Dyer 1982.
42. Hoskins 1953.
43. Gazetteer in Beresford and Hurst 1971, pp. 145–68.
44. Andrews and Milne 1979, Figs. 3 and 4.
45. See L. A. S. Butler in Hinton 1983 for work on churches in recent years.
46. West Whelpington was excavated by Professor M. G. Jarrett; Goltho and Barton Blount by Guy (no alias of M. W.) Beresford; Faxton by L. A. S. Butler; Upton by Professor Rahtz; and Hound Tor by Mrs Minter.
47. Mead 1954.
48. Thirsk 1964 and 1966.
49. Titow 1965.
50. In Rowley 1981, pp. 22–38.
51. Taylor 1974.
52. The metaphor is Professor W. R. Mead's.
53. Harvey 1978 and 1981; Sheppard 1976.
54. Beresford 1951a.
55. Baker and Butlin 1973.
56. Roberts 1982.
57. Taylor 1977; Hall in Rowley 1981, pp. 22–38.
58. In the actual lecture at Wolfson College I concluded by demonstrating briefly that there was life in the Old Guard yet, despite his recent defection to urban studies. I demonstrated the evidence for medieval peat workings over a wide area of Inclesmoor near Goole (North Yorkshire, once West Riding) on the basis of evidence to be published in P. D. A. Harvey, ed., *Local Maps* (Oxford University Press, forthcoming) from two plans drawn *c.*1407 which also include the earliest-known representation of a now deserted village, Haldenby.

References to Chapter 4 (pp. 106–128)

Allcroft, A. H. 1908, *Earthwork of England* (Macmillan, London).

Allison, K. J. 1976, *The East Riding of Yorkshire Landscape* (Hodder and Stoughton, London).

Andrews, D. D., and Milne, G. 1979, *Wharram, Domestic Settlement, 1: Areas 10 and 6* (Society for Medieval Archaeology Monograph Series: No. 8, London).

Baker, A. R. H., and Butlin, R. A. (eds.) 1973, *Studies of Field Systems in the British Isles* (Cambridge University Press, Cambridge).

—— and Harley, J. B. (eds.) 1973, *Man Made the Land* (David and Charles, Newton Abbot).

Beresford, M. W. 1941–2, 'The economic individualism [*recte* individuality] of Sutton Coldfield', *Transactions of the Birmingham Archaeological Society,* **64**, 101–8.

—— 1943, 'Lot acres', *Economic History Review,* **13**, 74–9.

—— 1946a, 'Commissioners of Enclosure', *Economic History Review,* **16**, 130–42.

—— 1946b, 'Deserted villages of Warwickshire', *Transactions of the Birmingham Archaeological Society,* **65,** 49–106.

—— 1947, *The Hedge and the Plough* (Public Library, Rugby).

—— 1948, 'Ridge and furrow and the open fields', *Economic History Review,* 2nd series 1,34–46.

—— 1950, 'Maps and the medieval landscape', *Antiquity,* **24,** 114–18.

—— 1951a, 'Glebe terriers, and open field Yorkshire', *Yorkshire Archaeological Journal,* 37, 325–68.

—— 1951b, 'The lost villages of Medieval England', *Geographical Journal,* 117, 129–49.

—— 1951c, 'The lost villages of Yorkshire, Part 1, *Yorkshire Archaeological Journal,* 37, 474–91.

—— 1952, 'The lost villages of Yorkshire, Part 2, *Yorkshire Archaeological Journal,* 38, 44–70.

—— 1953, 'The lost villages of Yorkshire, Part 3, *Yorkshire Archaeological Journal,* 38, 215–40.

—— 1954a, 'The lost villages of Yorkshire, Part 4, *Yorkshire Archaeological Journal,* 38, 280–310.

—— 1954b, *The Lost Villages of England* (Lutterworth Press, London; paperback ed. 1983, Alan Sutton, Gloucester).

—— 1957, *History on the Ground* (Lutterworth Press, London; paperback ed. 1984, Alan Sutton, Gloucester).

——, and Hurst, J. G. (eds.) 1971, *Deserted Medieval Villages: Studies* (Lutterworth Press, London).

——, and St Joseph, J. K. S. 1958, *Medieval England: An Aerial Survey* 2nd edn. 1979, (Cambridge University Press, Cambridge).

Cantor, L. M. (ed.) 1982, *The English Medieval Landscape* (Croom Helm, London).

Chalklin, C., and Havinden, M. (eds.) 1974, *Rural Change and Urban Growth: Essays in honour of W. G. Hoskins* (Longman, London).

Chambers, E. K. 1930, *William Shakespeare* (Clarendon Press, Oxford).

Clark (later Spufford), H. M. 1960, 'Selion size and soil type', *Agricultural History Review,* **8,** 91–8.

Clapham, J. H. 1949, *A Concise Economic History of Britain to 1750* (Cambridge University Press, Cambridge).

Crawford, O. G. S. 1925, 'Air photograph of Gainstrop (*sic*), Lincs.', *Antiquaries Journal,* **5,** 432–4.

——, and Keiller, A. 1928, *Wessex from the Air* (Clarendon Press, Oxford).

Darby, H. C. 1936, *An Historical Geography of England* (Cambridge University Press, Cambridge).

Dyer, C. 1982, 'Deserted medieval villages in the West Midlands', *Economic History Review,* 2nd series, **31,** 19–34.

Fowler, G. H. 1936, *Four pre-enclosure Village Maps,* Bedfordshire Historical Record Society, Quarto Memoirs, 2.

Harvey, M. 1978, *The Morphological and Tenurial Structure of a Yorkshire Township,* Queen Mary College Occasional Papers in Geography, 13.

Hinton, D. (ed.) 1983, *Twenty-five Years of Medieval Archaeology* (Department of Prehistory and Archaeology, University of Sheffield, Sheffield)

Hoskins, W. G. 1943, 'The reclamation of waste in Devon 1550–1800', *Economic History Review,* 1st series, **13,** 80–92.

—— 1945, 'The deserted villages of Leicestershire', **22,** *Transactions of the Leicestershire Archaeological Society,* **22,** 241–65.

—— 1946, *The Heritage of Leicestershire* (Backus, Leicester).

—— 1949a, *Midland England* (Batsford, London).

—— (ed.) 1949b, *Studies in Leicestershire Agrarian History* (Leicestershire Archaeological Society, Leicester).

—— 1953, 'The re-building of rural England', *Past and Present,* **4,** 44–59.

—— 1955/1970, *The Making of the English Landscape* (Hodder and Stoughton/Penguin, London).

—— 1956, 'Seven deserted village sites in Leicestershire'. *Transactions of the Leicestershire Archaeological Society,* **32,** 38–53.

—— 1973, *English Landscapes* (British Broadcasting Corporation, London).

Kerridge, E. 1951, 'Ridge and furrow and agrarian history', *Economic History Review,* 2nd series **4,** 14–36.

McCloskey, D. 1976, 'English open fields as behaviour towards risk', in Uselding, P. (ed.), *Research in Economic History,* **1,** 154–62.

Maitland, F. W. 1898, *Township and Borough* (Cambridge University Press, Cambridge).

Mead, W. R. 1954, 'Ridge and furrow in Buckinghamshire', *Geographical Journal,* **120,** 34–42.

Meitzen, P. A. 1895, *Wanderung, Anbau und Agrarrecht der Völker Europas nordlich der Alpen* (W. Herz, Berlin).

Mowat, J. L. G. 1888, *Sixteen Old Maps of Oxfordshire* (Clarendon Press, Oxford).

Muir, R. 1982, *The Lost Villages of Britain* (Michael Joseph, London).

Orwin, C. S. and C. S. 1938, *The Open Fields,* 3rd edn. 1967 with Introduction by J. Thirsk (Oxford University Press, Oxford).

Palliser, D. M. 1976, *The Staffordshire Landscape* (Hodder and Stoughton, London).

Pocock, E. A. 1968, 'The first fields in an Oxfordshire parish', *Agricultural History Review,* **16,** 85–100.

Postan, M. M. 1972, *The Medieval Economy and Society* (Weidenfeld and Nicolson, London).

Power, E. E. 1924, *Medieval People* (Methuen, London).

Roberts, B. K. 1982, *Village Plans* (Shire Publications, Princes Risborough).

Rowley, T. (ed.) 1981, *The Origins of Open Field Agriculture* (Croom Helm, London).

——, and Wood, J. 1982, *Deserted Villages* (Shire Publications, Princes Risborough).

Royal Commission on Historical Monuments 1968, *An Inventory of Archaeological Sites in Cambridgeshire,* Vol. 1, (RCHM, London).

—— 1975, *An inventory of Archaeological Sites in N.E. Northamptonshire* (RCHM, London).

Sawyer, P. H. (ed.) 1976, *Medieval Settlement: Continuity and Change* (Edward Arnold, London).

Seebohm, F. 1883, *The English Village Community* (Longman, London).

Sheppard, J. A. 1976, 'Medieval village planning in Northern England', *Journal of Historical Geography,* **2**, 3–20.

Spufford, M. H., *see* Clark.

Steane, J. M. 1974, *The Northamptonshire Landscape* (Hodder and Stoughton, London).

Steensberg, A. 1982, 'The development of "Open Area" excavation and its introduction into medieval archaeology', *Medieval Village Research Group Thirtieth Annual Report 1982,* 27–30.

Tawney, R. H. 1912, *The Agrarian Problem in the Sixteenth Century* (Longman, London).

Taylor, C. C. 1973, *The Cambridgeshire Landscape* (Hodder and Stoughton, London).

—— 1974, *Fieldwork in Medieval Archaeology* (Batsford, London).

—— 1977, 'Polyfocal settlement and the English village', *Medieval Archaeology,* **21**, 189–93.

—— 1983, *Village and Farmstead* (George Philip, London).

Thirsk, J. 1964, 'The common fields', *Past and Present,* **29**, 3–25.

—— 1966, 'The origins of the common fields', *Past and Present,* **33**, 142–7.

Titow, J. 1965, 'Medieval England and the open field system', *Past and Present,* **32**, 86–102.

Wilson, D. R. 1982, *Air Photo Interpretation for Archaeologists* (Batsford, London).

Notes to Chapter 5 (pp. 129–147)

1. For garlic, see the *Guardian,* 7 November 1979; for rabbits, *Oxford Mail,* 3 March 1981; for goats, the *Observer,* 1 August 1982; for ewes, *Sunday Telegraph,* 21 June 1981; for rapeseed, Godfrey Smith, 'Alarm clocks and milking as usual', *Sunday Times,* 18 May 1980.

2. Thirsk 1978, p. 67.

3. Thirsk 1978, pp. 70–1; Smith and Baker 1983, pp. 90, 106, 109.

4. Public Record Office (PRO), E134, 2 Car.I, Easter 19; Joint Record Office, Lichfield, Probate Inventory, 1698 R, Thomas Renshawe of Whitwell, yeoman; Worlidge 1687, p. 45; Malcolm Falkus, 'Lighting in the dark ages of English economic history: town streets before the Industrial Revolution', in Coleman and John 1976, p. 260.

5. Brace 1960, p. 28; Hugh Clayton, 'Future for oilseed rape is assured', *The Times,* 22 May 1978; Martin Wright, 'Somerset firm could help save the whales', *Guardian,* 3 January 1983.

6. Thirsk and Cooper 1972, p. 19; Hampshire Record Office (Winchester), J. L. Jervoise, Herriard Collection of Sherfield MSS, 44 M 69/XXXIII, *passim.* I am grateful to Mr Jervoise for permission to consult and quote from these papers; Larking, 1862, p. 154.

7. Sherfield MSS, 44 M 69/XXXIII; Blith 1653, p. 239; *Calendar of State Papers Domestic (CSPD),* 1636–7, p. 211; *CSPD,* 1637, p. 47; *CSPD,* 1635–6, pp. 292, 429, 552; PRO, SP 29/7, no. 136.

8. Blith 1653; Mortimer 1707, pp. 123–4; Miller 1758, pp. vii–viii.

9. PRO, E134, 31 & 32 Chas. II, Hil.6; *Impartial Considerations on the Cultivation of Madder in England* (1765), p. 1: I wish to thank Dr Dennis Baker for this reference; Jacob 1774, pp. 98–9; Hudson and Luckhurst 1954, pp. 59, 89–90: I owe this reference to the kindness of Dr Juanita Burnby.

10. Thirsk 1985, Vol. 5, Chapter 16.

11. Thirsk 1978, pp. 28–30, 98; Sherfield MSS, 44 M 69 XXX/76; 'The end of woad', *Sunday Telegraph,* 28 January 1979.
12. Smith 1956, pp. 257–60. I shall describe the geographical distribution of woad in a forthcoming book, *Alternative Agriculture in the Seventeenth Century.*
13. Thirsk 1978, pp. 29–30, 4–5.
14. See, for example, the parish registers of Bletchingdon, Oxfordshire, 3 October 1611, and Misterton, Leicestershire, 1662 and 1665. I wish to thank Dr D. M. Barratt and Dr John Goodacre for these references.
15. Tawney and Power 1924, Vol. 1, pp. 327, 330; Googe 1577, Epistle to the Reader; Plot 1686, p. 380 (call mark of Bodleian Library copy—Gough Stafford 1).
16. Googe 1577; Cartwright 1889, p. 166; Harvey 1972, pp. 90, 108; Jack Sutherland, 'Ripening grapes at Pilton', *Morning Star,* 6 September 1975; obituary of Mrs Margaret Gore-Browne, *The Times,* 26 August 1976; English Wine Centre 1981, p. 8.
17. Chadwick 1960, p. 7
18. This argument was substantiated in my Neale Lecture at University College, London, December 1982, to be published in Thirsk, *Alternative Agriculture.*
19. Henisch 1976, pp. 107–11; Dyer 1983, 'English diet in the later Middle Ages', in Aston *et al.* 1983, p. 208.
20. Heresbach's book was translated into English by Barnaby Googe and published as *Four Bookes of Husbandrie* (London, 1577). For these passages, see Googe 1577, pp. 48–48v.
21. Rye 1865, pp. 109–10.
22. Webber 1968, pp. 31–3.
23. Beutler 1973, p. 1287; Gairdner, 1882, Vol. 6, p. 72.
24. Googe 1577, p. 63; Moffet 1746, p. xii; OED under artichoke; Byrne 1981, Vol. 2, p. 203; Everitt 1966, pp. 32–3; Worlidge 1677, p. 186.
25. Thirsk 1985, Vol. 5, Chapters 18, 19.
26. Folkingham 1610, p. 42; Thirsk 1985. Vol. 5, Chapters 18, 19, 11; Coles 1657, p. 356; Thirsk and Cooper 1972, p. 179.
27. Coles 1657, Part 2, p. 33; Forster 1664, pp. 2–3, 4–7.
28. Gardiner of Shrewsbury 1603, *passim;* Thirsk 1985, Vol. 5, Chapter 19.
29. Thirsk 1985, Vol. 5, Chapter 19.
30. [Braddon] 1723, p. xiii.
31. *The Times,* 6 January 1983, from Lawrence D. Hills, Director of the Henry Doubleday Research Association.
32. Plucknett and Beemer 1981, *passim.*

References to Chapter 5 (pp. 129–147)

Aston, T. H., *et al.* (eds.) 1983, *Social Relations and Ideas* (Cambridge University Press, Cambridge).

Beutler, C. 1973, 'Un chapitre de la sensibilité collective: la littérature agricole en Europe continentale du XVIe siècle', *Annales Economies Sociétés, Civilisations,* **28**.

Blith, Walter 1653, *The English Improver Improved* (London).

Brace, H. W. 1960, *History of Seed Crushing in Great Britain* (Land Books Ltd., London).

[Braddon, Lawrence] 1723, *To Pay Old Debts without New Taxes . . .* (London).

Byrne, Muriel St Clare 1981, *The Lisle Letters*, Vol. 2 (University of Chicago Press).

Cartwright, J. J. (ed.) 1889, *The Travels through England of Dr Richard Pococke*, Vol. 2, Camden Society, NS 44.

Chadwick, Paxton 1960, *Flowers of the Cornfield* (Cassell, London).

Coleman, D. C., and John, A. H. (eds.) 1976, *Trade, Government and Economy in Pre-Industrial England* (Weidenfeld and Nicolson, London).

Coles, W. 1657, *Adam in Eden* (London).

Dyer, C. 1983, 'English diet in the later Middle Ages', in Aston 1983.

English Wine Centre 1981, *English Wine Then and Now* (Alfriston, E. Sussex).

Everitt, A. M. 1966, *The Community of Kent and the Great Rebellion, 1640–60* (Leicester University Press, Leicester).

Folkingham, W. 1610, *Feudigraphia* (London).

Forster, J. 1664, *England's Happiness Increased* (London).

Gairdner, J. 1882, *Letters and Papers of Henry VIII*, Vol. 6: *1533* (London).

Gardiner of Shrewsbury, Richard 1603, *Profitable Instructions for the Manuring, Sowing and Planting of Kitchin Gardens . . .* (London).

Googe, Barnaby 1577, *Four Bookes of Husbandrie* (London).

Harvey, John 1972, *Early Gardening Catalogues* (Phillimore, London).

Henisch, Bridget A. 1976, *Fast and Feast: Food in medieval society* (Pennsylvania State University Press).

Hudson, D., and Luckhurst, K. W. 1954, *The Royal Society of Arts, 1754–1954* (John Murray, London).

Impartial Considerations on the Cultivation of Madder in England 1765 (London).

Jacob, E. 1774, *The History of the Town and Port of Faversham in the County of Kent* (London).

Larking, L. B. (ed). 1862, *Proceedings principally in the County of Kent . . .*, Camden Society, OS 80.

Miller, Philip 1758, *The Method of Cultivating Madder as it is now practised by the Dutch in Zealand* (London).

Moffet, Thomas 1746, *Health's Improvement . . .*, ed. Oldys (London).

Mortimer, J. 1707, *The Whole Art of Husbandry* (London).

Plot, R. 1686, *Natural History of Staffordshire* (Oxford).

Plucknett, Donald L., and Beemer, Halsey L. (eds.) 1981, *Vegetable Farming Systems in China*, Westview Special Studies in Agricultural Science and Policy (Boulder, Colorado).

Rye, W. B. 1865, *England as seen by Foreigners in the Days of Elizabeth and James I* (London).

Smith, A. H. 1956, *English Place-Name Elements*, English Place-Name Society, **26**, Part 2. (Cambridge University Press, Cambridge).

Smith, A. Hassell and Barker, Gillian M. 1983. The Papers of Nathaniel Bacon of Stiffkey, Vol. II, 1578–85 (Centre of East Anglian Studies, University of East Anglia).

Tawney, R. H., and Power, Eileen, 1924, *Tudor Economic Documents*, Vol. 1 (London).

Thirsk, Joan, and Cooper, J. P. (eds.) 1972, *Seventeenth-Century Economic Documents* (Clarendon Press, Oxford).

—— 1978, *Economic Policy and Projects: The development of a consumer society in early modern England* (Clarendon Press, Oxford).

—— (ed.) 1985, *The Agrarian History of England and Wales,* Vol. 5: *1640–1750* (Cambridge University Press, Cambridge).

—— (forthcoming), *Alternative Agriculture in the Seventeenth Century.*

Webber, R. 1968, *The Early Horticulturalists* (David and Charles, Newton Abbot).

Worlidge, J. 1677. *Systema Horticulturae* (London).

—— 1687, *Systema Agriculturae,* 4th edn. (London).

Notes to Chapter 6 (pp. 148–167)

1. Illustrations of this theme go back to the classic works of C. Lyell (*Principles of Geology,* 1830–3, and *Elements of Geology,* 1838) and A. Geikie (*The Scenery of Scotland,* 1865). These works ran through many editions.
2. Core V28–239, at 3° 15′ N 159° 11′ E, where the ocean is about 3,500 metres deep, analysed by Dr N. J. Shackleton of the Palaeotemperatures Laboratory, University of Cambridge.
3. The methods of derivation of the temperatures displayed in Figures 6.3 and 6.5 have been described in my books *Climate: Present, past and future* (1972/1977) and *Climate, History and the Modern World* (1982).
4. See Lamb 1982.
5. Cf. Manley 1949.
6. Lamb 1982 and Lamb 1977.
7. Köppen 1923.
8. Features such as those mentioned in this paragraph are well illustrated in Sparks and West 1972.
9. Godwin 1956, p. 203.
10. Fraser 1970.
11. Scott (ed.) 1970.
12. Thackeray on George I in *The Four Georges* (1860).
13. Lamb and Weiss 1979.
14. These threats to the stability of our climate are reviewed in Lamb 1982.

References to Chapter 6 (pp. 148–167)

Fraser, Antonia 1970, *Mary Queen of Scots* (Weidenfeld and Nicholson, London).

Geikie, A. 1865, *The Scenery of Scotland* (Macmillan, London).

Godwin, H. 1956 (Second Edition 1975), *History of the British Flora* (Cambridge University Press, Cambridge).

Köppen, W. 1923, *Die Klimate der Erde* (Berlin/Leipzig); 2nd edn. 1931, entitled *Grundriss der Klimakunde* (Berlin).

Lamb, H. H. 1972/1977, *Climate, Present, past and future,* 2 vols. (Methuen, London).

—— 1982, *Climate, History and the Modern World* (Methuen, London).

——, and Weiss, I. 1979, 'On recent changes of the wind and wave regime in the North Sea and the outlook', *Fachliche Mitteilungen,* **194,** Amt für Wehrgeophysik (Traben-Trarbach).

Lyell, C. 1830–3, *Principles of Geology,* 3 vols. (London).

—— 1838, *Elements of Geology* (London).

Manley, Gordon 1949, 'The snowline in Britain', *Geografiska Annaler* (Stockholm), **36**, 179–93.

Scott, T. (ed.) 1970, *The Penguin Book of Scottish Verse* (Penguin Books, London).

Sparks, B. W., and West, R. G. 1972, *The Ice Age in Britain* (Methuen, London).

Thackeray, W. M. 1860, *The Four Georges* (London).

Notes to Chapter 7 (pp. 168–187)

1. William Cowper, *The Task,* Book 1: 'The Sofa' (1785), line 749.
2. Boswell's *Life of Johnson,* 20 Sept. 1777; Alexander Pope, 'A Farewell to London', 1.
3. D. H. Lawrence, *Nottingham and the Mining Country* (1929), in Clayre (ed.) 1977, p. 389.
4. Cited in Trinder 1982, p. 207.
5. The usage may be seen in Trinder 1982 and in Whitehand 1981.
6. Temple Thurston, *The Flower of Gloucester* (1911), quoted in Trinder 1982, p. 247.
7. H. G. Wells, *The New Machiavelli* (1911; Penguin edn. 1946), pp. 33–9.
8. It is impossible to offer exact figures for the increase in square footage occupied by the 'average' working-class house, even if such a thing existed. But the general tendency to more spacious houses and house plots is well attested: see, for example, S. M. Gaskell, 'Housing and the Lower Middle Class, 1870–1914', in Crossick (ed.) 1977, pp. 159–83; Muthesius 1982, especially Chapter 6.
9. The concept of an 'average' density of houses per acre is of uncertain value, for any date, since a 'house' is of extremely variable size. In any case, figures for densities are hard to come by, except by the indirect route, from census returns, of population densities per acre and average size of household (which itself might, or might not, be occupying a separate dwelling or tenement; a separate dwelling or tenement again might, or might not, be the same thing as a 'house', which is usually understood to be a structurally separate building). Nevertheless, indications of housing densities at different periods may be found, for example, in Corfield 1982, Chapter 10; Burnett 1978, pp. 175–6, 204, 219; and Thompson (ed.) 1982, pp. 220, 231–3, 247.
10. J. Guest (ed.), *The Best of Betjeman* (1978), 'The Metropolitan Railway', pp. 93–4; 'Slough', p. 24.
11. Gatrell 1977, p. 108, and Deane, 1965, p. 86, provide some of the data for this calculation.
12. Contemporary statisticians, economists, and officials were interested in recording people, production, houses, rooms, and administrative areas, not land use. Historians have followed the records, and their own concerns with the history of capital and labour, and have not been much interested in such matters as the surface area requirements of business enterprises.
13. These figures are most readily accessible in Harrison *et al.* 1977, and the following discussion is dependent on their data, particularly in Appendix I.4 and Appendix II.
14. Ernest de Selincourt, *Wordsworth's Guide to the Lakes* (1906), pp. 146–66.
15. Marshall and Walton 1981, Chapter 8; Bass MS, Bass Brewery Museum, Burton-on-Trent, works' outings programmes.
16. Statistics of industrial power capacity and utilization are in Musson 1976, pp. 415–39, and Kanefsky 1979, pp. 360–75. The estimate for 1850 in the text assumes 141,000 h.p. from

water power (26,000 in textiles, and 115,000 in other industries in 1870 [Kanefsky] assumed to be already in place in 1850) and 300,000 h.p. from steam power [Musson, p. 435].

17. The 1951 Census (*General Tables,* 1956, Table 3) recorded figures for the acreage and total population of both the LCC area (74,850 acres, 30,290 hectares) and the Greater London conurbation (461,824 acres, 186,890 hectares), which showed that in 1901 69 per cent of the population of Greater London were in the LCC part, and in 1951, 40 per cent. No retrospective estimates of the 'real' area of Greater London for pre-1951 census years were made, and figures of Greater London populations for the earlier years merely related to the population living in all the surrounding areas which had subsequently, by 1951, become part of the census concept of Greater London. The relationship between the two areas in 1951, therefore, bears no known connection with the relationship they had in 1901. The statement in the text, implying that 31 per cent of the 1901 population of Greater London, 2 million people, occupied about 75,000 acres surrounding the LCC area, is no more than a guess.

18. 1951 Census, England and Wales, *General Report* (1958), pp. 60, 83–4, and *General Tables* (1956), Table 3.

19. Swenarton 1981, p. 13.

20. 1901 Census, *Summary Tables* (1903), Table X. Anthony Sutcliffe (ed.) 1974, Introduction, p. 13, gives a hypothetical example of a density of 126 houses per acre in back-to-back development, allowing 'ample' space for access and refuse disposal.

21. The 22 largest county boroughs of the text are, more precisely, the 22 largest towns listed in the 1841 Census, *Enumeration Abstract,* Part I (1843), Table of the Comparative Population of the Chief Towns in England and Scotland, 1801–41, Preface, p. 10; and the same 22 towns, which had by then all become county boroughs (plus the LCC), extracted from the 1901 Census, *Summary Tables* (1903), Table XI. The 22 largest of 1841 were not exactly the same as the 22 largest of 1901, and notably Bath was in the first list but would have been dropped from any new list drawn up on 1901 figures, while Rochdale, Stoke-on-Trent, and Ashton-under-Lyne, although included in the 1841 Census list on grounds of population size, were excluded from the 22 of the text because no information was provided on their surface areas. The 6 largest Scottish towns, listed in the 1841 Census Table, are excluded from the group in the text because no information was given on their surface areas either. The administrative areas of the 22 towns of the text were:

  1841: 149,880 acres (60,653 hectares); population 3.6 million;
  1901: 294,261 acres (119,080 hectares); population 9.9 million.

22. Girouard 1979, pp. 299, 405, 409, 411, 420, 425.

23. Aslet 1982, pp. 317, 320, 323; *Country Life,* 31, 23 March 1912, p. 430 for Ewelme Down, described as a product of the motor car, since the magnificent site was previously inaccessible.

24. Howkins 1973, the best account of the grubbing-up of Wychwood is in *Select Committee on Crown Forests* (Parliamentary Papers, 1854, X), q.738, and Cluttons 1950, pp. 45–6.

25. Harrison *et al.* 1977, Appendix I.2.

26. HMSO 1968, pp. 5–11.

27. *The Best of Betjeman,* 'Slough', p. 25.

References to Chapter 7 (pp. 168–187)

Aslet, Clive 1982, *The Last Country Houses* (Yale University Press, New Haven & London).

Burnett, John 1978, *A Social History of Housing, 1815–1970* (David and Charles, Newton Abbot).

Clayre, Alasdair (ed.) 1977, *Nature and Industrialization* (Oxford University Press, Oxford).

Cluttons, 1950, *Some Historical Notes put together in 1948* (privately published, London).

Corfield, P. J. 1982, *The Impact of English Towns, 1700–1800* (Oxford University Press, Oxford).

Crossick, Geoffrey (ed.) 1977, *The Lower Middle Class in Britain, 1870–1914* (Croom Helm, London).

Deane, Phyllis 1965, *The First Industrial Revolution* (Cambridge University Press, Cambridge).

Gaskell, S. M. 1977, 'Housing and the Lower Middle Class, 1870–1914', in Crossick (ed.) 1977.

Gatrell, V. A. C. 1977, 'Labour, power, and the size of firms in Lancashire cotton in the second quarter of the nineteenth century', *Economic History Review,* 2nd series, 30, 108.

Girouard, Mark 1979, *The Victorian Country House* (Yale University Press, New Haven and London).

Harrison, Alan, Tranter, R. B., and Gibbs, R. S. 1977, *Landownership by Public and Semi-Public Institutions in the UK* (Reading University Press, Reading).

HMSO 1968, *A Century of Agricultural Statistics: Great Britain, 1866–1966* (HMSO, London).

Howkins, A. 1973, *Whitsun in Nineteenth-Century Oxford* (History Workshop, Oxford).

Kanefsky, John W. 1979, 'Motive power in British industry and the accuracy of the 1870 Factory Return', *Economic History Review,* 2nd series, 32, 360–75.

Marshall, J. D., and Walton, John K. 1981, *The Lake Counties from 1830 to the Mid-Twentieth Century* (Manchester University Press, Manchester).

Musson, A. E. 1976, 'Industrial motive power in the United Kingdom, 1800–70', *Economic History Review,* 2nd series, 29, 415–39.

Muthesius, Stefan 1982, *The English Terraced House* (Yale University Press, New Haven & London).

Sutcliffe, Anthony (ed.) 1974, *Multi-Storey Living* (Croom Helm, London).

Swenarton, Mark 1981, *Homes Fit for Heroes* (Heinemann, London).

Thompson, F. M. L. (ed.) 1982, *The Rise of Suburbia* (Leicester University Press, Leicester).

Trinder, Barrie 1982, *The Making of the Industrial Landscape* (J. M. Dent, London).

Whitehand, J. W. R. (ed.) 1981, *The Urban Landscape, Historical Development and Management* (Academic Press, London).

Index

Numbers printed in bold type indicate illustrations and their inscriptions.

afforestation, 158, 166, 186–7, 192, 193, 194
agriculture, 59, 70, 104, 129, 187, 201; agribusiness, 186, 190; alternative, 130–2; and landscape, 55, 68, 186, 191, 195; Continental influences, 132–7 *passim*, 142; effects of enclosure, 106; of mechanization, 189, 190; of Roman occupation, 63–5, 104–5; of temperature changes, 155; open-field system, 70, 89, 92, 100, 123–6, 125; self-image, 190; *see also* farming
air photography, 60, 61, 64, 106, 110, 117, 121
Alpine Mountain system, 21–2, 33, 47; upper tree-line, 151, 154
animals: and browse plants, 51–2, 53, 62; husbandry, 57, 58, 62, 83, 119, 122; cattle, 52, 53, 57, 62; deer, 51, 52, 73, 83; pig, 51, 62, 63, 83; sheep, 52, 53, 62–3, 73, 122, 158, 160
Arctic sea-ice, 152–3, 155
Atlantic Ocean, 22, 27, 29

Bedford, G., and madder-growing, 133–4
Beresford, M. W., *The Lost Villages of England*, 118–19
Black Death, and depopulation, 119, 165
Bristol Channel, 19, 24, 149
Britain, British Isles, 48–9, 191; coastal landscape, 3, 5, 19, 31, 41–4; erosion and, 45, 155,

159, 164, 166; forest faults, 19, 20, 21, 25; Lowland–Highland division, 15, 17, 18, 19, 22, 25, 26, 28, 30, 35, 40, 41; marine submergence, 25, 26, 27–8; orogenic episodes, 19, 20, 22, 25; Roman occupation, 63–7; tectonic development, *see* Earth's crust

canals, 45, 65, 175, 176
Chalk, denudation, 29–30, 30, 34; deposition, 25, 28, 32; distribution, 25, 26, 34; erosion, 29, 30, 59; transgressions, 33
chalklands, 12, 41, 61; sarsen stones, 34–5, 34; South Downs, 59, 63, 157, 161–2; Wessex, 53, 55, 59, 63, 65
Chalk Sea, 16, 17, 28–9
charters, Anglo-Saxon, 99–103, 101, 102
climate, 49, 197; and landscape, 8, 148, 150, 165; changes and fluctuations, 9, 10, 16, 17, 47, 160–3, 166; cold eras, 12, 41, 43; effects of deterioration, 57–9, 58; great frosts, 163–4; post-glacial, 12, 146, 148; record, 150–7; stages, 11, 148, 149; temperate, 35, 50; world classification by Köppen, 159
coalfields, 19, 108–9; and landforms, 45, 178, 179
countryside, 48, 148, 190–1; 197–8; cult of, 168–9; departure of industry, 185–6; London encroachment, 180, 181,

182; urban businessmen and, 184; wildlife impoverishment, 204
Cretaceous period, 27, 28; Late, 33; Upper, 25–8, 26
crops, 129, 165, 189; experimental, 138, 139, 140, 141; grain, 130, 138, 146, 189; jojoba, 132, 133; madder, 132–5, 134, 136, 140; rapeseed oil, 131–2; salt-flower, 135, 136, 140; woad, 136, 140; cropping systems, 111, 166

demography, 53; and man–landscape relationship, 49, 53, 55; agricultural workers, 190; effects of population growth, 4, 58–9, 130, 146, 172, 189; urban numbers (1901), 181, 182
denudation, 22, 28, 35; and landscape, 10, 12–15, 17, 19, 21, 36; by glaciation, 40; fluvial, 9, 31, 36, 41; rock resistance, 5, 29; during Quaternary and Tertiary, 12–14, 29
Domesday Book, evidence from, 75, 76, 80, 84, 85, 86, 94, 95, 96, 97, 100–2, 104, 139
Dover Straits, 5, 40, 43

EEC, 132, 189, 191, 204
Earth's crust, 19, 47; 'pulsed tectonism' process, 25, 35–6; 'silcrete' duricrust, 34; up-heavals, 19, 21, 149
earthworks, 45, 53, 110, 115, 117, 118, 122

enclosure, and landscape, 68, 84, 88–9, 93, 129

Enclosure Act, 68, 69, 84, 88–9, 93

energy landscape, 178, 179, 184

England, Anglo-Saxon, 104, 126; charters, 99–102; place-names, 97, 98, 99; *see also* Domesday Book

England, regional characteristics:

Cheddar Gorge, **14**, 41

Chilterns, 11, **33**, 38, 40

Cotswolds, 8, **24**, 41, 100, 113

Dartmoor, 8, 22, 50, 63, 73, 155, 163; denudation, 14, 29, 35; granite, 10, 12, 19, 31; settlement patterns, 55–6, **56**; Shaugh Moor project, 57–8, **58**

East Anglia, 4, 40, 44, 47, 50, 159, 199

Fens, 4, 44, 100, 144, 145, 151; drainage, 65, 131–2; Roman works, 65–6

Lake District, 4, 19, 22, 36, 47, 53–5, **54**, 155, 159, 176; Borrowdale and Great Gable, **15**; ice-moulded landscape, 12, 19, 36–8

Midlands, 5, 26, 38, 68, 104, 108, 113, 117, 186; landscape, 4, 17, 19, 25, 45

Peak District, 13, 35

Pennines, 4, 22, 50, 51, 115, 151; Millstone Grit and Limestone, 13, **14**, 19, **23**, **25**, 41; upwarp of tilted blocks, **20**, 25

Romney Marsh, 4, 44

South Downs, 4, **12**

South-East, 30, 32, 41–3

South-West Peninsula, 19, 21–2, 47; Bovey Basin, 29, 35

Weald, the, 9, 10, 15, 19, 25; –Artois Anticline, **20**, 21, 29, 31–3; flood-plains, **46**; Roman works, 66

England, Two Landscapes concept (AC and PC), distinctions, 69–70, **69**, **71**, **72**, 94, 96, 97, 100, **102**; placenames, 97, 98, **99**, **100**

English Channel, 11, 21, 40, 150

English Counties:

Bedfordshire, **108**, 111

Buckinghamshire, 89, 97, **109**, 138

Cambridgeshire, 11, 69, 70, 77, 104, 114; Gamlingay (1601/1900), **71**; Hayley Woods, **82**, 88, 92, 94; hedges, 89, **90**, 91, 92

Derbyshire, 93, 97, 132, 140; Barton Blount, 123; Winnats Pass, **14**

Devon and Cornwall, 4, 11, 14–15, **25**, 68, 97, 149; batholith, 21; Hound Tor, 123

Essex, 81, 83, 89, 97, 159; Earl's Colne, **89**; fields and roads, 102–3, **103**; Forests, 73, 80, 84, **85**, 86

Hampshire, 21, 25, 31, 33, 63, **64**, 100, 104, 137, 140, 193; Danebury, 60, 60–3; Tertiary sediments, 19, 28, 30, 34, 35

Herefordshire, 5, 68, 132, 169

Kent, 35, 41, 68, 145, **157**; gardens and orchards, 136, 142, 143, 144; Pegwell Bay, 31, **32**

Lancashire, 21, 144–5, 177, 178

Leicestershire, 97, 108, 109, 113, 115, 116, 118; Whatborough, **112**, 113, 117

Lincolnshire, 68, 75, 82, 97, 131–2, 138; Gainsthorpe, 110, 118; Golitho, 123

Middlesex, Enfield Chase, 84

Norfolk, 131, 144, 149, 161, 165; Breckland, **76**, 97, **158**; Broads, 45, 164; ice-sheet, 11

Northamptonshire, Bray-

brooke, 114–15; Faxton, 120, 123

Northumberland, Craigside, 184; West Whelpington, 123

Nottinghamshire, 87; Laxton, **107**, 114

Oxfordshire, 97, 111, 120, 138, 155; Blenheim Park, 86; Wychwood Forest, 84, 86; saltflower, **135**, 136; Victorian country houses, **183**, 184, 185

Rutland, Barnsdale (deer) Park, 84

Somerset, 94, 97, 99, 140; Levels, 4, 43, 132, **133**

Staffordshire, 97, 140, 184

Suffolk, 68, 77, 79, 81, 87, 89, 104; Breckland, **76**, 158; Lawshall (1611/1922), **72**; woods, **74**, 77, 78

Sussex, 78, 137; Downs, **12**

Warwickshire, 19, 100, 117; coalfield, 19, 108–9; Sutton Coldfield, 111, 114; Ilmington, 114

Wiltshire, 68, 99, 100, 104, 110, 162

Worcestershire, 97, 99, 100, 145; Milcote, 138–9

Yorkshire, 40, 50, 117, 132; deserted villages, 118–19; Towthorpe, **125**, 125; Wharram le Street, 120; Wharram Percy, 118–24, **119**, **121**

erosion, 8, 10, 45, 46, 149; Chalk, 29, 31, **33**; ice, 36, 40; sand, 130, 158, 164; 'stripped stratum planes', 10–11, 33

Europe, 52, 53, 140–1, 144; champagne regions, 88, 89; climate, 150, **152**, 164, 165; severance from Britain, 50; upper tree-line, 151, 154, 155

farming, farmers, 56, 57, 61, 63, 69, 186; and the countryside, 73, 186, 190–1, 195; field size

and cultivation, 70, 89, **91**,
92, 100, 102, **103**, 104–5,
115, 123–6, 129; food production, 48, 49, 51–3, 73, 79,
130, 141–6 *passim*, 164, 187,
189; self-image, 190–1, 194;
see also agriculture
fauna, 148; insect, 48, molluscan, 48, 53, 59
fire, 48, 49, 50
forests, forestry, 73, 195; and
the future, 188–9, 191, 192,
200; clearances, 45, 48, 50–5
passim, 66; croppings, 191,
192, 193; development, 50,
53, 151–2, 192, 193; management, 191–3; plantations, 73,
74, 200; retreat causes, 152;
Uganda experiment, 192; upper limits, 160, **161, 162**;
'wildwood', 70
Forestry Commission, 191, 192,
193
fossil data, 50; landscapes, 55

gardens, vegetable and herb, 130,
141–4; and plant survival, 149
Geological Column, **16**
glaciers, glaciation, 8, 38, 43,
150; and landscape, 12, **15**,
17, 38, 40, 41–4; deposition,
8, 38, 41, 43, 46; development
in Britain, 36–8, **37**, 39, 40;
periods, Anglian, 36, **37**,
38, 40, Baventian, **10**, 36,
Beestonian, 36, **37**, 40,
Devensian, **10, 11**, 37, 37–8,
44, Wolstonian, 36, **37**, 40;
Perth Re-advance, **37**, 38;
post-glaciation changes, 50,
70, 135, 157; relics, **153**,
160–1, **162, 163**; troughs, 12,
38
Godwin, (Sir) Henry, and pollen
analysis, 48, 50

hedges, 80, 87, 165–6; dating,
65, 88–94 *passim*, **91**; documentation, 92–3, 99, **101**,
102, 104; size of, 71, **72**, 89,
90, 91, 92

hill-forts, 59; Danebury, **60**, 60–
3; 218 n. 33
Holocene, Holocene/Recent, **15**,
44–5
Hooper, Dr Max, dating of
hedges ('hypothesis'), 93, 94
horticulture, 141–6
Hoskins, W. G., *Making of the
English Landscape*, 2, 4, 107,
108, 117, 122
housing, 172–3; suburban, 173;
types, 57, 117, **119**, village,
106–7, 122; Victorian, 170–1

ice, 5, 38, 40, **42**; and rock
formation, 5, 12, 41, 160;
snowmelt, **12**
ice-ages, 149, 150, 157, 160–1;
climax, **151**
ice-sheets, 9, 15, **27**, 36, 38–40,
42, 47, 160; of Britain, 11, 12,
37, 39, 50, 150, **152, 153**
industrial revolution, and landscape, 3, 45, 123, 170, 172,
173, 174, 178, 184; land-use,
174, 182; urban characteristics, 176, 177, 184–5; industries, cotton, 132–9, 173–4,
184, 185, manufacturing,
179, 184, mining, 174, 178,
wine, 139
Ireland, 29, 34, 144; ice-sheets
and glaciers, 150, **152**; Variscan episode, 21
Isle of Ely (Wisbech), 135, 136
Isle of Wight, 28–9, 45, 120

landforms, creation and survival, 5, 8, 9–12, 19, 36, 44, 149
Landsat, **24–5**, 47
landscape, evolutionary history,
1, 2–5, 33–5, 41–4, 47, 68–9,
110–11, 117, 160; English
characteristics, 1–5, 19, 20,
21, 39, 45–7, 152–5, **154**,
190; palimpsest imagery, 11,
47; topography, 10, **12**, 13,
149, 160
land-use, 55, 58, 173–4, 191,
198; settlement patterns, 50,

55, 55–6, 58, 63; State activities, 175, 179–81; tree-
systems, 70, **72**, 73, **74**, 75

Mackinder, H., 17–19, **18**, 22
man, chief agent of change, 17,
45–7; socio-economic sys-
tems, 57–8, 59
mapping, 71, 80, 89
marine environment, 5, 17,
30–1
Middle Ages, 120, 127, 166;
agriculture, 58, 59, 130, 141,
155; woodmanship, 73, 76–8,
81, 93–4
moorland, 21, 58, **58**, 108, 159
mountains, creation by denudation, 21; corries, **15**, 161;
folds and faults, 19, **20**, 21;
frost-shattering, 12, **15**;
orogenic episodes, 19, 21; valleys (dry), **24, 25**, 59, 63, **157**

nature conservation, 2, 4, 48,
68–9, 79, 167–8, 193–6
Neogene epoch, 32, 35, 36, 47
North Atlantic, palaeoclimatic
change, 17, 150, **151**, 153,
156; Basin, 16, 22; Drift, 150
North Sea, 22, 40, 44; Basin,
11, 22, 30, 35

oil: jojoba, 132, **133**; olive, 131;
rapeseed, 131–2
Oligocene epoch, 17, **26**, 35–6;
sarsen stones, 34–5
outcropping, 11, 17, **18**, 19

Pacific Ocean, 150
painting, landscape, 106, 153,
170, **180**
Palaeogene epoch, **16, 25**, 33,
33–5, 47; Sub-Palaeogene,
11, **33**
Palaeozoic floor, depth, 22, **23**,
30; Variscan structures, 22,
23
peat bogs, 52, 157, 159, 160
Permian period, 16; Permo-
Triassic rifting, 22, **25**

place-names, 97–9, **98–9**, 100, 102, 105

plant species, 81–2, 87, 142, 148, 158, 193; browse, 51–2; dye, 132–9, **137**; experimental, 132–6, **133**; farming, 52, 53, 57, 165; light-demanding, 50–1, 53; Pleistocene epoch, 1, 9, 10, 13, 16–17, 28, 35–40, 41, 47, 50; Plio-Pleistocene, 32, 33

Pleocene, 36

ploughing, 88, **107**, 122, 124; ridge-and-furrow, **77**, 81, 112, 114, **116**, 118, 123, 165

pollen analysis, and archaelogical research, 48, 50, 53, **54**, 57, 64, 70

pottery, 66–7, 126

Pre-Cambrian era, **16**, 19, 21

preservationism, 169, 177, 186, 194–5

Quaternary period, 9, 10, 12–14, 47

radio-carbon dating, 50, 54, 59, 157

railways, 79, 88, 94; cult of, 169, 176–7; land used, 175–6; 'Train landscape', **172**

rainfall, 8, 10, 13, **24**, 36, 46, 157, 159; denudation and topography, 9, 36, 40; drainage, **26**, 28, 31–3, 40; terraces, 41, 47

roads, motorways, 177–8; in Planned Countryside, 69, 103; Roman, 103

rocks, 5, 6, 7, 11, 17, **18**, **24**, 36; denudation and erosion, 12, 14, 36; formations, 5, 8, 10, 12, **13**, **14**, 21, 25, 32, 33, 43; granite, 8, 10, 12, 19, 21, 29; Pre-Cambrian, 19, **24**, 36; sandstone, **34**, 41, 149, 150, 160, 166; *see also* Chalk

Roman administration, 49, 81; impact on rural Britain, 63, **64**, 65–7, 104–5; villas, 65

Salt, Titus, 171, **174**

Scotland, 29, 192; Cairngorms, 160, **162**, **163**; climate, 153, 159, 165; glaciation, 12, 36, 37, 38; physical features, 19, 20, 29, 38, 149, **153**, 161, 166; upper tree-limits, 151, 155, 160, **163**

sea, the, 31; changes in level, 16–17, **27**, 36, 40–4, 47, 155; invasion by, 40, 44, 155; surface temperature, 153, **156**

sedimentation, 25, 28, 30–1, 34–5, 59; French classification, 45

soils, 48, 50–2, **56**, 59, 61, 63, 148, 149, **164**, 189; alluvium, **44**, 45, **46**; coloured, 5; fossil, 48; permafrost, **12**, 41, 157, 162

State activities, land ownership, 175–6, 177, 179

technology, 4, 49, 64, 106, 169, 189–90, 197

temperature, 153, **156**; severest oscillations, 152–3 (Little Ice-Age), **154**, 155; variations in, 50, 57–8, 150, **151**

Tertiary Period, 1, 13, 16, 19, 21; Britain's emergence, 16, 17, 28–9; denudation, 13, 14, 29–31, 30, **33**; Sub-Palaeogene, 11, 31, **33**

Thurston, T., *The Flower of Gloucester* (quoted), 171

tools, 48, 49, 55, 57, 64, 145

town/country, dichotomy, 183–4; symbiosis, 184–7 *passim*

trees, 53–5, 69, 148; management systems, 70, 73, **74**, 75, **75**; land-use 73, **73**, 75, 81; shelter-belts, 165–6; tree-line, 150–2; varieties, **74**, **76**, 77, 81, 87, 88, 94, 151–2, 158, 160

Triassic period, 16, 22, 59, 149

tundra, 12, 41, 159

turf mounds (*buttes gazonnées*), 8

United States, 1, 88, 104

Upper Cretaceous times, earth's submergence, 16

urbanization, 4, 45, 170, 182–3

vegetables, vegetable growing, 135, 140–6; as a food, 141–2, 144–5

vegetation, 3, 9, 50, 52, 148–51, **154**; zones, 158–60

Victorian Age, 94; housing, 181, 184; landscape, 170, 187; land use, 172–5

villages, 61, 63, **64**, 69, 99, 129, 199; deserted, 106, 107, 110, 115, 117, 119–23 *passim*; surviving, 106–7, 194

vineyards, 139–40, 163, 166

volcanism, 15, 19, 28, 29

Wales, 22, **25**, 149, 162, **164**; coalfields, 178; Marches 59; Variscan episode, 21; upper forest limit, 160, **161**; Snowdonia, 160

walls, 68, 88, 100, 106, 129

waterlogging, 52, 157, 166

water-table, flood-plains, 45, **46**; lowering effect, **12**

weather, 148, 149, 155, 164–6; weathering, 5, **15**, 29, 35

Wildlife and Countryside Act, 1982, 188, 195–7

wildwoods, 70, 81, 97

wind, 5, 157, 158, 160, 178

woodlands, 4, 53, 62, 63, 73–6, **75**, 77, 81, 86, 123, 129, 151

wood-pastures, 73, 83–4, 86–7, **87**, 97

woods, ancient, 68, 76–8, 80–1, 94–7, **95**, **96**; and woodmanship, 70–9 *passim*; timber and underwood, 70, 73, **74**, 75, 78, 81, 84; pollarding, **75**, 84, **86**, 87

wool, British, 62, 65, 130